Mauritius
De la
Reunion
Rodriguez

Archipel
Des Comores

MALAGASY

Bassas Da
India
Europa

NYASALAND

MOZAMBIQUE

RHODESIA

NORTHERN

SOUTHERN RHODESIA

BECHUANALAND

SWAZI

BASUTO

ANGOLA

SOUTH WEST AFRICA

SOUTH AFRICA

St. Helena

da Cunha

Prince Edward
Marion

miles

0   200   400   600   800

n, St. Helena, Mafia, Mauritius, Pemba, Socotra, Tristan da Cunha,
Gough, Seychelles, Amirante, Rodriguez.
India, Europa, De la Reunion, Archipel des Comores.
, Sao Tome, Cape Verde Islands, Madeira, Arquipelago dos Bijados.
, Canaries, Fernando Po. **Guinea:** Los.
Prince Edward, Marion. **Independent:** Malagasy.
Ethiopian: Dahalach Chebir.

AFRICA MUST UNITE

Africa Must Unite

KWAME NKRUMAH

FREDERICK A. PRAEGER, *Publisher*

New York

BOOKS THAT MATTER

Published in the United States of America in 1963
by Frederick A. Praeger, Inc., Publisher
64 University Place, New York 3, N.Y.

Library of Congress Catalog Card Number: 63–18462

Printed in Great Britain

Dedicated to
GEORGE PADMORE
(1900–1959)
and to
the African Nation
that must be

CONTENTS

INTRODUCTION

Freedom! Hedsole! Sawaba! Uhuru!

Men, women and children throughout the length and breadth of Africa repeat the slogans of African nationalism – the greatest political phenomenon of the latter part of the twentieth century.

Never before in history has such a sweeping fervour for freedom expressed itself in great mass movements which are driving down the bastions of empire. This wind of change blowing through Africa, as I have said before, is no ordinary wind. It is a raging hurricane against which the old order cannot stand.

The great millions of Africa, and of Asia, have grown impatient of being hewers of wood and drawers of water, and are rebelling against the false belief that providence created some to be the menials of others.

In this century there have already been two world wars fought on the slogans of the preservation of democracy; on the right of peoples to determine the form of government under which they want to live. Statesmen have broadcast the need to respect fundamental freedoms, the right of men to live free from the shadow of fears which cramp their dignity when they exist in servitude, in poverty, in degradation and contempt. They proclaimed the Atlantic Charter and the Charter of the United Nations, and then said that all these had no reference to the enslaved world outside the limits of imperialism and racial arrogance.

But in the course of fighting for their own freedom, they had, like Abraham Lincoln in fighting America's civil war, to enlist the aid of the enslaved, who began to question the justice of their being dragged into wars for the freedom of those who intended to keep them in bondage. The democratic enunciations of the world's statesmen came under the critical examination of the colonized world. Men and women in the colonies began to regard them as deceptions; clearly they were not to have universal application.

The realization was breaking upon the vast world of subject peoples that freedom is as much their inalienable right as it is of those who had set themselves over them on the pretext of bringing them christian light and civilization. The ideas of freedom and democracy, which the Western world was busily propagating to engage support for their cause, were being eagerly absorbed by those to whom freedom had been most strenuously denied. A boomerang to those who broadcast them, and 'dangerous' in those to whom they were not intended to apply, they were feeding the will to freedom in the overseas areas of the world where their meaning was most deeply felt and accepted.

Turned by the nationalist leaders to the interests of the struggle for political emancipation, they have helped to foment the revolt of the majority of the world's inhabitants against their oppressors. Thus we have witnessed the greatest awakening ever seen on this earth of suppressed and exploited peoples against the powers that have kept them in subjection. This, without a doubt, is the most significant happening of the twentieth century.

Hence the twentieth century has become the century of colonial emancipation, the century of continuing revolution which must finally witness the total liberation of Africa from colonial rule and imperialist exploitation. The independence of Ghana in 1957 opened wide the floodgates of African freedom. Within four years, eighteen other African countries achieved independence. This development is the unique factor in world affairs today. For it has brought about significant changes in the composition of the United Nations Organization, and is having a momentous impact upon the balance of world affairs generally. It has resulted in an expanded world of free nations in which the voice of Africa, and of the reborn states of Asia, Latin America and the Caribbean will demand more and more careful attention.

This expanding world of free African nations is the climax of the conscious and determined struggle of the African peoples to throw off the yoke of imperialism, and it is transforming the continent. Not all the ramparts of colonialism have yet fallen. Some still stand, though showing gaping rents from the stormy onslaughts that have been made against them. And we who have battled our way to independence shall not stand quiet until the last stronghold of colonialism has been laid to the ground in Africa.

For we have dedicated ourselves to the attainment of total African freedom. Here is one bond of unity that allies free Africa with unfree Africa, as well as all those independent states dedicated to this cause. My party, the Convention People's Party, fervently upholds, as an unquestionable right, the burning aspirations of the still subjected peoples of our continent for freedom. Since our inception, we have raised as a cardinal policy, the total emancipation of Africa from colonialism in all its forms. To this we have added the objective of the political union of African states as the securest safeguard of our hard-won freedom and the soundest foundation for our individual, no less than our common, economic, social and cultural advancement.

In my Autobiography, and to some extent also in another book of mine, *I Speak of Freedom*, I tried to show how, and why, the struggle for independence developed and succeeded in the then Gold Coast. My purpose now is to trace briefly the African background and the effects of centuries of colonialism on the political, economic and social life of Africa as a whole; to place developments in Ghana in the broader context of the African revolution; and to explain my political philosophy based on my conviction of the need for the freedom and unification of Africa and its islands.[1]

[1] The following are the islands of Africa: (1) Canary Islands Gran Canaria, Tenerife, Las Palmas, Ferro, Fuerte-Ventura, Lanzarote, *Spanish*; (2) Cape Verde Islands (Sto. Antão, São Tiago), *Portuguese*; (3) Madeira with Selvagens, *Portuguese*; (4) Arquipelago dos Bijagos (Caravela, Roxa), *Portuguese*; (5) Los Island, *Guinea*; (6) Fernando Po, *Spanish*; (7) Principe, *Portuguese;* (8) Sâo Tome, *Portuguese*; (9) Annobón, *Spanish*; (10) Ascension, *British*; (11) St. Helena, *British*; (12) Tristan da Cunha with Gough, *British*; (13) Prince Edward and Marion, *South African*; (14) Malagasy, *Independent*; (15) Bassas da India, *French*; (16) Europa, *French*; (17) De la Réunion, *French*; (18) Mauritius, *British*; (19) Rodriguez, *British*; (20) Archipel des Comores (Grande Comore, Moheli, Anjouan, Mayotte, Banc du Geyses, Glorieuses), *French*; (21) Seychelles (Bird, Denis, Silhouette, Praslin, Mahé, Platte, Amirante, Desroches, Bijoutier, Alphonse, St. François, Coetivy, Aldabra, Assumption, Cosmoledo, Astove, Providence, St. Pierre, Cerf, Farquhar, Agalega), *British*; (22) Socotra, *British*; (23) Dahalach Chebir, *Ethiopian*; (24) Zanzibar, *British*; (25) Pemba, *British*; (26) Mafia, *British*.

Out of this conviction, I am necessarily as much concerned with the problems of all the different countries which make up our great continent as I am with those of Ghana. I have, therefore, drawn for illustration upon all patterns of colonialism. If there does at times appear to be an emphasis upon the British pattern and upon events in Ghana, it is because these are part of my personal experience. They have been to a considerable extent the agencies that have moulded my intellectual processes and political philosophy. But I have also, as an African and a political being drawn into the vortex of African affairs out of my dedication to the cause of Africa's freedom and unity, sustained an indelible impression from the experience of my continental brothers under other colonial rulers.

Their history of colonialist subjection differs from ours only in detail and degree, not in kind. Some there are who make fine distinctions between one brand of colonialism and another, who declare that the British are 'better' masters than the French, or the French 'better' than the Belgian, or the Portuguese or the white settlers of South Africa, as though there is virtue in the degree to which slavery is enforced. Such specious differentiations come from those who have never experienced the miseries and degradation of colonialist suppression and exploitation. More frequently they are apologists for the colonialism of their own country, anxious out of jingoistic patriotism to make a case for it.

The colonial subject, the true bearer of the 'white man's burden', can have no such philosophical approach. He is, therefore, unable to judge the delicate difference between having to pass through a door marked 'natives' in any part of the world and one so marked in Johannesburg, simply because the latter would often be in a separate, segregated area.

Whatever the means used by the colonialists, the objective was the same. It was not that a nasty-minded bunch of men awoke simultaneously one morning in England, France, Belgium, Germany, Portugal, or in any other of the colonial countries, and decided that it would be a good thing to jump into Africa and grind the people's noses in the dust so that they could all of them retire to their homelands in due course, rich and happy from the Africans' hardship. It was a good deal more complex than that, despite the plundering compulsions that sent the Portuguese and others out as early as the fifteenth century to pluck Africa's gold and ivory, and later its human treasure, to enrich the coffers of Western monarchs and merchants.

When the great scramble for Africa began in the last quarter of the nineteenth century, colonies had become a necessary appendage for European capitalism, which had by then reached the stage of industrial and financial monopoly that needed territorial expansion to provide spheres for capital investment, sources of raw materials, markets, and strategic points of imperial defence. Thus all the imperialists, without exception, evolved the means, their colonial policies, to satisfy the ends, the exploitation of the subject territories for the aggrandizement of the metropolitan countries. They were all rapacious; they all subserved the needs of the subject lands to their own demands; they all circumscribed human rights and liberties; they all repressed and despoiled, degraded and oppressed. They took our lands, our lives, our resources, and our dignity. Without exception, they left us nothing but our resentment, and later, our determination to be free and rise once more to the level of men and women who walk with their heads held high.

When that time came and we showed our resolution to be rid of them as unbidden and unwelcome foreign intruders, they still refused to go until we forced the issue. It was when they had gone and we were faced with the stark realities, as in Ghana on the morrow of our independence, that the destitution of the land after long years of colonial rule was brought sharply home to us. There were slums and squalor in our towns, superstitions and ancient rites in our villages. All over the country, great tracts of open land lay untilled and uninhabited, while nutritional diseases were rife among our people. Our roads were meagre, our railways short. There was much ignorance and few skills. Over eighty per cent of our people were illiterate, and our existing schools were fed on imperialist pap, completely unrelated to our background and our needs. Trade and commerce were controlled, directed and run almost entirely by Europeans.

Of industries, we had none except those extracting gold and diamonds. We made not a pin, not a handkerchief, not a match.

The only cloth we produced was hand-woven *kente*, traditional and exclusive. We were without most of the raw materials necessary to industrial production. Though there had been geological surveys of our sub-soil, we were unaware whether these materials existed or not, as the reports had been scrupulously withheld. We were reliant upon the outside world, and more particularly upon the United Kingdom, for practically everything we used in our daily life.

Among our roads were those called 'political roads', the old, worn and sometimes untarred colonial roads. There were also the new roads, built since 1951, when my Party entered upon government. There was Takoradi harbour and the new harbour and port under construction at Tema. We had a telegraph and telephone system. We had an efficient administrative machine, but one adjusted to the needs of colonial rule and decidedly not the most suitable for the new requirements of independent statehood.

As a heritage, it was stark and daunting, and seemed to be summed up in the symbolic bareness which met me and my colleagues when we officially moved into Christiansborg Castle, formerly the official residence of the British governor. Making our tour through room after room, we were struck by the general emptiness. Except for an occasional piece of furniture, there was absolutely nothing to indicate that only a few days before people had lived and worked there. Not a rag, not a book was to be found; not a piece of paper; not a single reminder that for very many years the colonial administration had had its centre there.

That complete denudation seemed like a line drawn across our continuity. It was as though there had been a definite intention to cut off all links between the past and present which could help us in finding our bearings. It was a covert reminder that, having ourselves rejected that past, it was for us to make our future alone. In a way it hinged with some of our experience since we had taken office in 1951. From time to time we had found gaps in the records, connecting links missing here and there which made it difficult for us to get a full picture of certain important matters. There were times when we had an inkling of material withheld, of files that had strayed, of reports that had got 'mislaid'. We were to find other gaps and interruptions as we delved deeper into the business of making a going concern of the run-down estate we had inherited. That, we understood, was part of the business of dislodging an incumbent who had not been too willing to leave and was expressing a sense of injury in acts of petulance. On the other hand, there may have been things to hide. It was part of the price, like much else, that we had to pay for freedom. It is a price that we are still paying and must continue to pay for some time to come.

For freedom is not a commodity which is 'given' to the enslaved upon demand. It is a precious reward, the shining trophy of struggle and sacrifice. Nor do the struggle and sacrifice cease with the attainment of freedom. The period of servitude leaves behind tolls beyond what it has already taken. These are the cost of filling in the emptiness that colonialism has left; the struggle and the toil to build the foundation, and then the superstructure, of an economy that will raise up the social levels of our people, that will provide them with a full and satisfying life, from which want and stagnation will have been banished. We have to guard closely our hard-won freedom and keep it safe from the predatory designs of those who wish to reimpose their will upon us.

New nations like ours are confronted with tasks and problems that would certainly tax the experience and ingenuity of much older states. They would be difficult enough if we existed in a peaceful world, free of contending powers and interested countries eager to dabble in our internal affairs and manipulate our domestic and external relations in order to divide us nationally and internationally. As it is, our problems are made more vexed by the devices of neo-colonialists. And when we attempt to deal with them in ways which, having regard to all the facts that are known to us, seem most appropriate in the endeavour to maintain the internal unity upon which our viability and progress depend, we are misrepresented to the outside world to the point of distortion.

If that outside world refuses us its sympathy and understanding, we have at least the right to ask it to leave us alone to work out our destiny in ways that seem most apposite to our circumstances and means, human as well as material. In any event, we are determined to overcome the disruptive forces set against us and to forge in Africa a Ghanaian nation that will stand out as a shining example before the rest of the world of the African's ability to manage his own affairs.

That we shall succeed, I have no doubt. But years of toil and perseverance, of restraint and even privation, lie ahead. We have to free ourselves from the grip of economic imperialism, and protect our freedom. We have at the same time to work ceaselessly for the complete liberation and unity of Africa.

There is, in fact, an interacting relation in these objectives. Imperialism is still a most powerful force to be reckoned with in Africa. It controls our economies. It operates on a world-wide scale in combinations of many different kinds: economic, political, cultural, educational, military; and through intelligence and information services. In the context of the new independence mounting in Africa, it has begun, and will continue, to assume new forms and subtler disguises. It is already making use, and will continue to make use, of the different cultural and economic associations which colonialism has forced between erstwhile European masters and African subjects. It is creating client states, which it manipulates from the distance. It will distort and play upon, as it is already doing, the latent fears of burgeoning nationalism and independence. It will, as it is already doing, fan the fires of sectional interests, of personal greed and ambition among leaders and contesting aspirants to power.

These and many others will be the devious ways of the neo-colonialism by which the imperialists hope to keep their stranglehold on Africa's resources for their own continued enrichment. To ensure their continued hegemony over this continent, they will use any and every device to halt and disrupt the growing will among the vast masses of Africa's populations for unity. Just as our strength lies in a unified policy and action for progress and development, so the strength of the imperialists lies in our disunity. We in Africa can only meet them effectively by presenting a unified front and a continental purpose.

We have to be constantly on the alert, for we are steadfastly resolved that our freedom shall never be betrayed. And this freedom of ours to build our economies, stands open to danger just as long as a single country on this continent remains fettered by colonial rule and just as long as there exist on African soil puppet governments manipulated from afar. Our freedom stands open to danger just as long as the independent states of Africa remain apart.

At this very moment, the Union of South Africa is building up a military machine comparable with those of the foremost nations of Western Europe. This presents a most ominous danger, not just to the struggle of those African peoples still fighting for freedom, but to the very existence of the independent African states. Unless we meet this obvious and very powerful threat with a unified African front, based upon a common economic and defence policy, the strategy will be to pick us off and destroy us one by one.

Our essential bulwark against such sinister threats and the other multifarious designs of the neo-colonialists is in our political union. If we are to remain free, if we are to enjoy the full benefits of Africa's rich resources, we must unite to plan for our total defence and the full exploitation of our material and human means, in the full interests of all our peoples. 'To go it alone' will limit our horizons, curtail our expectations, and threaten our liberty.

But since we cannot sit idly by waiting for the consummation of our hopes for the earliest unification of Africa, we in Ghana are making our plans and shall strive unremittingly to raise our people to such higher levels of civilized living as we are able to do by our own exertions. At the same time, we shall never relax our efforts to bring total independence and unity to this African continent, for the greater good of all Africa and of each of us as component members of African Union.

CHAPTER ONE

THE AFRICAN BACKGROUND

COLONIALISM and its attitudes die hard, like the attitudes of slavery, whose hangover still dominates behaviour in certain parts of the Western hemisphere.

Before slavery was practised in the New World, there was no special denigration of Africans. Travellers to this continent described the inhabitants in their records with the natural curiosity and examination to be expected of individuals coming from other environments. It was when the slave trade and slavery began to develop the ghastly proportions that made them the base of that capital accumulation which assisted the rise of Western industrialism, that a new attitude towards Africans emerged. 'Slavery in the Caribbean has been too narrowly identified with the man of colour. A racial twist has thereby been given to what is basically an economic pheno-menon. Slavery was not born of racism: rather, racism was the consequence of slavery.'[1] With this racial twist was invented the myth of 'colour' inferiority. This myth supported the subsequent rape of our continent with its despoliation and continuing exploitation under the advanced forms of colonialism and imperialism.

It was during the period that has come to be called 'the opening up of Africa' that there began to spring up a school of what some fervid African nationalists have dubbed 'imperialist anthropologists', whose ranks extend down to the present time. Their works are aimed at proving the inferiority of the African. Anything of value that has been uncovered in Africa is attributed by them to the influence of some allegedly superior group within the continent or to people from outside Africa. The idea that

[1] Dr Eric Williams: *Capitalism and Slavery*, University of North Carolina Press, Chapel Hill 1944, p. 7.

Africa can have exerted any civilizing influence over other
people is shunned or denied.

Of late, another school of thought is re-assessing the evidence
and applying more objective standards of judgement. Some
historians and anthropologists think that civilization dawned
contemporaneously in Africa and in China. Very much exploration for further evidence which will determine the early
history of man in Africa remains to be done.

L. S. B. Leakey[1], has this to say:

> In every country that one visits and where one is drawn into
> conversation about Africa, the question is regularly asked by
> people who should know better: 'But what has Africa contri-
> buted to world progress? . . . not the wheel, not writing, not
> mathematics, not art . . . not this, not that and not the other
> thing . . .' These critics of Africa forget that men of science
> today are, with few exceptions, satisfied that Africa was the
> birth-place of man himself, and that for many hundreds of cen-
> turies thereafter Africa was in the forefront of all world progress.

It is certain that the origins of European culture trace their
roots to the ancient civilizations of the Nile valley. Early
geographers and chroniclers speak of well organized African
states and empires on both sides of the continent. North Africa,
before the Islamic invasion inhabited by the Tuareg and
Berber people, maintained flourishing societies and centres of
trade. It was with the spread of Islam that the mass Arab drive
reached into Africa's northern belt as well as Egypt. From the
discovery of written records in Arabic going back as far as the
ninth century, we are learning something of Africa's past. They
tell us that Ghana was already a centralized state in A.D. 800.
This kingdom, whose centre lay some 200 miles north of the
watershed between the Senegal and Niger rivers, was one
of the earliest of West African kingdoms. Though Ghana
was seriously weakened by the Almoravid invasion of the
eleventh century, its traditions of government and empire did
not die. They reached even greater heights in its successor state
of Mali, which flourished in the fourteenth century, and which
possessed intellectual centres, such as Djenné and Timbuktu,

---

[1] *The Progress and Evolution of Man in Africa* (O.U.P. 1961): Lecture 1, The
Progress of Man in Africa, p. 1.

whose colleges could exchange scholars with Spain and other parts of the Muslim world. When Mali declined, it was replaced by the just as splendid Songhay empire of Gao, while farther to the east lay the great state of Kanem, with a monarchy, almost as ancient as that of Ghana, which continued steadfastly into the nineteenth century.

Books like the *Tarikh es Sudan* and the *Tarikh el Fettach*, written by the African scholars of Timbuktu in the sixteenth and seventeenth centuries, give graphic descriptions of still existing Sudanese states of power and prestige. One of the great writers of Islam, Ibn Battuta, touring through Mali in the middle of the fourteenth century, observed of its peoples that they

> are seldom unjust, and have a greater abhorrence of injustice than any other people. Their sultan shows no mercy to anyone who is guilty of the least act of it. There is complete security in their country. Neither traveller nor inhabitant in it has anything to fear from robbers or men of violence. They do not confiscate the property of any white man who dies in their country, even if it be uncounted wealth. On the contrary, they give it into the charge of some trustworthy person among the whites, until the rightful heir takes possession of it.[1]

Could as much be said for our European contemporaries of that time? Europe was then passing into its Renaissance; it was awakening from the social torpor of medievalism and divided into petty and quarrelsome kingdoms. Capitalism was on the uprise and seafaring adventurers were starting out on their centuries-long search for gold and spices and silks, slaves and ivory, that they might plunder them for money-hungry monarchs and traders. These voyages brought them to the coast of Africa. Originally, the African coastline was explored by Phoenician and Greek sailors and there is growing knowledge of Chinese contact with the east coast going back at least to the early twelfth century. The modern period of exploration may be said to have begun with the Portuguese voyages during the time of Prince Henry the Navigator (1394–1460). Bartholomew Diaz sailed round the Cape of Good Hope in 1488, and some ten years

---

[1] *Ibn Battúta: Travels in Asia and Africa* 1325–1354, translated by H. A. R. Gibb (Routledge 1929) pp. 329–30.

later Vasco da Gama touched on the Kenya coast on his way to
India.

What kind of people, what kind of cities did these plunderers
find? Basil Davidson, adducing evidence from authentic records
of the time, sums up the scene thus:

> They anchored in havens that were thick with ocean shipping.
> They went ashore to cities as fine as all but a few they could have
> known in Europe. They watched a flourishing maritime trade in
> gold and iron and ivory and tortoiseshell, beads and copper and
> cotton cloth, slaves and porcelain; and saw that they had
> stumbled on a world of commerce even larger, and perhaps
> wealthier, than anything that Europe knew.

> To these European sailors of the last years of the fifteenth
> century the coast of eastern Africa could have seemed no less
> civilised than their own coast of Portugal. In the matter of wealth
> and knowledge of a wider world it must have seemed a great deal
> more civilised. They were repeatedly surprised by the ease and
> substance of the ports and towns they saw and sheltered in and
> plundered. They found themselves repeatedly disregarded as
> strange and uncouth. 'When we had been two or three days at
> this place,' says the laconic log-book of da Gama's flagship, the
> *São Gabriel,* of an encounter at a port that was probably Queli-
> mane [above the Zambesi river], 'two *senhores* of the country
> came to see us. They were very haughty; and valued nothing
> which we gave them. One of them wore a cap with a fringe em-
> broidered in silk, and the other a cap of green silk. A young man
> in their company – so we understood from their signs – had come
> from a distant country, and had already seen big ships like
> ours.'[1]

This was the Africa these plundering sailors found, an Africa
of fair and thriving cities, whose inhabitants allowed them un-
impeded entry, to their own undoing. For the strangers,

> schooled in the bitter rivalries of Europe . . . fell upon these
> tolerant and easy-going civilizations of the Indian Ocean with a
> ferocity and violence that were like nothing seen there through
> many centuries. . . . All this was as easy for the Portuguese, and
> for much the same reasons, as it was in India whenever they met

[1] Basil Davidson: *Old Africa Rediscovered,* Victor Gollancz Ltd. 1959, p. 165.

with resistance to their greed and theft. They were better armed.
They were trained to ruthlessness. They wanted more than a
simple monopoly of trade, ruinous though that would be for the
coastal cities: they wanted loot as well. African warfare, like
Indian warfare, was designed to minimize casualties, not
maximize them. These invaders had no such care.[1]

It is well worth dwelling upon these facts when we recall the
pretexts on which later European colonization of Africa was
justified. Assuming the Christian responsibility of redeeming
Africa from the benightedness of barbarism, the ravages of the
European slave trade were forgotten; the enormities of the
European conquest were ignored. Maps prepared in Europe
which had borne the names of Mali and Songhay were lost.
Records of the African kingdoms were left to gather dust and
crumble away. The achievements of states that had manufactured in iron and gold and carried on lucrative international
trade were expunged from memory.

They had disappeared as a result of the continuing European
penetration and spoliation. For on the heels of the Portuguese
there quickly followed Dutch, Spanish, Danish and English and
French sailors and traders. Their purposes were the same, their
methods, too. They set up forts and trading posts at various
points along our coasts, and added a living commodity to the
other items of plunder. For over three hundred years the slave
trade dominated Africa's history; and, in fact, influences it still
today through our diminished population and its brutalizing
and retarding effects upon our socio-economic order. It does
not require a very perceptive mind to appreciate the disastrous
consequences it has had upon African development. Whole
villages were frequently left empty of inhabitants either through
capture or flight. The number of inhabitants drawn off the
African continent as slaves has been variously put between
twenty and fifty million.

In Ghana, there exist many reminders of those days. Christiansborg Castle, which the Danes built in the seventeenth
century, still stands. So also do forts at Cape Coast, their guns
still facing out to sea, where they once were used to ward off

[1] Basil Davidson: op. cit., pp. 168–70.

attacks by other Europeans who wanted to plunder gold and ivory, and to share in the rich slave trade.

It was the Portuguese who, in the fifteenth century, discovered gold in the area between the Ankobra and Volta rivers and called the country Mina, 'the mine', or the 'Gold Coast'. They were the first to build fortified warehouses along our shores for the protection of their trade. But soon Spanish, English and Dutch ships also began to explore the Guinea Coast, as they came to call it, and more forts were established. Towards the end of the sixteenth century the Gold Coast was exporting about ten thousand slaves a year, and more than half the trade was in British hands. In 1808, Britain stopped trading in slaves, and in 1874 the Gold Coast colony was established, thirty years after the 'Bond' signed by our chiefs gave Britain her first real political influence in the country.

The notorious 'scramble for Africa' began in the last quarter of the nineteenth century. At that time, Great Britain, France, Germany, Spain, Portugal, Belgium and Italy embarked on a race for colonies. In 1881, France extended her colonial sway over Tunis, and in the following year Britain secured control over Egypt. In 1884, the first German colony was established at Angra Pequena on the coast of South-West Africa. The occupation of Togoland and the Cameroons in West Africa followed. A French force seized the territory between the Cameroons and the Portuguese colony of Angola, which became the French Congo. In 1894 the tricolour was hoisted over Timbuktu, Dahomey and the Ivory Coast. The whole of the western Sudan was soon occupied by France. In 1885 a protectorate was established over Madagascar.

Then ensued the Anglo-French jealousy which culminated in a crisis in 1898 when the occupation of the Sudanese post of Fashoda threatened to upset Britain's colonial position within that area. War between France and Britain appeared to be imminent, but the French force withdrew. France then turned her attention to Morocco. There she came up against German ambitions. A conference of colonial powers was called in Algeciras in 1906, with the result that French and Spanish claims to interfere in Moroccan internal affairs were recognized.

In 1876 the Congo International Association was formed

under the direction of Leopold II of Belgium for the occupation of the Congo Basin. Among the declared objects of the Association was the intention 'to open to civilization the only part of our globe where it had not yet penetrated'. At the Berlin Conference of 1884–85, when the European powers divided most of Africa up between them, Leopold obtained permission to form the Belgian settlements into a 'Congo Free State' under his personal suzerainty.

Italy, coming relatively late into the scramble for colonies, occupied, among other places, Assab and Massawa (on the African shore of the Red Sea); and in 1889 the colony of Italian Somaliland was formed. Thus, by the beginning of the twentieth century, Africa, apart from South Africa which developed differently, was largely divided up between the various European powers. Africa's people, mineral resources, harbours, rivers, forests – all were to be used to build up the economic and political strength of the colonial powers.

Some of the territories changed hands after the First World War, when former German colonies were distributed among the victors as mandated territories under the League of Nations. Britain received German East Africa, a quarter of Togoland and a piece of the Cameroons. France took over the remaining three-quarters of Togoland and the greater part of the Cameroons, while Belgium got a slice of German East Africa. The Union of South Africa received German South-West Africa.

Just as when the colonies were originally seized, the rights of the indigenous peoples were completely disregarded. Territorial boundaries were confirmed or freshly delimited in accordance with the new 'share out' in a quite arbitrary fashion. They had no relation to ethnic realities. In many cases boundaries cut across tribes and even villages. Problems resulting from the cynical parcelling-out of Africa still remain, and can only be settled by continental union.

The reasons which led the nations of Europe to seek colonies have been explained, with differing emphasis, by many historians. Most seem to agree that the colonial powers were guided primarily by economic, political and military considerations, probably in that order. Although certain individuals may have come to Africa from purely altruistic motives the general ideas of the European 'civilizing mission' and the 'white man's burden' have at last been largely abandoned, even by the most rabid of imperialists.

CHAPTER TWO

THE COLONIAL IMPRINT

THE TERM 'colony' originally meant a settlement of immigrants in a foreign land. In the political sense, a colony is either a settlement of the subjects of a nation or state beyond its own frontiers; or a territorial unit geographically separated from it, but owing allegiance to it. In modern colonial history, two types of colonies have grown up, owing in the main to climatic conditions. There is the 'settlement' colony in which climate and geographical environment have favoured the establishment of sizeable European communities; while the others, regarded formerly, before the discovery of prophylactic drugs and the clearance of jungles, as inimical to the health of Europeans, usually gathered relatively small groups of business men, administrators, soldiers and missionaries, all of whom lived in an environment quite different from that of the 'mother' country.

These two different forms of colony have been responsible for the evolution of different systems of government. In fact, there has been no uniform system of colonial government in Africa. The pattern has varied according to the policy and traditions of the different colonial powers, as well as to the existence and size of a settler community.

France, the colonial power which ruled over the largest area of territory in Africa, followed a policy of assimilation aimed at producing an élite class. She hoped by introducing a favoured class of Africans to French culture and civilization and raising them to the status of Frenchmen, to avoid the rise of African nationalism in the territories under her rule. The class of élites, however, always remained relatively small, and outside it the bulk of the Africans remained 'subjects', to be exploited and maltreated at the will of on-the-spot Frenchmen, both high and low.

'What was French administration like in practice?' I asked a Moroccan friend when I visited the country some years ago.

He shrugged his shoulders, and proceeded to tell me how the French had never allowed a national election in Morocco, or indeed any form of democratic assembly. No Moroccan sat in the French Assembly or Senate. There was no question of training Africans to manage their own affairs, even in the field of government. There was no freedom of the press. Patriotic organizations, like Istiqlal, were driven underground.

'It was practically impossible for a Moroccan child to get a decent education,' he said. 'As for economic matters, the wealth of the country was almost entirely in French hands.'

But French policy can perhaps best be studied in Algeria. There the French really tried to make the country an integral part of France. The Departments of Algiers, Constantine and Oran had the same status as Departments inside France itself; and the African inhabitants of Algeria had, if they renounced Muslim law, the same rights as citizens of France. Yet the utter failure of French policy in Algeria is apparent to the world. The reason is simple. Algeria forms part of the African continent. It could never be part of France. It was just self-deceit to talk of French Algeria; for there is only one Algeria, and that is Algerian.

I have publicly stated Ghana's position towards Algeria. We supported the Algerian nationalists publicly. The argument that the European settlers had made Algeria their home and regarded themselves as Algerians, is irrelevant. If they had been truly patriotic Algerians, they would not have opposed the Algerian nationalists: they would not have killed and terrorized, and broken the provisions of the Franco-Algerian peace agreements. To the African, the European settler, whether living in South Africa, Kenya, Angola, or anywhere else in Africa, is an intruder, an alien who has seized African land. No amount of arguing about the so-called benefits of European rule can alter the fundamental right of Africans to order their own affairs.

In the areas of settlement, the Europeans, in order to buttress their domination and entrench their economic hold, alienated the land from the Africans and then raised poll and other taxes upon them in order to drive them out to work for starvation wages. They erected barriers of race to enforce segregation on grounds of the inferior social development of the indigenous people, and made this a reason for enforcing their right to rule. There is no logic except the right of might that can accept the undemocratic rule of a majority by a minority. The predominant racial group must, and will, provide the government of a country. The race that is in the majority is the possessor of the land it occupies, irrespective of the annexations made by a minority of settlers. It is obvious that unhappiness, friction and fear must prevail when a minority settler group tries to take possession of a land, or to dictate to a majority, as in the cases of South Africa, Algeria, Kenya, or the Central African Federation.

The first step towards testing the right of rule in communities of mixed races and creeds is to give every adult, irrespective of race and creed, the right to vote. When each citizen thereby enjoys equality of status with all others, barriers of race and colour will disappear, and the people will mix freely together and will work for the common good.

Portugal, like France, has also pursued a colonial policy of assimilation in its African territories, though of a rather different kind. Mozambique and Angola are regarded as integral parts of Portugal, administered by the Ministerio do Ultramar in Lisbon. The press is censored, and all national movements suppressed. Mozambique, where the Portuguese have been for over 450 years, has a Governor-General's Council, with equal numbers of official and non-official members, and sends two deputies to Lisbon. But the Portuguese have never intended to allow any development towards self-government. Likewise in Angola, everything is run from Lisbon.

Portugal is at home an old-fashioned despotic oligarchy established and maintained in the interests of a small group of extremely wealthy families. It is at the same time one of the poorest of European countries. There is, therefore, a potentially revolutionary situation in Portugal itself. All those who are afraid of social change in Europe thus become the allies of Portuguese colonialism, since its maintenance appears to be the only method by which Portugal itself can be saved from revolution.

Although there is no official colour bar in the Portuguese colonies, conditions both in Mozambique and Angola are among the worst in Africa. In recent years, the average African wage in Mozambique was about ninepence a day. Education has been shamefully neglected. In 1955, there were only 68 African high school students in the whole of Angola.

But the system of forced labour, which still operates, is perhaps the worst blot on the Portuguese record in Africa. It amounts to a form of slavery. Men are treated not as men, but as chattels, to be pushed around from place to place at the whim of the local Chefe do Posto, or district officer. The 'assimilado' or 'civilizado' system, whereby an African may, by process of law, become in effect a 'white' man, if he comes up to certain European standards, demonstrates yet another aspect of the Portuguese brand of colonialism. Quite apart from the arrogant assumption of racial superiority implied in the idea that every African would *wish* to become 'white', is the insidious effect of a policy aimed at deliberately trying to turn Africans into Portuguese. I am reminded of the African from Lourenço Marques who said: 'The Portuguese think that it was a mistake on the part of God to make the African, African. Their assimilado policy is an effort to correct this divine error.'

I intend to discuss the social and economic effects of colonialism as a whole in a later chapter. It is sufficient at this point to state that all the injustice, social degradation and slavery of the Portuguese régime in Africa reached a climax at the time of the 1961 revolt in Angola. The Angola people have entered the African nationalist revolution, and the country will never be the same again.

Doubtless the ending of Belgian rule in the neighbouring Congo encouraged the rise of nationalism in Angola. The vast country of the Congo, about 77 times the size of Belgium, was between 1876 and 1908 the exclusive property of one man, King Leopold II of Belgium. He became one of the richest men in the world by mercilessly exploiting the country. African workers were mutilated or shot if they failed to bring in the required amount of rubber or ivory, the two chief objects of value in the Congo at that time. A reliable source has put the cost of lives of Leopold's régime at between five and eight million. In 1908, as a result of a Commission of Enquiry set up to investigate atrocities, the Congo Free State became a colony under the

Belgian Government. A Governor-General was appointed, responsible to the Belgian Parliament, but he had no Legislative Council or Assembly to check his power, and no Congolese sat in the Brussels Parliament. Nobody in the Congo, white or black, could vote, and the Congolese had few, if any, civil rights. The essence of the Belgian colonial system, as later developed, was to buy off any discontent by giving a certain amount of economic opportunity.

Belgian district commissioners ruled their various localities in the same authoritarian manner as the Governor-General in Leopoldville. The Roman Catholic church and big business were the other, no less, powerful rulers of the Congo. The Belgian Government, in fact, shared considerably in the investment holdings of the interlocking combines which monopolized the Congo's economy, often to the extent of as much as fifty per cent.

The belated attempts of the Belgians to prevent mounting national feeling in the Congo from expressing itself in violence, by holding carefully controlled and limited municipal elections, failed. The Congo became independent in June 1960, and tragic subsequent events showed that the Belgians never intended that Congolese independence should, in fact, become effective. There were practically no experienced Congolese politicians or civil servants, and no African officers in the *force publique*. The persistent interference of Belgian big business interests in Congolese politics has further complicated an extremely difficult situation.

In South Africa a different, though no less dangerous, state of affairs exists. There, government policy can be summed up in the one word, *apartheid*, which involves social, political and economic segregation on a basis of race. The Union of South Africa, when it was formed in 1910, was a sovereign, independent state within the British Empire.

It is now a Republic, no longer a member of the Commonwealth, and the only independent country in Africa governed by its white minority. The problem in South Africa is basically the same as that in other settler territories in Africa. In these countries there is a European minority, settled over a considerable period of time, which claims by virtue of race the right to rule for ever over the majority of the inhabitants.

The ruling class in South Africa consists of some three million persons of European descent. This ruling class controls the armed forces, which are armed and trained specifically to deal with civil disturbance. The opponents, the remaining twelve million inhabitants of South Africa, are unarmed and lack the elaborate political and economic organization which the ruling class has built up. It is because of this that the ruling class consider that their position is safe and that they can continue indefinitely to pursue their *apartheid* policy.

History has shown that such a calculation is entirely false, and if we look below the surface it can, I think, be shown that the position of the South African Government is fundamentally weak. There has been a significant repudiation of the régime by a section of the intellectual class, significant in the context of the South African situation, where even the slightest liberalism in race relations brings down the wrath of the Government. It is the cloud the size of a man's hand seen by the Prophet Elijah, the inevitable approach of the storm.

A second sign of trouble to come is the division in the ruling class itself. The two main political parties in South Africa, the United Party and the Nationalists, though both dedicated to the maintenance of racial inequality, differ about how this inequality should be maintained. The significance of the division is that it runs deep enough to have split the unity of the wielders of South Africa's intensive racialist policy, and the Government cannot, therefore, claim undivided loyalty.

Also significant in recent years is the emergence of the Progressive Party, an organization of persons of goodwill allied to some of the shrewdest financiers in the country. These financiers are mainly of British stock and represent mining, manufacturing and commercial interests, concerned with the erection of a wider internal market and easier international relations than the Boer-controlled *apartheid* policy allows. The intellectuals within the party realize that there is something deeply wrong with South Africa, and that if the Union is to survive, radical changes must be made. Ultimately, however, they all fight shy of the only change which can solve the South African situation, the establishment of the principle of one man one vote, irrespective of colour or racial origin. Like most reforming parties which spring up on the eve of revolution, they see an abyss opening up before them, but are unable to formulate any decisive alternative.

Against the disrupting tendencies in the Union itself stands the tremendous unfolding of the African Revolution, which has spread with remarkable swiftness out towards the east, centre and south, so that it is now almost at the frontiers of South Africa. 'Why are you so certain that there will soon be a change of régime in South Africa?' a member of the Ghana National Assembly asked me shortly after South Africa left the Commonwealth. I replied: 'Because of the strength of the African Revolution which has already transformed most of Africa; and because the South African régime shows exactly those symptoms which have invariably preceded revolutions elsewhere.' South Africa is a country timed for explosion, like Haiti before its revolt, and for the same reasons: racial tyranny and fear.

Not surprisingly, therefore, discontent mounts in the Union, as also in the South African administered territory of South-West Africa.

Labour disputes often end in strikes and demonstrations; sporadic outbreaks of violence increase in size and number. These in themselves may not be enough to disrupt the South African economy, but if a sufficient number of countries boycott South Africa, the total effect is bound to be considerable. Already the Union government is dangerously isolated politically, cut off from the sympathy of its African neighbours, and deprived, because of its *apartheid* policy, of the moral support of most of the world.

The South African question is one upon which African states have proved that they have a unity of approach, and it should not be difficult to devise an appropriate line of policy which could attain universal African support. Plans must certainly be made to train Africans from South Africa to be ready to take over positions of responsibility once the existing government has been overthrown.

British colonial policy has assumed various forms in different parts of Africa. A full description would fill several books, and I can mention only what I consider to be some of the more significant and characteristic aspects of it. The avowed British policy has been to guide the colonial territories to responsible self-government within the Commonwealth. The late Ernest Bevin defined the reasons for this policy as 'Give . . . and keep.' It seems he meant that by voluntary withdrawal at a suitable time the British would retain the goodwill of the African, strengthen the Commonwealth, earn the praise of the rest of the world, and at the same time keep maximum political and economic advantages. The British, though liking to pose as dreamy idealists who, through absence of mind, achieved an empire, are in my experience the most hard-headed of realists. They know that Africa must inevitably be ruled by Africans, and they want to come out of the business in the best possible way.

From early days internal self-government was granted to colonies of settlement, but in the case of colonies where there was no strong European settler community to run affairs, political development was much slower. Unlike France, Britain did not consider her colonies an extension of the homeland. No colonial constituencies have at any time been represented in the House of Commons in London.

Generally, a Governor was placed over each colony. He was responsible to the Secretary of State for the Colonies, who in turn was responsible to the House of Commons, the Cabinet, and ultimately to the Crown. He was not responsible to a *local* electorate; and here the truly authoritarian nature of the régime becomes apparent.

Although most colonies had an Executive Council (Exco), this was usually appointed by the Governor, and again was not responsible to any locally-elected assembly. In some colonies unofficial members were in due course appointed. European unofficial members sat on the Executive Council in Kenya after 1919; and Africans on the Executive Councils of the Gold Coast (Ghana) and Nigeria after 1942. These Councils had advisory power only; and their proceedings were secret.

Under the Executive Council was the Legislative Council (Legco), which passed the Budget and certain laws. It could debate and vote on legislative proposals put before it, and could question the government. But the government was not bound to take its advice. Before the Second World War no Africans sat in Legislative Councils in East Africa. In 1944 one was nomi-

nated to the Kenya Legislative Council; the following year three
were appointed in Uganda; and in 1946, two in Tanganyika.
Progress was faster in West Africa. The first African member of
the Legislative Council in the Gold Coast was nominated in
1861.

The power of the Legco varied in different countries according to the ratio between official, unofficial (i.e. appointed), and
elected members. Where the elected members were out-
numbered by the official and unofficial members, the assembly
was controlled, in fact, by the Governor. But, in any case, the
Legco could not cause the government to resign, even if it out-
voted it on some Bill. The Governor had certain 'reserved
powers' by which he could invalidate legislation; and he could,
in time of extreme emergency, suspend the constitution and rule
by decree. This was actually done not long ago in British
Guiana.

There have, of course, in recent decades been progressive
revisions of the constitutions of almost all United Kingdom
dependencies, and those which are not already independent
have advanced constitutions which place responsibility for their
own affairs largely in the hands of the local people. The evolution towards parliamentary government on the Westminster
model has been marked by an obstinate refusal to grant, particularly in areas of white settlement, universal adult suffrage,
the keystone, after all, of true democracy.

In spite of the moralizings of British colonialists who argue
that political reform is granted as and when the colony is ready
for it, change has, in fact, come mostly as a result of pressure
from below. In the case of Ghana, a vigorous campaign waged
by my party, its slogan 'Self-Government Now', was needed
before independence could be achieved. As I said in the National
Assembly on 10 July 1953, when presenting the historic motion
for independence:

> There comes a time in the history of colonial peoples when
> they must, because of their will to throw off the hampering
> shackles of colonialism, boldly assert their God-given right to
> be free of a foreign ruler. . . . If there is to be a criterion of a
> people's preparedness for self-government, then I say it is their

readiness to assume the responsibility of governing themselves.
For who but a people themselves can say when they are prepared?

I know of no case where self-government has been handed to a
colonial and oppressed people on a silver platter. The dynamic
has had to come from the people themselves. It is a standing joke
in Africa that when the British start arresting, independence is
just around the corner.

The principle of indirect rule adopted in West Africa, and also
in other parts of the continent, allowed a certain amount of
local self-government in that chiefs could rule their districts
provided they did nothing contrary to the laws of the colonial
power, and on condition they accepted certain orders from the
colonial government. The system of indirect rule was notably
successful for a time in Northern Nigeria, where the Emirs
governed much as they had done before the colonial period. But
the system had obvious dangers. In some cases, autocratic chiefs,
propped up by the colonial government, became inefficient and
unpopular, as the riots against the chiefs in Eastern Nigeria in
1929, and in Sierra Leone in 1936, showed.

In wide areas of East Africa, where there was no developed
system of local government which could be used, headmen or
'warrant' chiefs were appointed, usually from noble families.
They were so closely tied up with the colonial power that many
Africans thought chiefs were an invention of the British.

The alliance of the governing power with the privileged classes
tended to slow up or put a break on social change and progress,
as both had an interest in maintaining the *status quo*. In Ghana,
the position of chiefs is entrenched in our Constitution, and they
still play an important part in the life of the country. Chiefs in
some parts of Africa have been, and still are, in the forefront of
nationalist movements. In Tanganyika, for example, the Tanganyika African National Union (TANU) claimed that not a
single chief supported the government; they were all supporters
of TANU. But by and large, the system of indirect rule, where
chiefs were paid to administer their areas under the supervision of
the colonial power, did lead frequently to divided loyalties, as
well as to the slowing down of democratic processes.

The establishment of local councils, like those in Kenya in 1924, was an improvement, but their powers were strictly limited. The District Officer was the *ex officio* President and retained all executive power. The Councils had treasuries, but received no share of the general tax.

When the Councils were reconstructed, in 1950, as African District Councils, the presidents and members were to be appointed by the Provincial Commissioners. The latter invariably appointed District Commissioners as presidents, though they usually allowed a majority of the members of each council to be elected by the people.

Dedicated to the complete destruction of colonialism in all its forms, I can hold no brief for any colonial government, whatever its pattern. British, French, Portuguese, Belgians, Spanish, Germans, Italians, all at one time or another ruled parts of Africa or still continue to do so. Their methods might have varied, but their purpose was the same: to enrich themselves at the expense of their colonies.

CHAPTER THREE

COLONIAL PATTERN OF ECONOMICS

MANY HAVE argued that the resources of Africa were useless to the native inhabitants until they were developed, and they could not have been developed without European capital and skill. It has even been said that 'the European investor, however self-interested he may have been, was serving Africa.'[1] This sort of argument reminds me of the man who, having found buried treasure in his neighbour's garden, took it away and then told his neighbour that he was doing him no harm, because, until then, he was unaware of its existence. In any case, he did not own a spade. To those who study the facts fairly, it must surely be clear that the European occupation of Africa was carried out for the benefit of Europeans. Concern for the welfare of the African peoples hardly entered into the matter.

Jules Ferry, Premier of France in 1885, gave the dominant reasons for the European quest for colonies in Africa, when he spoke in the Chamber of Deputies in defence of the colonial policy of the French Government.

He said:

Is it not clear that the great states of modern Europe, the moment their industrial power is founded, are confronted with an immense and difficult problem, which is the basis of industrial life, the very condition of existence – the question of markets? Have you not seen the great industrial nations one by one arrive at a colonial policy? And can we say that this colonial policy is a luxury for modern nations? Not at all, gentlemen, this policy is, for all of us, a necessity, like the market itself.

Today, as you know, the law of supply and demand, freedom

[1] A. J. Hanna: *European Rule in Africa* (1961). Hist. Assoc. Pamphlet G.46, p. 17.

of exchange, the influence of speculations, all these move in a circle which extends to the ends of the world.

Colonies are for rich countries one of the most lucrative methods of investing capital. . . . I say that France, which is glutted with capital, and which has exported considerable quantities, has an interest in looking at this side of the colonial question. It is the same question as that of outlets for our manufacture.

Colonial policy is the offspring of industrial policy, for rich states in which capital is abundant and is rapidly accumulating, in which the manufacturing system is continually growing and attracting, if not the most numerous, at least the most alert and energetic part of the population that works with its hands, in which the countryside is obliged to industrialize itself, in order to maintain itself, in such states exportation is an essential factor of public property. . . . The protective system is like a steam boiler without a safety-valve, unless it has a healthy and serious colonial policy as a corrective and auxiliary. European consumption is saturated, it is necessary to raise new masses of consumers in other parts of the globe, else we shall put modern society into bankruptcy and prepare for the dawn of the twentieth century a cataclysmic social liquidation of which we cannot calculate the consequences.

Albert Sarraut, French Colonial Secretary of State in 1923, spoke in even stronger terms, at the Ecole Coloniale in Paris:

What is the use of painting the truth? At the start colonization was not an act of civilization, nor was it a desire to civilize. It was an act of force motivated by interests. An episode in the vital competition which, from man to man, from group to group, has gone on ever increasing; the people who set out to seize colonies in distant lands were thinking primarily of themselves, and were working for their own profits, and conquering for their own power.

Sarraut concluded his speech with these words: 'The origin of colonization is nothing else than enterprise of individual interests, a one-sided and egotistical imposition of the strong upon the weak.' He thus exposed the falsehood of the theory of the 'white man's burden' and the *mission civilisatrice*.

The Marxist-Leninist view supports the stand of Jules Ferry, which argues that the most determined imperialists are frequently concealed Marxists and abler exponents of Marxist analysis than many self-styled socialists. According to the Marxist-Leninist view, imperialism is the development of the capitalist system to its highest stage. Its most important feature is that of *monopoly*. The concentration of production and capital has developed to such a degree that it has created monopolies which play a decisive role in economic life. National monopolies have linked up internationally to share the world among themselves, and the territorial division of the globe is completed. Banking capital has reached the stage where it dominates production capital; and the export of investment capital has become as vitally necessary as the export of commodities. It is true that excess capital could be invested at home in the improvement of agriculture, but the profits are not by any means as large as those obtained from overseas investment in 'backward' countries, where labour and land costs are minimal. The annual returns on overseas investment (one of the chief hidden benefits of colonies) are often several times the volume of trade and shipping with the 'backward' areas. As a result of intensive production, there is keen competition for raw materials.

It was at the juncture where production was dominated by industrial combines and the shortage of raw materials was becoming acute, that the possession of colonies became imperative, as controlled sources of raw materials and outlets for manufactured goods and finance capital. On the colonial scene, the stage opened with the appearance of the missionaries, the traders and the administrators. While missionaries implored the colonial subject to lay up his 'treasures in Heaven, where neither moth nor rust doth corrupt', the traders and administrators acquired his minerals and land. There was no intention of processing locally the discovered raw materials. These were intended to feed the metropolitan mills and plants, to be exported back to the colonies later in the form of finished commodities.

The simple two-way traffic is implicit in colonial trade. In her African colonies, Britain controlled the export of raw materials by preventing their direct shipment to foreign markets. After satisfying the demands of her home industries, she sold the surplus to other nations and netted the profits herself. The colonial farmer and worker had no share in those profits. Nor was any part of them used in providing public works and social services in the colonies. There is a belief that the British Government contributed to the costs of administration and public services in their colonies. This is a fallacy. Each colony raised its own budget out of taxes and revenue, and the first charge upon it was the salaries of the European officials of the administration. The construction of railways, harbours and roads was met out of loans raised from local sources, and was undertaken largely to meet the transport and communications requirements of the colonialists. For example, diamonds and gold lay at the basis of South Africa's railway system. Gold prospecting, the finding of coal at Wankie, and the opening up of the copper belt fixed the pattern of Rhodesia's first railways. Our own railways in Ghana were laid down in order to take out minerals and timber from areas of production to the harbour at Takoradi.

Immense profits have been, and are still being, taken out of Africa. Important mineral deposits in various parts of Africa have attracted foreign capital, which has been used mainly to enrich alien investors. The rich copper mines of Northern Rhodesia are a case in point. The Anglo-American Corporation of South Africa with its associated diamond combine, besides having a practical monopoly of all the diamonds produced in Africa, and owning many gold and coal mines in South Africa, has a large stake in the Rhodesian copper belt.

Much of the great mineral wealth of Africa, which ought to have been kept in Africa to develop basic industries here, has been systematically shipped away. The process is still going on, even in the independent countries. There are those who argue that the conditions and resources of Africa are not suited to industrialization. In this way they seek to excuse the economic policy of the colonial powers and support the infiltration of neo-colonialism. The argument falls to the ground when the facts are examined.

We have here, in Africa, everything necessary to become a powerful, modern, industrialized continent. United Nations investigators have recently shown that Africa, far from having inadequate resources, is probably better equipped for industrialization than almost any other region in the world. Potential reserves of iron ore, for instance, would last some two thousand years. Coal deposits are estimated at 4,500 million tons. The Sahara's oil reserves are thought to be as great as those in the Arabian peninsula. Natural gas abounds in the bowels of the Sahara. Northern Rhodesia is reported to have the second largest vanadium deposits in the world. Potential hydro-electrical power is almost limitless. In Ghana we have bauxite reserves estimated at some 200 million tons. I have mentioned only a few of our natural resources; many other figures, equally impressive, could be given. When the whole continent has been geologically surveyed, immense new riches will undoubtedly be discovered.

The true explanation for the slowness of industrial development in Africa lies in the policies of the colonial period. Practically all our natural resources, not to mention trade, shipping, banking, building, and so on, fell into, and have remained in, the hands of foreigners seeking to enrich alien investors, and to hold back local economic initiative. Out of £148,000,000 allocated between 1946 and 1956 under the U.K. Colonial Development and Welfare Aid, only £545,000, less than half per cent, was directly used for industrial development.[1]

Capital investment from outside is, of course, required in Africa. But only if there is real political independence can the profits from the investment of this capital be shared in a way which is fair both to the outside investor and to the people of the country where the investment is made.

The way in which many foreign companies obtained their concessions in Africa was often sordid, to say the least. A Commission of Enquiry, set up to investigate the granting of concessions in the Gold Coast, recently discovered some very revealing facts.

These concessions were secured by local agents persuading the chiefs, the custodians of tribal and Stool lands, to sign away the mineral and timber rights of their people for purely nominal sums. Some money, a few hundred yards of cloth, a few cases of whisky and gin, were usually sufficient inducement to secure the

[1] *Special Study on Economic Conditions in Non-Self-Governing Territories.* United Nations, 1958.

marks of the chiefs to legal documents which they could neither read nor understand.

One of Ghana's best known chiefs, Nana Sir Ofori Atta I, told the Legislative Council in 1939 how six of his brother chiefs had been deceived when they signed away concessions to the largest of the mining companies. One, he said, got £66, another £133, a third and a fourth received £50 each, and the fifth and sixth £200 and £100 respectively. 'These rents,' he added, 'are payable to chiefs in respect of the Ashanti Goldfields Limited, and nothing goes to any of the chiefs on the profits that are earned.'[1] The chiefs tried to get the then Governor, Sir Arnold Hodson, to support a Bill which would require the company to pay the Native Authorities a royalty on their profits. He refused, giving the reason that it would be shortsighted and extremely harmful to interfere because capital was very sensitive, and it might have the effect of driving it away to other parts of the world.

At the end of the Ashanti wars, about 300 British concerns secured mining and timber concessions which, according to Lord Hailey,[2] amounted to about a third of the total land area of the Gold Coast Colony, and about one-eighth of Ashanti.

With all the wealth drawn from our mineral resources, it may come as a shock to some to learn that, except for a small annual tribute from the gold mines, no mining company in the Gold Coast ever made any contribution by way of direct taxes to the country's revenue, until my government introduced its new taxation measures in 1952, and these made no noticeable impression upon the distributed profits of these companies. I often wonder just how much the Union Minière du Haut-Katanga paid for its concessions in the Belgian Congo!

Commercial exploitation in our country has a long history, as long, in fact, as European contact with the West African coast. In keeping with the imperialist policy of fostering single crop agriculture in the colonies, our farmers, having found that cocoa did well in our soil and climate, were encouraged to concentrate on its production to the neglect of local food crops and a diversity of cash crops. The encouragement of mono-crop cultivation was not, however, accompanied by stable prices. The price of our

[1] *Gold Coast Legislative Council Debates*, 1939, No. 1.
[2] Lord Hailey: *African Survey*, Oxford University Press, p. 778.

cocoa was manipulated by European and American buyers, who
included, besides the large chocolate manufacturers, the big im-
porters and distributors of food products, farm implements and
manufactured goods. Joined together in their association, they
forced down the price of cocoa, while the cost of imported commodities, upon which our people became more and more
dependent, as a result of single-crop farming, remained stable.

During the war, the British Government set up group marketing boards in the West African colonies as agencies for the bloc
purchase of raw materials by the Ministry of Supply in London
as part of its planned arrangements for satisfying the metropolitan rationing system. Our present Cocoa Marketing Board,
which operates our bulk purchasing and selling of the crop,
developed out of these wartime arrangements. This system of
planned purchase and sale enables us to give the farmers a
guaranteed price fixed to prevent a domestic inflationary spiral.
There has been a steady elimination of the predatory middlemen
who used to act as the agents of the big merchant firms and
chocolate manufacturers, while the foremost of the trading firms
has itself retired from this sphere of activity. But the twin purpose
for which our economy had been geared under imperialist rule,
of providing markets for British products and mercantile
services, and the export of cocoa, and mining commodities, on
the basis of low-paid labour, cannot overnight be replaced by
one more suited to the needs of modern Ghana. The pattern of
its monopolistic control was firmly set in the first quarter of the
present century, when the pioneering firms and our own African
'merchant princes', as they were called, were either forced out of
business or absorbed by the giant companies. A substantial
volume of petty trade came to be carried on by thousands of
women street hucksters and market vendors. These women, a
few of whom have accumulated some sizeable capital, play an
important part in our internal trade distribution. But they are
reliant for their supplies on the monopoly firms, for whom they
provide the cheapest kind of retail distributive system it has been
possible to devise.

Under colonial rule, foreign monopoly interests had our whole
economy completely tied up to suit themselves. In a country
whose output of cocoa is the largest in the world, there was not a

single chocolate factory. While we produce the raw materials for the manufacture of soap and edible fats, palm products, the manufacture of these items was discouraged. A British firm owning lime plantations here, as it does in the West Indies, actually expresses the juice from the fruit before shipping it in bulk to the United Kingdom and exporting it back to us, bottled, to retail in stores at a high price. Though we had the raw materials needed for their manufacture, every bottle used in this country was imported. These facts have a kind of Alice in Wonderland craziness about them which many will find hard to accept. But they are implicit in the whole concept and policy of colonialism. Native initiative, where it was likely to endanger the interests of the colonial power, was quickly stifled.

We import a lot of soap and, as I have already said, we have the raw materials right here. Indeed, the overseas manufacturers get their vegetable oils from us. It seemed quite a sound idea for a Ghanaian to establish a soap factory here in Ghana. Not so sound, though, for the British firm which manufactured soap, or for those who shipped it to us and imported it, especially when they were tied up together. A Ghanaian factory was started, but the machinery ordered was of the wrong type, designed for animal rather than vegetable fat. The automatic cutter produced bars of laundry soap larger than those imported. There were constant break-downs with the machinery, and the larger soap bar could not retail at a price above that charged for the imported soap. Inevitably the Ghanaian factory was forced to close down, and soap continued to be imported.

I cannot understand why so many people in the United Kingdom still refuse to admit that local industry was deliberately discouraged in many of the colonies. After all, they learn in their school history books that the Americans complained of the same sort of thing in the eighteenth century. They, too, were not allowed to manufacture any commodity which might compete with industries in the metropolitan country. If the American colonists had genuine economic grievances, why not us? Why not Africa?

In his book, *West Africa*, F. J. Pedler admits that the colonial governments prevented industries from being introduced, but gives the strange reason that: 'They have wished to safeguard the social system of the African tribes against disintegrating influences of urban conditions.'[1] And yet so many historians regard the industrial revolution as one of the best things that ever happened to Britain.

The view that the African must be spared the dangers of industrialization and town life used to be very widely held. Many a district officer under the colonial régime sincerely believed it, and would have been genuinely hurt if it was suggested that his belief sprang from an inner conviction that the Africans were an inferior people, capable only of primitive village life. It is understandable that histories of Africa, until recently written almost entirely by Europeans, should give the European viewpoint. But it is time that some of the popular and most glaring misconceptions about colonialism were cleared up. The system must be examined in the light of the facts, and from the point of view of those who suffered under it.

Not least among our worries in planning the economic development of our country has been the whole question of communications. Before we took office in 1951, there was no direct railway between Accra and Takoradi, our capital city and our main port. Passengers and freight had to travel by way of Kumasi. This was because Kumasi was the centre of the cocoa, timber and mining industries. We have now built a railway line from Achiasi to Kotoku, thus linking Accra to Takoradi by a direct route. Another line links Accra with the new harbour at Tema.

Similarly with roads; there were relatively few before 1951. Farmers found it difficult to get their produce to market, because of the lack of feeder roads from farm to main highways. Few of our villages had any regular transport to a main road or station. In the towns, one was lucky if one happened to live near a 'mammy lorry' route. For the most part our people walked from place to place.

The colonial administration would, no doubt, have claimed that they were working to a specific budget, a budget strictly related to the revenue. But our revenue in no way reflected the volume of the country's production, its trade and commerce.

[1] *Home Study Books*, 2nd edition, Methuen, 1959, p. 93.

Income tax was kept at a deliberately low level, when it was steadily rising in the United Kingdom. Worse than that, the British companies operating in the Gold Coast were registered in England, which received the tax benefits from the enormous profits made out of our wealth and labour. It was not our farmers and workers who shared the profits made, but the British shareholders to whom dividends were exported. It is estimated that during the last thirty years of British colonial administration, British trading and shipping interests took out of our country a total of £300,000,000. Just imagine what might have been done by way of development if only part of these gigantic transfers of profit had been retained and used for the benefit of our people.

I have already referred to the grim emptiness that faced us on our assumption of independence, the gaps and deficiencies. Behind it all was the refusal to use our wealth for our development. Not only were our natural resources extracted but the benefits of their exploitation came, not to us but to the metropolitan country. This is the answer to those economists who maintain that imperialism should be judged not on what it takes away but on what it leaves behind, as well as to those who parade the heritage of the schools and hospitals and roads that the missionaries and our colonial rulers left to us. They have no case against the actualities that I am describing.

Under the British there was no poultry farming to speak of; there was no proper dairy farming, and the ordinary Gold Coast family never saw a glass of fresh milk in its life. There was no raising of beef cattle. There were no industrial crops. Climate, plant and cattle disease, are the least of the reasons for this deplorable neglect, for the Ghana Government is going ahead with precisely these agricultural projects, with considerable success. The British sent out a few good veterinary doctors and botanists, who carried out a certain amount of field work and experiments. These, however, were isolated, and remained mostly unapplied at the practical level. Somehow or other, useful and necessary knowledge seldom seemed to percolate down to the local farmer.

The administrators who should have used their scientific results as the basis of a thorough-going agricultural development policy

were either too lethargic or too uninterested to take action. It
may be that they were reluctant to do anything which might
interfere with the import of agricultural products at monopoly
prices. Whatever the reason, local agriculture was discouraged
and imports swelled.

During the war, British troops were stationed in the Gold
Coast. Everyone knows that potatoes are to the British what
bread is to the French. A meal is not complete without them.
Under wartime conditions, shipping was severely restricted, and
it looked as though the British soldiers would have to go without
their potatoes. It had always been maintained that our climate
was not suitable for growing them. But the administration,
moved at the thought of British servicemen being deprived of
their staple food, began a 'grow potatoes' campaign. Before long,
our hitherto 'unsuitable' climate was producing magnificent
crops. Once the war was over, however, and normal shipping
facilities were resumed, the Department of Agriculture changed
its tune. Gold Coast potatoes, we were told, were unfit for
human consumption. The result was that potatoes disappeared
from our fields and once more figured among our imports.

We have wide savannahs in the north, ideal with the right
irrigation for the growing of cotton. Yet for many years we spent
millions of pounds importing richly-patterned cloths from
abroad. We have made plans for irrigating these savannahs, and
have projects for cotton-growing and textile-making, and our
experiments are going ahead. We have had to do everything from
scratch, but in spite of this great progress is being made.

Similarly with the fishing industry, we hope in due course to
make up for lost time. Here, too, the colonial régime failed. In
the absence of cattle farming, fish was the most important source
of animal protein in the country, and there are plenty of good
fishing grounds near our coasts. A comparatively small expenditure of money on refrigeration and on motorized boats
would have provided for a sufficient quantity of fish to be caught
and brought home in good condition to cover the local market
and leave some over for export. Throughout the entire period of
British administration, even though malnutrition figured as a
basic cause of a number of the country's diseases, and was
certainly a contributory factor in low productivity, no attempt

was made to initiate such a project. On the contrary, the Gold Coast annually imported large quantities of fish.

The failure to promote the interests of our people was due to the insatiable demands of colonial exploitation. However wise, enlightened and good-hearted certain individual officers may have been, their functions and authority fitted into a pattern of colonial administration which was itself conditioned by the central and over-all need to extract the riches of the colonies and transfer them overseas. If in the process it was necessary to build some roads, to construct a harbour, or to educate some Africans, well and good. The point I want to make is that any welfare activity for the benefit of our people was little more than incidental. It was far from being the underlying purpose of colonial rule.

CHAPTER FOUR

SOCIETY UNDER COLONIALISM

THERE IS growing up in Ghana a generation which has no first-hand knowledge of colonial rule. These boys and girls, born since Independence, will find it difficult to believe that there was a time when Africans could not walk in certain parts of every town, unless they had business there as servants. The limitations on our freedom, the crimes against our dignity as human beings, will seem to them remote and unreal. It is cheering to think that when they meet a European it will never occur to them to touch the imaginary forelock, or bow in servility, as some of our older men still do, so hard is it to break long-established habits.

The social effects of colonialism are more insidious than the political and economic. This is because they go deep into the minds of the people and therefore take longer to eradicate. The Europeans relegated us to the position of inferiors in every aspect of our everyday life. Many of our people came to accept the view that we were an inferior people. It was only when the validity of that concept was questioned that the stirrings of revolt began and the whole structure of colonial rule came under attack.

Signs like NO AFRICAN ALLOWED, or FOR EUROPEANS ONLY could at one time be seen in practically every part of Africa. Now they are fast disappearing, though still much in evidence in the Republic of South Africa and in Southern Rhodesia. I can well imagine what the reaction of an Englishman would be if he came across signs proclaiming NO BRITON ALLOWED in any part of Europe, or even in one of the newly-independent African states. Africans, however, were expected to put up indefinitely with such treatment in the land of their birth.

The colour bar, where it has operated strongly, has been responsible for much of the bitterness, which has, in some areas, entered into African nationalism. This is hardly surprising. But what is perhaps more remarkable is the moderation of most African political leaders. Not a single one has advocated any kind of policy founded on racial discrimination. All have stressed the need for co-operation between races, based on the rule of the majority. We have seen too much of racialism to want to perpetuate the evil in any way.

Of course, it will be some time before all traces of colonialism will disappear from our society. Problems connected with health, education, housing and living conditions generally, continue to remind us of the colonial period. We have much ground to make up, as a result of long years of being treated as an inferior people fit only to provide cheap labour for foreign employers. We were supposed not to be able to appreciate, or to need, any real measure of social improvement.

It is true that shelter in a tropical climate is a less urgent problem than it is in a cold or temperate climate. It is also true that Africans do have improvised homes. This, in fact, was the housing position in the Gold Coast under colonial administration. But Africans did not live in shacks and mud huts because they preferred them to proper houses. They had no choice. They had neither the jobs nor the resources to enable them to build. And it never occurred to the administration to do what most advanced countries perform as an automatic service, undertake a popular housing programme for the people. Nor were there any building societies to help folk without ready capital to acquire homes. Thus the people of this country lived as they had always lived, crowded together in hovels as far removed from the dream of living in a three-roomed abode with normal conveniences as a London messenger boy is of owning Buckingham Palace.

There was once in England a similar prevailing upper-class view of workers who lived in slums. 'They enjoy it,' was the sentiment expressed. 'They like to live crowded together. If we did give them up-to-date houses with bathrooms, they wouldn't know what to do with them. They would use the bath to store coal.' Strangely enough, this was not merely a justification for the Conservative Governments of the time to do nothing to meet general housing needs. Some really believed that only the educated upper class wanted and knew how to appreciate a decent house.

With the close of the Second World War there followed a change in the official outlook on these matters. Most established countries brought about tremendous alterations in the social pattern of their people by clearing slums and launching vast housing schemes for the working population. These new ideas of popular housing, however, never reached Africa. We could go on living as we had always lived. We knew no better. What had been good enough for our great-grandparents could go on being good enough for us and our children.

The housing situation when we took office was shocking. It reflected what appeared to be a standard European view of the African attitude towards domestic shelter: anything that keeps off the rain and offers shade from the sun is good enough. The white man, living in his stone, brick or concrete house, seemed to think that the African 'native' neither wanted nor needed an elaborate structure in which he and his family could live in comfort. It was considered enough for a few palm fronds and thatch to give shelter to the family living in the village and for an improvised shack with corrugated iron roof to serve the towns-folk. This assumption was just another facet of the contemptuous regard of the African as a creature devoid of human sensibility.

In all the years that the British colonial office administered this country, hardly any serious rural water development was carried out. What this means is not easy to convey to readers who take for granted that they have only to turn on a tap to get an immediate supply of good drinking water. This, if it had occurred to our rural communities, would have been their idea of heaven. They would have been grateful for a single village well or stand-pipe.

As it was, after a hard day's work in the hot and humid fields, men and women would return to their village and then have to tramp for as long as two hours with a pail or pot in which, at the end of their outward journey, they would be lucky to collect some brackish germ-filled water from what may perhaps have been little more than a swamp. Then there was the long journey back. Four hours a day for an inadequate supply of water for washing and drinking, water for the most part disease-ridden!

This picture was true for almost the whole country and can be explained by the fact that water development is costly and no more than a public service for the people being administered. It gave no immediate prospect of economic return. Yet a fraction of the profits taken out of the country by the business and mining interests would have covered the cost of a first-class water system.

Under the colonial administration there was, until more recent times, discrimination in the Gold Coast health services. For example, there were seven hospitals in the country which catered for under 3,000 Europeans as against thirty-six for about 4,000,000 Africans. We all remember when the Ridge hospital in Accra was reserved for whites and when only in very special cases any of our own people were admitted there. Korle Bu, the principal Accra hospital, was always over-crowded. Even at that, it was considered one of the best in Africa. In fact, as with education, so the public health and medical services of the Gold Coast were rated to be well ahead of those in most other colonies.

Yet the services they provided were hopelessly inadequate. Some attempt had been made by the administration to raise health standards, and medical men and nurses had been brought in from Britain to complement the medical services which had been started by the missions. The budget, however, was terribly restricted and practically nothing was done by way of preventive medicine. The greatest scourge of our people is malaria, which is almost endemic. It is extremely debilitating and one of its effects is sterility in women. To get rid of malaria one has to rid the country of the anopheles mosquito. Other diseases, like tuberculosis, yaws, and kwashiorkor, take a shocking toll of life and energy, and are immediately ascribable to poor nutrition, over-crowded living conditions and bad drinking water. Infant mortality rates are appallingly high, and many surviving children are crippled or invalid.

Attempts were being made to bring about some amelioration, through the health services, but administrative policy did nothing to eliminate the economic conditions which assisted the incidence of death-dealing and energy-depriving diseases and maladies. To some degree lack of education can also be blamed, because without knowledge superstition persists. Health and education most certainly go hand in hand, and many of our people resisted the 'white man's medicine', because they suspected it of being evil rather than good. Acceptance of twentieth-century medical techniques demands a certain level of education, and without this many of our people accepted death and disease as part of an ordained pattern.

Just as the colonialists failed to develop our countries, they did little to enlarge our intellectual and social horizons. The reasons they gave for this were as much resented by us as the denial of the advantages. The African, it was maintained, would not appreciate better conditions. He was incapable of education beyond certain limits; he would not respond to the incentives of higher standards of life. All these arguments, produced over and over again in the past, have since been shown to be no more than slander and calumny.

In many parts of our continent, Africans were deliberately barred from attaining necessary skills to raise wages and standards of living. An industrial colour bar has existed. Africans and Europeans doing the same job, as in the Copper Belt, are given very different pay; in most cases Africans are getting about one-tenth of the European equivalent. Conditions in South Africa are too well known to need illustration, though it may come as a surprise to some to learn that in Cato Manor, a suburb of Durban, about 95 per cent of the inhabitants live permanently below the bread line. Even on the Reef, the richest part of the country, 70 per cent have incomes below the essential minimum.[1]

A World Health Organisation report by Dr J. A. Munoz[2] has revealed that in Basutoland the already low standard of living seems to be sinking even lower. The birth-rate which was 30.6 per thousand in 1951, had dropped to 22 per thousand in 1957, it being thought that infertility was due to lack of food. The infant mortality rate doubled between 1951 and 1957, when it reached 116 per thousand children.

European colonization has been responsible for much of the suffering of so many Africans. A recent writer has gone so far as to say that 'imperialist rule, far from bringing about progress, has

[1] Ronald Segal: *The Agony of Apartheid*.
[2] Patrick Duncan: *Contact*, 9 January 1960. Quoted *Africa Digest*, February 1960.

led to a catastrophic *decline* in the standard of living of the African people.'[1] In many parts native agriculture was discouraged in favour of cash crops; soil was ruthlessly exploited, sometimes causing erosion; and millions were turned into low-paid workers. For example, when Dutch settlers first appeared in South Africa they found native tribes of strong, healthy people, who lived by raising cattle, growing corn and hunting wild game. Today the diet of these tribes is almost exclusively corn. 'Laboratory rats fed on a typical African's diet,' according to an article in the *New Scientist*,[2] 'will eat their own offspring.'

It has been argued that Africans are poor because they do not produce enough. But their *capacity* to work must be examined. It is now generally agreed that malignant malnutrition is a major cause of African fatigue. If African labour is 'poor' it is because wages and conditions are poor.

There is, too, the question of incentive. What incentive had the African worker under colonial rule, when his efforts only served to enrich non-Africans? During the last twenty years, African miners have steadily increased the output of copper in Northern Rhodesia; yet every penny of increased wages had to be bitterly fought for. African workers, once they are liberated from colonialism, will soon show the world what they are capable of, in the same way as workers in Russia and China have done. Under the old régimes, Russians and Chinese were thought to be incapable of running a modern industrialized country.

Under colonialism, African workers have no effective bargaining power. Trade unions are frequently disallowed by law, and they are largely unorganized. They have either to accept the pitifully low wages offered to them or suffer the consequences of being without work, which, in certain régimes, makes them liable to a variety of punishments. In South Africa, under the gruesome regulations of *apartheid*, the African worker is hounded and forced into conditions of helotry. Shameful as these are, conditions for Africans in the Portuguese territories probably surpass them though they have not so far received such attention from critics.

For the Portuguese colonies in Africa are slave states, and have

[1] Jack Woddis: *Africa, the Roots of Revolt*, Lawrence & Wishart 1960, p. 166.
[2] 20 August 1959.

always been slave states. Though theoretically abolished in 1875, slavery was still continued by various methods which a Portuguese law of 1899 put into definite legal shape. This law, which is still in force in Angola, provides that 'all natives', that is to say, all Africans, are subject to a 'moral and legal obligation' to acquire by labour the means of subsisting or 'bettering their social condition'. Under this law every African male in Angola, which is in practice interpreted as those above the apparent age of ten years, may be obliged to show any time either that he has worked for six months in the year previous or that he is working. Employers who want forced labour indent to the Governor-General for 'a supply', the term used indiscriminately of goods and men. The Governor-General then allocates a calculated number. Local administrators up and down the country are sent orders to round up the numbers, which is done by threatening the chiefs and headmen. When the required numbers have been brought to the collecting centres, the District Officer enforces a collective contract, which is entered into on behalf of the workers by the chiefs and headmen who have produced the specified numbers.

Less than half of the labour employed in Angola is officially classified by the Portuguese authorities as contract labour, that is, forced labour. Over half of it is theoretically voluntary labour, but in practice the position of the voluntary labourer is not better than that of the forced labourer.

The voluntary labourer cannot leave his job because if he does he will become liable to be classed as 'idle' and therefore subject to forced labour. His only chance of escape is by slipping out of the Portuguese territory and attempting to obtain work in other neighbouring states. Portuguese sources have estimated that in the ten years previous to 1947 over one million people had left the Portuguese colonies by way of clandestine emigration. But not all the people can go, and those who are left behind often bear the brunt for those who have gone. And they have no medium through which they can make their grief known, their sorrows heard; nowhere to turn for mitigation of their plight. When others have been in the same position, there have been those who have raised their voices for them. All over the world we have heard cries for people who are reputed to exist in conditions which would be paradise to the Africans of the Portuguese colonial territories.

In an attempt to cover up this system of slavery, the forced workers are, in theory, paid wages. In fact, however, three-quarters of these wages are deferred until the end of their contract period and are not handed over until the Government has deducted taxation. This is so high that at the end of their period of employment they are left with scarcely any balance at all. For example, in one authenticated case, a man employed in the fishing industry had, after he had worked for four years, a final balance of £3 2s. 6d.

The indescribable misery of Angolan conditions has continuously been brought to the notice of the Portuguese Government, but nothing except paper reforms has been carried out. In 1947 Captain Henrique Galvao, Deputy for Angola in the Portuguese National Assembly and Senior Inspector of Overseas Territories, investigated these conditions on the request of the Portuguese Government and submitted a comprehensive report.

Galvao had been appointed because the Portuguese Government expected from him, as a fervent Government supporter, a whitewashing report which they could use in the United Nations and elsewhere. In fact, Captain Galvao was so shocked by what he saw in Angola that he changed his political views and submitted an honest and balanced account of what was taking place in the Portuguese possessions overseas. As might be imagined, the Portuguese Government did everything possible to suppress the report and Captain Galvao was thrown into prison for his presumption in telling the truth. Ultimately he escaped from Portugal to appear dramatically on the scene in 1961 when he led a band of seventy brave men to seize the Portuguese liner *Santa Maria*.

One of Captain Galvao's chief criticisms of the Portuguese régime was its deceit. In theory and on paper it had abolished forced labour on behalf of private firms and individuals. In fact forced labour was being stepped up. Captain Galvao wrote:

> In some ways the situation is worse than simple slavery. Under slavery, after all, the native is bought as an animal; his owner

prefers him to remain as fit as a horse or an ox. Here the native is not bought, he is hired from the State, although he is called a free man. And his employer cares little if he sickens or dies, once he is working, because when he sickens or dies his employer will simply ask for another.

These opinions he backs up with horrifying statistics showing in some cases a death rate of 40 per cent among the forced labourers.

The situation has recently been made much worse by the introduction of a large settler class. The precarious state of the Portuguese economy at home makes it necessary for Portugal to export its own poverty and to compensate citizens for the work which the State cannot provide them with at home, by dispossessing the African population of the colonies and by providing for Portuguese immigrants land and cheap African labour. Just as the farmers of South Africa are even harsher and crueller employers than are the mine owners and big industrial magnates, so are the Portuguese settlers, in the main, even more ruthless and cruel than the international big-business men who have established themselves in Angola.

The Portuguese consider the continuance of forced labour essential as it helps to feed the neo-colonial economy of neighbouring states and territories. In 1959, the last year for which we have statistics, only one-third of the labour force of nearly half a million workers employed in the South African mines came from within the borders of South Africa.

At the beginning of the century, in the early days of South African mining and before pass laws and the policy of repression of Africans generally had really got under way, it was impossible to recruit in South Africa free labour to work in the mines. The Portuguese colony of Mozambique was used, therefore, as a source of forced labour and in 1903, for example, provided no less than 89 per cent of the total labour force of the South African mines. This supply of conscript labour is still an economic necessity to South Africa if wages are to be kept down and trade unions prohibited.

Accordingly, the South African Government has entered into an actual treaty with the Portuguese Government to supply labour for the mines. The basis of the agreement is that in return for an undertaking by the Portuguese Government that the South African Chamber of Mines shall be the sole recruiting agency in Mozambique for mines labour, the South African Government formally undertakes that 47.5 per cent of the seaborne import traffic to the mining areas of South Africa shall go through the Portuguese harbour of Lourenço Marques. Originally, the maximum figure for labour recruits under the Convention was 90,000 a year. In 1940, however, the Portuguese Government agreed to raise the total to 100,000 a year in return for an Agreement by the South African Government to export 340,000 cases of citrus fruit a year through Lourenço Marques.

The mines where this contract African labour from the Portuguese territories works may be situated in South Africa or in the Rhodesias, but the main shareholders are large financial and commercial groups in the United States, in the United Kingdom, in France and in Belgium. There are, therefore, powerful forces in these and in other countries who are determined to use their political influence to ensure that their countries support Portugal in maintaining its forced labour system and all the tragedies that flow from it.

What happens in regard to labour for the mines so far as South Africa is concerned is merely, of course, an example. The existence of the Portuguese colonies makes cheap labour possible, not only in South Africa, but in all the neighbouring colonial territories and is an important element in the profits not only of mining, but of many other industries, including plantation farming. All those with a financial interest in such enterprises cannot therefore allow Portugal to lose her colonial possessions.

Much of the investment in the Portuguese colonies is not Portuguese at all, but international. The Benguela railway was built largely by British interests to bring out ores from the mines of Katanga. Traversing the great Angola plateau, it passes to a point above Elizabethville in the Congo, and then links up with the Rhodesian railway system, after which it passes on to Beira. Ninety per cent of the stock of the Benguela railway is held by the British holding company of Tanganyika Concessions, domiciled since 1952 in Southern Rhodesia.

Tanganyika Concessions is linked up with the copper interests of Northern Rhodesia and with Union Minière and other industrial concerns in the Congo. Through interlocking directorates, this company is linked with Forminière and certain diamond interests which, together with De Beers, the great South African mining company, control the Angola Diamond Company with mines in the Luanda province. This company is a state within a state. It possesses a prospecting monopoly over five-sixths of Angola and a labour conscription monopoly over most of the Luanda province, one-third the size of Ghana. One half of its profit goes to the state, the other half to the private shareholders. No wonder it can influence policy whichever way it likes and holds in its hands the lives of the Africans of the Luanda province.

For these economic reasons, Portugal can count on heavy backing from vested financial interests throughout the world. Her position in maintaining her colonial dictatorship is, in addition, immensely strengthened by her membership of the North Atlantic Treaty Organization (N.A.T.O.).

It remains to be seen what the effect will be of the vote in the United Nations General Assembly urging Portugal to prepare for self-government in Angola. Experience has led us not to place too much hope in resolutions and votes, but to rely more on positive action. The people of Angola themselves must provide the motive power, and we, the independent African States, must do all we can to help them.

The struggle for independence in the Portuguese colonies has come relatively late partly because of the exceptionally poor state of education there. In Mozambique, the 1950 census revealed 99 per cent illiteracy. In 1954, out of 6 million Africans only 5,000 were in primary schools, 73 in secondary schools, and 42 in industrial training classes. Portuguese officials have boasted that white rule would last longer in their colonial territories, because education has been deliberately held back. An official of the Education Ministry in Lourenço Marques has been quoted as saying: 'Frankly we do not want *many* educated natives, until they have an appropriate social background. They have no place to go. They become dissatisfied. What we want here is a stable society, a stable state. So we move very, very slowly.'[1]

[1] John Gunther: *Inside Africa*, Hamish Hamilton 1955, p. 581.

CHAPTER FIVE

THE INTELLECTUAL VANGUARD

THE HISTORY of human achievement illustrates that when an awakened intelligentsia emerges from a subject people it becomes the vanguard of the struggle against alien rule. There is a direct relation between this fact and the neglect of the imperial powers to provide for the proper growth of educational facilities in their colonies. I saw this connection quite soon in my career, and it was one of the main reasons why I became a teacher for a time.

The tremendous enthusiasm for education in Africa never fails to impress visitors. A schoolboy once wrote: 'I think the happiest event in my life was the day when my father told me to go to school.'[1] Another said: 'The most unfortunate thing that could happen to me would be to have had no education, or to be sent away from school now, for then all my life would be wasted.'[2] The burning desire for education among both children and adults received little encouragement from the colonial powers, and one of the worst legacies of colonialism has been the absence of a trained body of African technicians and administrators.

A brief glimpse at the educational position in various parts of Africa will illustrate my point. In Northern Rhodesia, in 1960, only 43 per cent of African children of school age were at school; and only 1.1 per cent of those who reached the eligible age for secondary education received it. The 1954 report for Southern Rhodesia showed only 16.5 per cent of the school potential actually at school. In Kenya, the Government provided hardly any schools for Africans until the 1930s, so the Kikuyus created their own. They formed the Kikuyu Independent Schools Association. To provide teachers, Peter Koinange founded the

[1] Jack Woddis: *Africa, the Roots of Revolt*, Lawrence & Wishart 1960, p. 157.
[2] *ibid.*

Kenya Teachers' College at Githunguri, where Jomo Kenyatta later became Principal. Not surprisingly, these Kikuyu schools turned out keen nationalists, and they were suppressed by the British after the Mau Mau outbreak in 1952. In 1955 there were only 35 high schools in the entire country for 5½ million Africans.

In the whole of French Equatorial Africa there were about 850 elementary schools, and most of them were badly equipped and staffed. Of the children of school age, only about 18 per cent went to school at all.

As for higher education, until the foundation of the University College at Salisbury incorporated in 1955, Makerere College, founded in 1922, was the only school with university rank in the whole immense distance between Khartoum and Johannesburg. In all the British colonies put together, there were only three other colleges similar to Makerere: Achimota in Ghana, then the Gold Coast, Ibadan in Nigeria, and Fourah Bay in Sierra Leone. In French Africa, south of the Sahara, there was one; in Portuguese Africa, none. The Sudan had Gordon College, and the Belgians opened a small Roman Catholic University outside Leopoldville, at Lovanium.

In the Union, where little more than 30 per cent of African children go to school, there are now very few opportunities for higher education, because the Afrikaner nationalists fear African progress. There were once four universities which accepted Africans, though the total number of graduates every year probably did not exceed 400. But in December 1953 Dr Malan, pursuing the policy of *apartheid*, announced that the Universities of Capetown and Witwatersrand would no longer accept Africans. In May 1955 the all-African College at Fort Hare was closed down as the result of an alleged 'secret authority' among the students.

The problem of education was uppermost in my mind and in the minds of my party when we had our first meeting after taking office under the colonial administration. The fact that most of my colleagues had, like me, been trained as teachers reflected their faith, too, in education as the key to our liberation and advance.

Before we could embark on our plans, we made a review of the situation as we found it. It was not heartening. The picture had changed little since a foremost British authority on colonial affairs, Mr Leonard Barnes, writing in the nineteen-thirties, had this to say about education in the Gold Coast:

> In 1913 education there cost £25,000: in 1931, the peak year, it cost just over a quarter of a million. This is ten times as much, and there can be no objection to calling it such, or to calling it an increase of 900 per cent, if you prefer. The same fact can be stated, though less impressively, by saying that educational expenditure took eighteen years to rise from 3 per cent to 7 per cent of Government revenue. Both forms of statement omit another fact, which is equally relevant, namely, that even in 1931 four Gold-Coast children out of five were receiving no schooling of any kind, and less than half per cent got past the primary stage.... Authorities have calculated that at our present rate of progress it will be 700 years before the natives of even the Gold Coast can read and write their own language. *Note*: Or 3,500 years, if the natural increase of population is taken into account.[1]

It is difficult to appreciate from these observations that the educational system in the Gold Coast was considered to be one of the most advanced in tropical Africa. Our primary education, in fact, goes back as far as 1752 and was begun by missionaries and continued by them for a very long time. After a long period, they received grants-in-aid from the local government, but a good part of the money was used for purely religious purposes and in paying for the salaries of European missionaries. Unfortunately, too, they paid the local teachers irregularly and enforced upon them the purely religious duties of lay preachers, catechists and Sunday school teachers. These faults aside, it must be admitted that we owe a considerable debt of gratitude to the missionaries for the contribution they made to such education as the country received. On their side, however, they did not lose, for in addition to the grants received from government, they charged school fees, and some of them set up bookshops for the sale of religious literature and school text-books. A few, like the Basel Mission, even branched out into trading and have developed into not inconsiderable business concerns. Today the mission bookshops more or less control the importation and

[1] Leonard Barnes: *Empire or Democracy?* Victory Gollancz, Ltd, 1939, p. 141.

distribution of school books, and my Government is faced with the task of establishing other means of getting text-books to our school population which will not be subject to the kind of manipulation which now creates a scramble for these books and a too heavy financial burden upon parents.

There did come a time when colonial administrators found that it was too expensive for the local budget to import British officers for the lower grades of the service, and when the European trading communities discovered a need for African workers with some degree of literacy. The colonial administration then took a hand in providing facilities at primary and secondary levels, though they were niggardly, especially in regard to secondary schools. Little attention was given to technical training, and as a result educated Africans have acquired a bias towards clerical work and a contempt for manual labour.

A fateful consequence of this accent upon a literary education has been the denial to our country of a skilled labour force. I do not refer here to highly qualified specialists, but to our general body of workers. There were no university facilities in the Gold Coast until the college started at Achimota in 1948 and later removed to Legon. Those of our young men who could collect the resources to enable them to pursue higher studies in the United Kingdom in the main went in for law. Apart from the fact that they found an attraction in the wig and gown which are the emblem of this profession, the industrial backwardness of our country, coupled with the reality that they could not find places in the administration – the almost sole employer of such skills – as engineers, doctors, pharmacists, agronomists, accountants, architects, and the rest, discouraged them from training for these professions. Other considerations were the higher cost and increased length of study required for these professions as compared with those required for training in law.

This lopsided state of affairs has created for us one of the biggest of our problems: that is, how to create a skilled labour force and a body of trained technicians in the many fields of modern agriculture, industry, science and economics in the quickest possible time.

When my colleagues and I came into office in 1951, we found some government schools in the principal towns of the country.

But they served only a small part of the urban populations and a minute section of the rural areas. The villages, where most of our people live, boasted few schools; such as there were, were operated mainly by the missions. The number of secondary schools was limited, being based mainly in Cape Coast. These, too, were largely the products of missionary endeavour. There was the large semi-governmental institution at Achimota.

When we confronted the colonial administration with this appalling situation on taking office at the beginning of 1951, they told us that the budget was limited and time was needed. Time, they said, was required to train the army of teachers needed for the education of all the children. They did not look very happy when we pointed out that they seemed to have had time enough to allow the traders and shippers and mining companies to amass huge fortunes. As for the budget, we made the point that it did not seem inequitable to use part of those fortunes to educate the children of the land from which they had been drawn. We were determined, we said, to press for increased expenditure on social services.

I cannot say that in the six years in which we formed a token government under British administration, we were able to register unqualified success with our educational plan. We certainly did go some way towards laying the foundations of a country-wide educational system. The plan which we proposed in the Legislative Assembly in August 1951 provided for the abolition of school fees in the primary schools as an initial step towards a more comprehensive policy of free education. The Roman Catholic hierarchy strongly resented our decision to discontinue the subsidizing out of public funds of new schools owned and managed by religious bodies. It was not our aim, as we pointed out, to prevent the establishment and maintenance of new schools by denominational bodies through voluntary contributions, but they could not look to government for financial support.

At the beginning of 1951, primary school enrolments stood at 125,000. At the beginning of 1952, there were 270,000 children enrolled in our primary institutions and we estimated that this number would reach 400,000 by the beginning of 1957. Actually, at the time of independence in March 1957, the figure had

c

expanded far beyond half a million. We had hoped that by that time our educational programme of teacher training and the erection of buildings and equipment would be able to cater for the anticipated increase. But the increase was greater than we had expected and our output of trained teachers and buildings had not, unfortunately, kept pace with it, even though the training college enrolment had more than doubled over the period.

We had established a system of scholarships and had planned for additional secondary schools. We established the College of Arts, Science and Technology at Kumasi, now the Kwame Nkrumah University, which will provide accommodation for 2,000 students and offer courses in building, engineering, accountancy, agriculture, science and commerce, among other subjects. Teacher training institutions in 1951 produced some 700 new teachers annually, a far too inadequate figure. We managed to establish twelve new training colleges and to double the capacity of four. By 1957, we were turning out some 4,000 new teachers each year, but this left us far behind the 70,000 teachers required to serve the national needs of elementary education.

We achieved some headway in trade and technical education, increasing the annual enrolment in six years from 600 to some 2,000, a considerable gain, but woefully short of need. With secondary school education we could do very little. Administrative budget for these needs was minimal, and we just did not have the time to train teachers to the standard required for secondary school instruction. The two institutions of learning, the University College at Legon and the College of Technology at Kumasi, continued to take in more students each year and we were able to improve and expand their services.

There was enough material in these records from which attractive brochures could be compiled by the Colonial Office to present to the United Nations showing how much was being done to introduce education to the 'primitive peoples of West Africa'. They were often accompanied by pretty pictures of schools and happy children at play in the grounds. They may well have impressed the outsider. They were of small comfort to us, when we sat down in March 1957 to consider, not what we had done, but what remained to be done to give every child in Ghana his real birthright of independence – a basic education.

Over and beyond this, we needed to plan an educational system that will be more in keeping with the requirements of the economic and social progress for which our new development plans are aiming. Our pattern of education has been aligned hitherto to the demands of British examination councils. Above all, it was formulated and administered by an alien administration desirous of extending its dominant ideas and thought processes to us. We were trained to be inferior copies of Englishmen, caricatures to be laughed at with our pretensions to British bourgeois gentility, our grammatical faultiness and distorted standards betraying us at every turn. We were neither fish nor fowl. We were denied the knowledge of our African past and informed that we had no present. What future could there be for us? We were taught to regard our culture and traditions as barbarous and primitive. Our text-books were English text-books, telling us about English history, English geography, English ways of living, English customs, English ideas, English weather. Many of these manuals had not been altered since 1895.

All this has to be changed. And it is a stupendous task. Even the ordering of text-books is an involved matter that makes the introduction of new ones with a Ghanaian character a prolonged affair. This is something that we are, however, getting on with, as it is vital that we should nurture our own culture and history if we are to develop that African personality which must provide the educational and intellectual foundations of our Pan-African future.

CHAPTER SIX

FREEDOM FIRST

IT IS my deep conviction that all peoples wish to be free, and that the desire for freedom is rooted in the soul of every one of us. A people long subjected to foreign domination, however, does not always find it easy to translate that wish into action. Under arbitrary rule, people are apt to become lethargic; their senses are dulled. Fear becomes the dominant force in their lives; fear of breaking the law, fear of the punitive measures which might result from an unsuccessful attempt to break loose from their shackles. Those who lead the struggle for freedom must break through this apathy and fear. They must give active expression to the universal longing to be free. They must strengthen the peoples' faith in themselves, and encourage them to take part in the freedom struggle. Above all, they must declare their aims openly and unmistakably, and organize the people towards the achievement of their goal of self-government.

The essential forger of the political revolution is a strong, well-organized, broadly based political party, knit together by a programme that is accepted by all the members, who also submit themselves to the party's discipline. Its programme should aim for 'Freedom first'. 'Seek ye first the political kingdom,' became the principal slogan of the Convention People's Party, for without political independence none of our plans for social and economic development could be put into effect.

There has been a good deal of talk about dependent territories making themselves viable before attempting to take upon themselves the responsibilities of self-government. That is precisely what they cannot do. As long as the government of less developed countries remains in the hands of colonial administrators, their economies are set to a pattern determined by the interests, not of the indigenous inhabitants but of the national beneficiaries of the ruling country. Improvement in living conditions for the bulk of the people will not come until political power passes into their hands.

Thus, every movement for independence in a colonial situation contains two elements: the demand for political freedom and the revolt against poverty and exploitation. Resolute leadership is required to subordinate the understandable desire of the people for better living conditions to the achievement of the primary aim of the abolition of colonial rule.

Before the Second World War, a number of political demonstrations and strikes took place in various parts of colonial Africa. The most common demands were for reforms; few people envisaged at that time the emergence of national political parties demanding independence.

During the 1940s, however, many African national organizations were formed. For example, in 1944, the National Council of Nigeria and the Cameroons was founded, and, in the same year, the Nyasaland National Congress.[1] Two years later, the Kenya African Union was formed; and the Rassemblement Democratique Africain, a federation of the various organizations which had developed throughout the French colonies in West and Equatorial Africa. There followed, in 1947, the formation of the Northern Rhodesian African National Congress;[2] and, in our country the United Gold Coast Convention, with its aim: self-government in the shortest possible time. On 12 June 1949, came the split with the U.G.C.C. when I founded the Convention People's Party with the declared aim of achieving 'Self-Government Now'.

The 1950s saw the emergence of the Uganda National Congress (1952), the Tanganyika African National Union (1953), and the African National Congress in Southern Rhodesia.[3] There were also national organizations formed in the

[1] This was banned in 1958 and the Malawi Congress Party set up in its place.

[2] When the Central African Federation was formed in 1953, this party split up, and others emerged, e.g. The United National Independence Party under Kenneth Kaunda in 1958.

[3] This was originally founded in 1920. It was banned in 1959, and the National Democratic Party was formed.

Congo. In Portuguese Africa, the União dos Populacãos de Angola and the Movemento Popular de Libertacão de Angola were formed. Eventually, in 1959, they merged to form the African Revolutionary Front Against Portuguese Colonialism. This organization includes supporters in Mozambique and Portuguese Guinea.

I have mentioned only a few of the many African political organizations formed during and after the Second World War. There are many others. Their structure, organization, and the quality of their leadership, have varied, but all have had in common the determination to struggle for the abolition of colonial rule and the improvement of economic and social conditions.

On the eve of the Second World War, only Liberia, Ethiopia and Egypt were independent. But by the end of 1959, that is, twenty years later, there were nine independent African States: Egypt, Sudan, Morocco, Tunisia, Libya, Liberia, Ethiopia, Ghana and Guinea. In 1960, Nigeria, the Congo, French Togoland, French Cameroons and Somalia achieved independence. They were followed, in 1961, by Sierra Leone, Tanganyika, Uganda and Nyasaland. The independence of Kenya, Northern Rhodesia and Zanzibar cannot long be delayed.

This fundamental change in the African situation has been brought about by the struggles and sacrifices of the African peoples themselves, and nothing can now stop the rushing tide of nationalism. As long as a single foot of African soil remains under foreign domination, the battle must continue.

It may be that the time has come to have a common political party with a common aim and programme. For instance, instead of the Convention People's Party in Ghana, there might be the Ghana People's Party. In Kenya, the progressive party could be the Kenya People's Party; in Guinea, the Guinea People's Party, and so on; each party having one common aim and objective, the freedom and unity of Africa.

The various People's Parties, with their common aim, would co-operate with each other. A central organization would undoubtedly be necessary, and also a highly-trained headquarters staff. If this kind of solidarity on the party political level could be achieved, it would surely strengthen African continental freedom and unity.

Party leaders in countries which are still not free would be able to derive strength and inspiration from close association with their opposite numbers in independent countries. Though beset by difficulties, they would gain confidence from being part of a strong continental organization with immense resources, which they could draw upon in time of need. From its inception, the Convention People's Party declared in its constitution that it would 'seek to establish fraternal relations with, and offer guidance and support to all nationalist, democratic and socialist movements, in Africa and elsewhere, which are fighting for national independence and self-determination!'

Among independent countries the common party would act as a unifying force. Also, if a common domestic policy could be worked out it would help immeasurably in the planning and development of the African continent as a whole, in the economic and social spheres.

The unevenness of development in Africa, both political and economic, is a major problem. Some countries are poor in natural resources; others rich. Some achieved independence comparatively easily, and peacefully; others are still struggling. The obvious solution is unity, so that development can be properly and cohesively planned.

Countries under alien rule achieve independence in different ways. India was promised freedom by 'steady evolution towards self-government in ordered constitutional stages'. In fact it took twenty-seven years of civil commotion and passive disobedience for India to achieve her aim. Libya was granted independence by the United Nations Organization as a direct result of Italy's defeat in the Second World War. The Portuguese colony of Goa was liberated by India. Several countries in the Middle East owe their existence as separate states to the Western powers, when they carved up the Ottoman Empire after the First World War.

In Africa, the nature of the freedom struggle has varied according to the background conditions against which it has had to operate and the position of the international scene at a given time.

Generally, in territories where there is a settler problem, the struggle has been more prolonged and sometimes violent, as in Kenya during the Mau Mau period. Where there is no settler problem, as in West Africa, the struggle has been hard, though on the whole peaceful and constitutional. I have already told how independence was achieved in Ghana.[1]

Looking back, and trying to determine the reasons for the successful outcome of our struggle for freedom, one factor stands out above all others, namely, the strength of a well-organized political party, representative of the broad mass of the people. The Convention People's Party represented the ordinary, common folk who wanted social justice and a higher standard of living. It kept in daily, living touch with the ordinary mass of people it represented, unlike the opposition, which was supported by a galaxy of lawyers and members of other conservative professions, the self-styled 'aristocracy' of the Gold Coast. They did not understand the new mood of the people, the growing nationalism and the revolt against economic hardship. Thinking that their lofty assertions were enough to win adherents to their ranks, they made little effort to come into close contact with the masses in the way that I had done in my early days as secretary of the U.G.C.C., and continued through my years of leadership of the C.P.P. As a matter of fact, when the leaders of the U.G.C.C. discovered that I had spearheaded a mass movement, they recoiled in fright. That was something they had not bargained for. They had wanted me to build up a movement whose ranks would not question their self-assumed right to political leadership, but would nevertheless provide a solid enough base for them to pose as the national champions in pressing for constitutional change. It was when the leaders of the U.G.C.C. demanded I get rid of the mass following I had built up, that I withdrew from their secretariat, and formed the Convention People's Party. Unwilling to come down to the masses, whom they scorned as 'flotsam and jetsam', it was not surprising that those leaders failed to make headway with the ordinary people, and were constantly rejected by them.

In the early years of the C.P.P., and frequently since, I urged members to follow the advice of the Chinese:

[1] In my autobiography, *Ghana*. Thomas Nelson & Sons 1957.

Go to the people
Live among them
Learn from them
Love them
Serve them
Plan with them
Start with what they know
Build on what they have.

This would be my advice to members of any nationalist and progressive Party.

The campaign of the Convention People's Party was helped by the press. On the very day I left the U.G.C.C. the first issue of my paper *The Accra Evening News* was published, with its challenging motto: 'We prefer self-government with danger to servitude in tranquillity.' I reached a wide circle of readers through the columns of this paper, and hammered home the message of full self-government and the need to organize for victory: 'The strength of the organized masses is invincible. . . . We must organize as never before, for organization decides everything.'[1]

The whole question of publicity, the spreading of information about the aims and achievements of any political party, is of supreme importance. In the struggle for independence, where the colonial government controls the major avenues of information and gives its blessing to the reactionary press, the mechanics of propaganda employed by the freedom movement are vital. The reach of the press is, of course, narrower in areas where there is a high degree of illiteracy; but even in those areas the people can always be reached by the spoken word. And frequently the written word becomes the spoken word.

A popular anti-colonial press developed in Africa during the 1930s. In 1932, Habib Bourguiba founded the *Action Tunisienne*. In Morocco, the *Action du Peuple* edited by Muhammad Hasan el-Ouezzani appeared in August, 1938; the editorial committee contained the nucleus of the leadership of Morocco's Comité d'Action Marocaine. In the Ivory Coast *L'Eclaireur de la Côte d'Ivoire* began in 1935. Three years later, in 1938, Dr Nnamdi

[1] The *Accra Evening News*, 14 January 1949.

Azikiwe's *West African Pilot* prepared the ground for the independence movement in Nigeria.

These, and other newspapers, have undoubtedly helped in the spread of African nationalism. They have emphasized the need for 'freedom first' and then development. If we are to banish colonialism utterly from our continent, every African must be made aware of his part in the struggle. Freedom involves the untiring efforts of every one engaged in the struggle for it. The vast African majority must be accepted as the basis of government in Africa.

CHAPTER SEVEN

ACHIEVING OUR SOVEREIGNTY

IT IS becoming axiomatic that colonial powers do not willingly retire from political control over any given land. Before they go they make superhuman efforts to create schisms and rivalries which they hope to exploit after they have gone. India, with its division into two separate parts, leaving its sad legacy of communalism and religious feuding, is the most glaring example. But the rifts in Burma, Ceylon, The Cameroons, Viet-Nam, the breaking down of the two federations of French West Africa and French Equatorial Africa into separate states of the French Community, all stand as eloquent witnesses to this extended policy of 'divide and rule'. So also does the federal division of Nigeria into three regions, where the British administration had previously most carefully built up a unitary form of government out of a vast conglomeration of different peoples.

Looked at superficially, it is difficult to understand the ways of the colonial powers. They will not leave Africa alone, even when they realize full well that they are clutching at a straw in trying to prevent the total and final liquidation of the colonial system. They act as if the right to meddle in the internal affairs of newly-emergent states is still theirs, and even presume to dictate which things are right and which are wrong among the acts performed by us. Examined closely, these manœuvres are seen to be part of the strategy of 'divide and rule', wielded from afar.

During our struggle for independence, and even after, all the armoury of the British press was brought into play against me and against the Convention People's Party. Special correspondents were sent to discover that we 'were not only Communist, but deep in bribery and corruption'. They came to interpret the tussle between the C.P.P. and the National Liberation Movement over the issue of our Constitution as one of dictatorial ambition on our part against the disinterested effort of our opponents to secure a democratic form of government. The raising by the N.L.M. of the demand for federation was eagerly seized upon as a hopeful means of fragmenting our small and largely homogeneous country.

In April 1955, I had put the issue of a federal form of government before a Select Committee, after having allowed the Opposition the privilege of five seats in our Constituent Assembly when they were legally entitled to two. The Committee's report decided against a federated government. In order to ensure the widest democratic acceptance of a constitution for independence, I sought a Constitutional Adviser through the British Government and in September, Sir Frederick Bourne came to advise on the devolution of powers and functions to the regions. We agreed that there should be decentralization of certain powers to the regions and, on the basis of Sir Frederick's work, we felt confident of majority support for our proposals when we put them forward. The Secretary of State had laid down two conditions as the prerequisite for the grant of independence: that a substantial majority of the people should show their desire for independence in the very near future and that they should agree upon a constitution that would meet their needs and be workable. Sir Frederick Bourne came back again as Constitutional Adviser to the conference which opened at Achimota on 16 February 1956 to examine his recommendations. All political parties, traditional councils and other appropriate bodies were invited to attend. The conference report agreed upon almost all of Sir Frederick's recommendations and made the proposal that there should be a House of Chiefs in each region of the country to discuss social and cultural legislation.

However, the N.L.M., in spite of the untiring efforts I made to secure their co-operation, had refused to take part in the deliberations and absented themselves from the proceedings. The terms of the Secretary of State, therefore, had not been fully met, which had been the opposition's purpose. Hence we were made to submit to the general election of 1956, which confirmed the C.P.P. ascendancy and the desire of the overwhelming majority of the people for independence and a unitary form of government, which was the platform on which we went to the country.

People who are independent, free and sovereign make their own constitution. Although Ghana achieved what is called 'full independence' on 6 March 1957, there were certain provisions in the constitution imposed on us which limited the full employment of our freedom, which were an affront to our sovereignty, a fetter upon our free development. These were the entrenched clauses which the British Government insisted upon writing into the constitution as a condition of our accession to independence. We raised our arguments against their inclusion, but the concern in British official quarters for the protection of minority rights and the welfare of British civil servants in Ghanaian employ outweighed consideration for the prerogatives of our independence and the expressed will of our people. Our resentment at being forced to accept what was partially a dictated constitution in order to keep the time-table of independence that we had given to our people, was made quite plain by me and my Government, as was our determination to divest ourselves of the objectionable clauses as soon as we were in a position to do so constitutionally.

When it was found in 1956 that it would be impossible to delay full independence much longer, negotiations were started to frame the constitution by which an independent Ghana would be governed. My Government was then a Government largely in name, ultimate power residing in the Governor of the Gold Coast, who really represented the Colonial Office on the spot. Until the moment when the instrument of independence was actually placed in our hands, freedom could be denied us. Our stand that independence involved the right of the local population alone to determine the nature of the laws, regulations and procedures of their State through their parliamentary institutions, was discountenanced. The British argument was that they held in sacred trust the rights of all the people in the Gold Coast, and it was incumbent upon them to safeguard the position of a section of the population, albeit a minority, which might be opposed to the existing Government. This we considered a somewhat grotesque premise and sought in vain for a precedent in special protection of minority opposition to the reigning Government of Britain. We protested our ability to safeguard the rights of our own people and were resentful of the doubts cast on our intentions. I posed the suggestion that if my Government could be suspected of ulterior intentions towards our political opponents, we were equally open to the suspicion that we might abrogate the imposed constitution on the morrow of British departure. Where, then, was the purpose of negotiating a constitution? Why not let us frame our own Constitution?

The British Government was adamant. They made it un-equivocally clear that unless we entered into constitutional negotiations they would take no further steps towards the grant of independence. This was the atmosphere in which we met and the mood in which the constitution emerged that was to tie the future of Ghana. It saw the light of day, indeed, not as a legal instrument from our own Ghanaian Assembly, but as a British Order in Council. Its official title was 'The Ghana (Constitution) Order in Council, 1957' of the British Government. It was published by the British Government on 22 February 1957.

Some might charge that there was a good deal of emotionalism involved in our attitude to the manner of the framing of our constitution for independence. Reviewing it with the dis-passionate objectiveness of three years of government under its provisions, we are reinforced in our conviction that only im-perialist arrogance could have decided that entrenched clauses are irremovable, even under such constitutional stringencies as those by which the British sought to tie us down. Perhaps we were regarded as too stupid to be able to extricate ourselves by constitutional means from the strait-jacket of the 'Special procedure for passing Bills relating to the Constitution and other important matters', in which the British strapped us with the freedom that they 'gave'. The British Government had decided that constitutional change should be made as difficult as possible for us, indeed almost impossible.

Clause 32 of our independence constitution allowed that

No Bill for the amendment, modification, repeal or re-enact-ment of the constitutional provisions of Ghana . . . shall be presented for Royal Assent unless it has endorsed on it a certi-ficate under the hand of the Speaker that the number of votes cast in favour thereof at the third meeting of the Assembly amounted to not less than two-thirds of the whole number of Members of Parliament.

In short, a simple parliamentary majority could not change any part of the constitution, nor even a two-thirds majority of members present and voting. There had to be a supporting vote from two-thirds of the total membership of the Assembly. Our opposition was not even obliged to be present at the debate on a Bill for constitutional change. Merely by the fact of being an opposition it could, if its numbers were large enough, destroy any likelihood of constitutional change. This is surely giving an odd twist to the democratic principle.

As a matter of fact, the popularity of the Government in the country, and the strength of the C.P.P. in the National Assembly, were such that we could have changed its terms absolutely in accord with the constitution, shortly after becoming free in 1957. The C.P.P. enjoyed a parliamentary majority which would have given us the required over-all two-thirds vote; and that majority increased as time went on. We would have been well within our rights to present a Bill to the Assembly scrapping 'The Ghana (Constitution) Order in Council, 1957'. This, however, I was reluctant to do. Public opinion, both at home and abroad, is not normally so well-informed and so equipped with detailed information on constitutional matters that it would have understood the absolute legality of our action. The issue would at once have become controversial and the idea spread that we were guilty of a breach of faith. It was no part of my purpose to start our existence as an independent country clouded by the suspicion that we had broken a contract, irrespective of the moral duress under which we had signed it. Knowledge of this duress, in any event, was not public. Having consideration for all the factors involved, we decided that we would let the constitution stand and respect all its clauses. We would proceed to procure its alteration when the appropriate occasion presented itself, in conformity with its terms.

Meantime, our first duty was to ensure the unity of the nation and its tranquillity, in order to go forward with our tasks of development.

The unrest which prevailed in certain parts of the country at the launching of our independence was not made any less by the provisions relating to the setting up of Regional Assemblies and the powers to be invested in them. The British negotiators of our constitution were more amenable to the federal aspirations of the Opposition than to the C.P.P. which represented the wishes of the majority of the people. The Opposition view was prompted by motives of political separatism, and these were reflected in the constitutional clauses relating to the establishment of Regional Assemblies.

In the same way, every opportunity was provided by the constitution for cramping our development endeavours. In communications, for instance, the Government might decide on a trunk road that would pass through several Regions. Opposition by the Regional Assembly of one affected Region could hold up the project indefinitely. As part of its national health scheme, the Government might determine the sites on which hospitals and clinics should be built. The Regional Assemblies could object to and obstruct these plans, in keeping with their constitutional authority over the regional health and medical services.

It was laid down that 'in each Region there shall be a Head of the Region, who, except in the case of the Ashanti Region, shall be chosen by the House of Chiefs in the Region'. No democratic principle was to be employed but use made instead of the outmoded procedure current under the colonial system of Indirect Rule which gave authority to compliant chiefs. If the chiefs of a certain Region happened to be opposed to modern health methods and medical practices, they could effectively block any Government programmes involving up-to-date treatment of disease in their area, for the restrictions of the constitution would safeguard them. Extend this to education, public works, housing, agricultural and industrial development, and it can be accepted that the central Government would have been in the position of possessing merely token sovereignty. Our hands and feet would be virtually bound the moment we attempted to govern.

The ground, it can be seen, was well laid for the promotion of disunity and fragmentation. The clue to the British purpose was really contained in the phrase, 'except in the case of the Ashanti Region'. Throughout the provisions relating to Regional

Assemblies, Ashanti was omitted and special regulations were introduced giving it powers superior to those of the other Regions. Everywhere else the head of the Region was to be chosen by the House of Chiefs. In Ashanti, the constitution specifically stated that 'the Asantehene shall be the Head of the Ashanti Region'. What kind of democracy were the British laying down on the eve of their departure, in designating the person who was to be the effective governor of a particular Region? Where was the respect for our sovereignty? Our independence was supposed to give us sovereignty over our own affairs. But there we were, a democratic Government, limited by constitutional provisions, designed by the retiring power, to a designated individual to conduct the highest executive post in the most delicate national territory. It was so openly a device to concede to the opposition party the opportunities they had been deprived of by their defeat at the polls that it was difficult to believe the British could have been so deceitful to their much-vaunted respect for democracy.

The choice of the Asantehene for this special elevation was deliberate. He was known to share the views of the National Liberation Movement, whose politics of violence had made our final steps to independence so immensely difficult. Considerable suspicion as to his original connections with the Movement had been current since its inception, because his chief linguist, the man closest to him in the affairs of the Ashanti state, was a founder member and its Chairman. The Asantehene had worked well with the British, even though his uncle Prempeh I had fought them in the Ashanti wars earlier in the century and had been exiled to the Seychelles islands for his African patriotism. For his services to the British in carrying out their colonial rule, the Asantehene had been knighted. His position as the spiritual and temporal head of Ashanti gave him the influence of a feudal lord over all the chiefs of the Region and over the local people, and made him extremely powerful. By seeking to safeguard his continued authority in the new Ghana through specific clauses in the constitution, the British were not only repaying him for services rendered and making good in part the promise of the N.L.M. to crown him King of Ghana, but were entrenching the greatest focal point of disintegration within our new state. This was a most dangerous situation and a limitation upon our power as a fully independent Government that we could not accept. It would have amounted to the exclusion of Ashanti from the sphere of Ghana's sovereignty. It was unthinkable we should lay ourselves open to this possibility and so endanger the future of the country.

Observing the provisions of the constitution, which set out that Regional Assemblies 'shall be established by act of Parliament in and for each Region', I named a commission of inquiry to examine the means by which they should be set up and the most efficient methods for their conduct. The commission took some time making its considerations and reporting back, and meantime we proceeded in Parliament with other, more urgent matters. Among these, regional needs were well to the forefront, and I am certain that the development schemes we have introduced so far in each of the Regions go far beyond anything that would have been accomplished if left solely to local initiative.

Old-established democracies are equipped for wide decentralization. They possess skilled and experienced local bodies to carry out urgent development tasks that would otherwise be the concern of the central Government. A new country, where there is strong national but limited local leadership and vigour, cannot afford to gamble on the ability or incompetence of a regional body to develop its Region. A new country needs to initiate central nation-wide planning fitting the required activities of each Region into the over-all programme. It cannot allow the programme to be held up by a dilatory or backward or obstructive Regional Assembly. Provision must naturally be made for local authorities with powers to carry out local development projects in co-operation with or under the guidance of the central Government. We suggested this to the British during our constitutional negotiations, but they insisted on the creation of Regional Assemblies with powers wide enough to impinge on those of the central Government, and with tight safeguards making modification virtually impossible. The only thing they failed to do was to include a date by which the Assemblies were to be established, and this was the loophole that we used to allay the tensions in the country and prepare the ground for the removal of what we regarded as an obstructive mechanism in the way of our development.

By the time the commission of inquiry into the setting up of Regional Assemblies had made its report and the Assemblies were established, the strides which the country was making in all directions and the mood of the people had brought most of the chiefs to a recognition of the sincerity of the Government and its development aims. Even the Asantehene began to show a startling change in attitude, and I know that he is now completely identified with our independence and shares the hopes and aspirations of the new Ghana. In this atmosphere of national unity, the newly-created Regional Assemblies met and voted themselves out of existence. Through the constitutional procedure, which we faithfully followed, the instruments were eliminated which the British had devised to keep us divided and backward. The establishment and dissolution of the Regional Assemblies opened the way to constitutional changes in other directions.

CHAPTER EIGHT

PROBLEMS OF GOVERNMENT

IN OUR struggle for freedom, parliamentary democracy was as vital an aim as independence. The two were inseparable. It was not our purpose to rid the country of the colonial régime in order to substitute an African tyranny. We wanted to free our people from arbitrary rule, and to give them the freedom to choose the kind of government they felt would best serve their interests and enhance their welfare. Our struggle was fought to make our people free to practise the religion they chose, to give them the liberty to associate in whatever groups they wished, to create an atmosphere in which they could say, write and think freely, without harming their neighbour or jeopardizing the state.

We introduced principles basic to the settled and established democracies of the world, such as the separation of powers between the executive, the legislature and the judiciary. As the repository of the people's will, the legislature is supreme. It is sovereign and unlimited in its enactment of laws, which are binding upon the people and the government. Election to the legislature is by universal adult suffrage, and men and women enjoy equality of rights and duties. That all persons in the state are equal before the law is another principle well enshrined in our constitution.

The government on the other hand has the responsibility of directing the affairs of the state and of initiating and executing policy. It is, however, at all times answerable to the legislature and could not rule unless it commanded a majority in parliament. For all legislation it initiates becomes the law of the land only if approved by parliament, and parliament can at any time it wishes throw out the government.

All of this is the recognized machinery of parliamentary rule in the old-established democracies. In our conditions, as an ex-colonial country, with our existing pattern of tribal loyalties and traditional customs strained by the superimposition of other loyalties and practices, it could not be regarded as extraordinary if the pattern proved too tight here and there, or too loose in other places. Members of the maturer democracies will tend naturally to equate our conditions with those current in their own country, forgetting the time it took their nation to evolve to its present standard, and forgetting, too, the economic and social conditions of our people. It is natural for people to look at another country through their own telescope and quite human to judge another's achievements or failings by their own experience.

There is a tendency to forget that Britain's evolution into democracy was not altogether peaceful. It was a little over three hundred years ago that they chopped off the head of a king, made their middle-class revolution and installed Cromwell as their dictator. The feudal ties were not completely broken and it required another revolution more than two centuries later, with its accompanying social jolts, to secure the base of that parliamentary democracy which the British people today mistakenly assume as a merit inherent in their national character. The states of America fought a bitter civil war, whose memories still condition attitudes and thinking, to impose their union. Its constitution, based upon the affirmation of the equality of all men, took several years to find full acceptance, and even today its tenets are disregarded in many parts of the country. There is still strife in America over the application of the essence of democracy to all of its members.

Conditions in Ghana today are comparable with those prevailing in Britain or France or America at the time when they were struggling to establish a free form of government, rather than those which currently obtain in those countries. It would be fairer, therefore, to ask what was the nature of the régime in those countries then and make the appropriate adjustments for the development of liberal ideas in the world since those days. The economic position of our people is no better than that of the workers in Britain at the same stage of their social and political development, perhaps a little worse in some aspects. Their social services were just as primitive, their country-wide educational

standards just as low. I think no one would deny that the maintenance of a democracy by the people of Europe and America
at the parallel stage would have been a massive task. Yet it is the
task we faced in Ghana on our assumption of independence.

This task might have been eased a little had we been blessed
with a reasonable and not violently destructive opposition. A
serious, well-intentioned opposition keeps a government alive
to its responsibilities, guarantees extreme care in the preparation and formulation of programmes, and underlines the
need for sponsors of legislation to be able to justify their proposals.

The essence of such discussion, if it is to be of benefit, is that it
must be constructive. This is the strength of the opposition in the
established democracies of the world. They recognize that they,
together with the government of the day, proceed from the
major premise that they have a joint aim, to advance the welfare
of the people. Both have a vital part to play in the building of
their country and the speeding of its development. The government initiates; the opposition is constructively critical.

Unfortunately this has not been the case in Ghana. The
narrowest interpretation of the term 'opposition' has been the
guiding principle for the opposition party both inside and outside Parliament. Their repeated rejection by the electorate convinced them that the possibility of gaining office by constitutional means was remote. They therefore embarked on a policy of
obstructing the government, without devising a programme on
which they would base an alternative one. Their politics have
been narrowly regional in concept, and often violent, abusive and
terroristic in action. Within Parliament, the castigation of the
cabinet has been, to them, an end in itself rather than an instrument for securing better conditions for the people. The measure
of their intent is that they seek to add to the difficulties of government and heighten the obstacles which need to be overcome so
that, with a breakdown in administration, they may get a chance
of grasping the reins of office.

It may be argued that some of these characteristics are present
in any opposition party. This is true, but not to the same extent
as in Ghana. Elsewhere they are set in the context of an alternative over-all programme of government. The Labour Party
in Britain, for example, follows a political doctrine opposed to

that of the Conservative Party. Ideologically they are widely removed. There are clashes over such concepts as nationalization. There remain, however, broad areas of internal and foreign affairs where there is a community of view. The opposition will make helpful suggestions but will not irresponsibly oppose. Therein lies the strength of that democracy.

The opposition in Ghana cannot boast this same sense of responsibility and maturity. So far it has been mostly destructive. We have seen the historic reasons for this in the revulsion of the United Gold Coast Convention leaders from the mass movement I had achieved as their secretary, and the subsequent formation of the Convention People's Party to embrace that mass movement as the instrument for the achievement of freedom. The U.G.C.C. leaders never forgave me and my associates for proving the rightness of our policy of 'Self-Government Now' in the results of the 1951 election. Thereafter their opposition amounted to a virtual denial of independence and a reluctance for the British to leave. They were prepared to sacrifice our national liberation if that would keep me and my colleagues out of government.

In colonial countries endeavouring to throw off the yoke of imperialism, the upsurge of nationalism finds expression in a major movement embracing the popular aspirations for freedom and a better way of life. Even where there is some disagreement among different local groups over the means to be employed in the attainment of freedom, the force which is brought into operation by the presiding power frequently secures their union on a broad national front. Thus the nationalist movement represents the majority of the population. Those dissident groups pursuing individual or particularist aims opposed to the nationalist objectives are doomed to frustration. It is inevitable, therefore, that on a free franchise of universal adult suffrage, the nationalist party gets elected with a majority that makes it appear to those accustomed to the more evenly balanced bipartisan politics of, for instance, Britain and America, that intimidation has been used.

I am reminded of the words of Julius Nyerere when he spoke of the overwhelming support of the nationalist movement by the people of Tanganyika: 'The Nationalist movement which fights

for and achieves independence inevitably forms the government of the new state. It would surely be ridiculous to expect
that a country should voluntarily divide itself for the sake of con-
forming to a particular expression of democracy, and to do so
during a struggle which calls for the complete unity of its people.
No one should jump to the conclusion that such a country is not
democratic or does not intend to be democratic.'[1]

The popularity of the party that brings freedom continues
into the period of full independence and is even enhanced where
improvements in economic and social conditions are obtained
under its government, and its majority grows. Since this overwhelming majority in parliament carries through the government's policy almost without exception, it gives the appearance
of a one-party regime. This is the pattern which has resulted in
the states emerging from colonialism, a pattern which I have
termed a People's Parliamentary Democracy and which the
people of Ghana have accepted.

However, to level against us, as a result of this situation, the
criticism of authoritarianism, as has been done, would seem to
suggest a contradiction in the Western idea of what constitutes
democracy. Democracy, if we are to accept the Aristotelian
description, is the law of the state that directs 'that our poor
shall be in no greater subjection than the rich; nor that the
supreme power shall be lodged with either of these, but that both
shall share it. For if liberty and equality, as some persons suppose, are chiefly to be found in a democracy, it must be so by
every department of government being alike open to all; but
as the people are a majority, and what they vote is law, it follows
that such a state must be a democracy.' This description has not
been invalidated because our modern world has outgrown the
city state and 'all the people' can no longer conveniently participate in government but delegate their right to their parliamentary representatives. The description has, indeed, been re-
validated and enlarged to its widest extremity in Lincoln's concept of 'government of the people by the people for the people'.

The impression that my Party and I drew from much of the
criticism levelled against us was that we should have divided up
the mandate given to us by the people and handed over part of

[1] James Cameron: *The African Revolution*, Thames & Hudson 1961, p. 186.

it to an opposition. If the will of the people is democratically expressed in an overwhelming majority for the governing party, and thereby creates a weakening of the accepted two-party pattern, as, for instance, in Ghana, we, the government, are obliged to respect the will of the people so expressed. We have no right to divide our mandate in defiance of the popular will.

The opposition, deprived of popular support, looked around for a means to undermine our authority. They found it in separatism. They demanded the virtual secession of Ashanti, the Northern Region, and what was formerly British Togoland, from the sphere of central Ghanaian authority. It was not their first attempt to cut off the nose and ears of the Motherland in order to spite the face of the C.P.P. In 1956, when there was a plebiscite in British Togoland to determine whether it was to continue as a British Trust territory or to join with the Gold Coast and soon become a part of independent Ghana, the opposition party proclaimed its support for Togoland's continuance as a British Trust territory. The people of Togoland proved to be more freedom-minded than our opposition and the plebiscite result was union with us. When we gained full independence, British Togoland became a part of free Ghana.

There followed after the plebiscite the general election of 1956, to which I had reluctantly agreed in order not to prejudice the early grant of independence. This election brought the C.P.P. back for the third time with an overwhelming majority. The opposition had not done as well as they maintained they would do in Ashanti and the Northern Territories, even though these were their major strongholds, where they had the backing of the Asantehene and other leading chiefs. The C.P.P. gained more than a third of the seats in Ashanti and almost half in the Northern Territories. In the rest of the country we had a landslide. We had proved indisputably that we were the only party qualified to speak in a national sense. The British Government could not deny this proof, and independence followed.

CHAPTER NINE

BRINGING UNITY IN GHANA

THE RESOUNDING victory of the C.P.P. at the 1956 polls so weakened the opposition that they decided to assert themselves outside the democratic framework. Their agitation in Ashanti, in the Northern Region and in Togoland, had already led to serious clashes, often developing into armed violence, in which some C.P.P. workers were actually murdered. As our independence dawned, we were placed in the anomalous position of having to send the forces of law into now free Togoland to quell armed disturbances. These outbreaks were fomented with the purpose of discrediting me and my government. They gave the impression that we were not in control of the country, that we were not a popular government, that there was widespread discontent.

In a country just emerging from colonial rule, there are many ills to right, many problems to solve. Time and money and expert knowledge are required to deal with them. The end of the colonial administration in Ghana left us, moreover, with a low level of education among the bulk of our people, and no system of universal education. Such a public is easy prey for unscrupulous politicians. It is amenable to demagogic appeals and readily exploitable by eloquence that arouses the emotions rather than reason. It was not difficult for the opposition in these conditions to discover grounds of dissatisfaction in which to plant and water the seeds of resentment and grievance. In Accra, they worked upon the tribal feelings of the Ga people and related them to the shortage of housing. They encouraged the formation of the Ga Shifimo Kpee, a strictly tribal organization, in our capital that was fast becoming cosmopolitan; they fomented separatism in Ashanti and dissension in the North. They tried to demonstrate to the world that they, the opposition, had been right in insisting that we were not ripe for independence.

Ghana was the cynosure of all eyes, friendly and unfriendly. The world's press was represented in our capital, and what they missed the opposition filled in for them with their own explanations. No occasion, no event, was too small to exploit in order to discredit both Ghana and the government before the world and reduce the high prestige which our struggle and attainment of freedom had won for Ghana. Not often, surely, has an opposition been so active in sacrificing the interests of its country to serve its own ends in disrupting the essential national unity.

I saw the state being undermined, its independence in danger of destruction, all in the name of democracy and freedom of expression. Our opposition used the press as a forum in a way that it had not been used in Europe, to vilify and attack us as a means of destroying our young state. To have served writs upon them for libel would have kept us busy in the courts to the exclusion of our proper duties. Though under extreme pressure from my party, I was still hesitant to take action. Having placed our faith in the working of a liberal democracy, I ardently desired to give it every chance, even at the risk of some abuse to which I knew it was open, especially in the absence of a legal code such as operated in the United Kingdom but had not been applied to the archaic laws of the Gold Coast. We were finding that an administrative and legal pattern under which a colonial régime could contrive to maintain itself required constant piecemeal adaptation to deal with the very different problems of our need to bring order and unity within a democratic framework and to establish a firm base for our national development.

Our toleration of the disruptive excesses of the opposition was accepted not as an expression of good faith in the democratic process but as a mark of weakness, and stimulated them to ever bolder action. The disinclination to take salutary measures was also being misunderstood abroad, where it was being regarded as a trial of strength between us, the lawfully constituted government, and the subversive non-governmental elements. We watched the antics of the foreign press with misgiving. It seemed as though our overseas critics were intent upon destroying us

before we ever got started. Nothing was too small to be twisted
as evidence in misrepresenting the strength and quality of my
government or to support the fiction of the growing strength of
the opposition.

In times of national emergency, the Western democracies
have been compelled to limit their citizens' freedom. We were
facing a time of national emergency. We were engaged in a kind
of war, a war against poverty and disease, against ignorance,
against tribalism and disunity. We were fighting to *construct*, not
to destroy. We needed to secure the conditions which would
allow us to pursue our policy of reconstruction and development.

My government brought in the Avoidance of Discrimination
Bill to deal with the control of political parties based on tribal or
religious affiliations. Its full title was 'An Act to prohibit organizations using or engaging in racial or religious propaganda to
the detriment of any other racial or religious community, or
securing the election of persons on account of their racial or
religious affiliations, and for other purposes in connection there-
with'. The effect was to bring the formation of the various
opposition parties into a United Party. Oddly enough, our show
of firmness was reflected in a temporary change in the tone of
the foreign press.

The Economist, for instance, summed up the negative position
of the opposition in a leading article:

> The criticism that has always been levelled against the
> N.L.M., and which is much more applicable to the present
> assorted bunch of critics (the United Party), is that while accus-
> ing the government of corruption, totalitarianism, destructive-
> ness and inefficiency, it has offered no alternative policies of its
> own. The opposition has two rather contradictory answers to
> this: first, that the United Party is soon to announce a con-
> structive policy (which has never come) and, second, that its
> programme has to be vague or the government will appropriate,
> and spoil, its ideas. In Ghana this fear is not altogether base-
> less. The only fundamental difference of opinion between the
> government and the opposition is over the relative power of the
> centre and the regions. Since there is no basic difference in their
> approach to, say, employment, education and housing, the

opposition can only criticize in a rather woolly way, saying, in effect, that they would do the same things, only better and more honestly.[1]

Unfortunately, the fundamental difference over the relative power of the centre and the regions went deeper than *The Economist*'s passing reference to it would suggest. It was the core of dissension between the Government and the opposition. It involved the whole question of our continuance as a unitary state exercising the democratic principle of majority rule. The opposition was employing the lever given to it by the constitutionally entrenched clauses enthroning the special position of Ashanti, to force by disruptive measures the secession of the region.

Here was the root cause of the bitter feuding that had gripped our beloved country on the eve of independence and continued to mar and harass our days of freedom. The N.L.M. had based its support on the Asantehene and other autocratic chiefs anxious to retain the special privileges and powers which the British colonial practice of Indirect Rule had conferred upon them. Their confidence in the success of their coercive methods was sustained by the willing allies they found among imperialist groups. It has been the unfortunate experience in all colonial countries where the national awakening has crystallized into a popular movement seeking the fundamental democratic right to the rule of the majority, that vested interests have come to the aid of minority separatist groups.

These governments have often shown a touching concern for the rights of these minorities. In fact, their concern has in some cases been so great that it has overlooked entirely the rights of the majority. Examples of this attitude may be seen in the exercise of *apartheid* in South Africa and the enforcement, for many years, of the Central African Federation against the wishes of the Africans of Northern and Southern Rhodesia and Nyasaland. It was the operative principle in Kenya, which supported the supremacy of the European minority over the African majority and was implicit in the view that the rights of that alien

[1] *The Economist*, 16 November 1957.

minority needed armed protection against the indigenous majority. *In fledgeling states, imperialist interests flourish where there is an atmosphere of dissension. They are endangered in an atmosphere of national unity and stability.*

For two and a half years of difficult state-building my government took no action to limit the freedom of the press. The opposition was quick to exploit this freedom and soon debased it into licence. Each day, its newspapers came out with screaming headlines about the perfidy of the government. They heaped abuse and libel upon my colleagues and me. They wrote and preached, they called press conferences with local and foreign correspondents, they addressed public meetings all over the country, stigmatizing the government and singling out me and my immediate associates for special attack, abuse and ridicule.

During the struggle for independence we had emphasized the need for national unity for the attainment of freedom, and for the enormous responsibilities of statehood that would follow. These call for a supreme effort on the part of every citizen. How could our people pull their weight with zeal and dedication when it was ceaselessly being drummed into them that their government was unscrupulous, inept and corrupt; that their leaders were venal and power-thirsty, and that the national effort was invoked, not for the greater glory of Ghana but for the personal glory of Kwame Nkrumah? This was not freedom of expression. This was irresponsible licence, and if allowed to continue unbridled, it could have undermined our state, our independence and the people's faith in themselves and their capacities.

This was the internal picture. The impact on the movements for liberation in the rest of Africa could be just as unfortunate. It was likely to cause despondency in their ranks and friction between us and their leaders, who might have no means of recognizing the falsity of opposition attacks upon us. The colonial powers would also not be unmindful of these happenings and possibly use them as a pretext for delaying their departure from trust and colonial territories by citing the magnified political 'battle' in Ghana as a frightening example of premature independence.

We came to the point where it was obvious that the government must take action if we were to avert the dangers inherent in a false situation. The imposition of any form of press censorship was an idea most repugnant to me, since it ran counter to everything I had always believed in, everything for which I had struggled in my life. Freedom of expression had been one of the essential rights for which I had fought. I had gone to prison for daring to say things the colonial administration had not liked.

Our fight had been the fight for the freedom of our people, and the native inhabitants of the land, against an alien régime that denied freedom. Now that we had won our emancipation and launched our national existence, were we to allow our independence to be endangered by the very people whose speech and action had abetted the colonial régime? We had embarked upon a course that aimed to push forward the clock of progress. Were others to be given the freedom to push it back? We had to face up squarely to the question whether a seedling less developed state, eager to modernize itself in the interests of the community, threatened by the unpatriotic deeds of a minority opposition, could permit itself all the forms which established democracies have taken generations to evolve. A young state has to work doubly hard, has to deny itself many of the trimmings that have become the accepted norm in the older nations.

Our experience is proving that democracy as a functioning system in newly emergent states must inevitably undergo many stresses. Its machinery and pattern of government are being superimposed upon social structures different from those in which they originally developed. Democracy has undergone development to its present accepted forms in the advanced countries in circumstances of compulsion that have yet to be reached in the young nations now attempting to throw themselves apace out of a stagnating economic backwardness into modern industrialized settings able to provide wide material and social benefits for all the people. It is not at all accidental that the great exponents of democracy are precisely those countries where industrial growth has achieved its highest levels within free development. That growth, accompanied at periods by social distress and discontent, was based upon vast private accumulations of capital and proceeded at a pace which was slower in the countries that embarked earlier upon the industrial road and faster in those that started later.

Recently emergent states like Ghana are having to tackle the task of industrialization at the period of its highest development in the old-established democracies, in conditions which have precluded the amassing of large capital reserves in the hands of private citizens. Upon the government, therefore, devolves the task of planning and establishing the main base of economic development and of pushing it through at a speedy rate against the formidable odds of an uneducated population devoid of technical and scientific knowledge, and the lack of even the most primitive industrial foundations. Time is the essence of our problem, and we are in duty bound to use the overwhelming mandate given to us by our people to advance their standards of life, to employ time for the purpose of securing the quickest possible economic and social development for our country. This duty resolves itself into the obligation to use the power bestowed upon us by the majority decision of the people to the limit of the task it imposes. To abdicate any part of that power to an opposition that has been repeatedly rejected by the people and engages itself in activities prejudicial to the independence, safety and forward growth of the State, would, I submit, be a betrayal of the popular will and trust. It would be completely incomprehensible to our people, and in the present state of their educational development would place our whole future in jeopardy. We intend to preserve the rights and freedom of our people, so long as these are exercised within the limits of the law, and without threat to the security of the nation. We welcome criticism, but we will not tolerate subversive and terroristic activities against the State, and illegal acts designed to promote the selfish greed of a dissident minority, supported by alien interests.

CHAPTER TEN

OUR GHANAIAN CONSTITUTION

EVERY SOVEREIGN people undoubtedly possesses the sovereign right to introduce changes in the regulations by which they are governed, to keep pace with the dynamic changes wrought by social, political, economic and technological progress. Such changes should not be arbitrary, nor should they be effected except through the chosen instrument of the people, Parliament, or, in matters of vital moment, through the direct expression of the people's will by plebiscite, or referendum. No one would dream of justifying Ghanaian subservience for eternity to regulations passed by a British Parliament before we achieved independence.

In the three years that we worked under the constitution arranged for us by the retiring imperialist power, we found that change was necessary. We were not concerned with change for the sake of change, simply because distasteful clauses had been imposed upon us against our will, or because the constitution as a whole had not been of our making. Our basic consideration was that certain parts of the constitution were found to be hampering our free development. We even found that some of its provisions with which we had fully agreed at the time of negotiation, and which we might well have introduced ourselves without imposition from others, were now outdated and no longer suited to the realities of Ghana.

The year 1960, after three years of independence, seemed an appropriate time to introduce the necessary changes in our constitution, suited to the mood of the times, the temper of the people, the political and cultural patterns of the country, the urgent need to develop our land and advance the liberation of the African continent. These factors were reflected in the fundamental articles of the new constitution. The most important

D

change was the conversion of Ghana from a monarchy to a republic. Since people have an essentially personal attitude towards the monarchy, I decided that in addition to introducing a Bill to parliament for its abolition and securing the necessary two-thirds majority, I would also submit the issue to the nation in a referendum. The National Assembly passed the Bill with an overwhelming majority. The referendum was held in three stages over the country during an eight-day period and resulted in an equally heavy majority for the republican constitution and the continuance of the C.P.P. government under my presidency.

I well knew what a hornet's nest I would be stirring up when I decided that it was incompatible with full independence for Ghana to continue to pay allegiance to the British Crown as Head of State. I knew that my action would be understood by all the republics of the world, and they form the bulk of the United Nations' members. I also knew that this action would find little sympathy in Britain and in the other countries of the Commonwealth.

It cannot be claimed that the people in those countries have always shown sympathetic understanding of every major act of policy which Ghana has followed since it became independent. There are of course among them many men of goodwill, but quite a lot seem still to resent the fact that we are no longer governed from Whitehall. We have the impression that subconsciously they would like us to fail. At all events, they are quick to ascribe uncharitable motives to any of our actions which they feel touch them on a tender spot. And the monarchy in Britain is a very tender spot. There is a certain mystique about the British monarchy, whose influence is intangible but very real. I would venture the thought that there is hardly a serious anti-royalist in Britain. There appears to be no consciousness of anything paradoxical in a highly advanced democracy maintaining an hereditary monarchy. If I were a Briton living in the United Kingdom, I might feel the same.

However, I am an African, a member of a country which has but recently broken the shackles linking it to Britain. We had, however, retained the link with the monarchy, but our orientation towards the continent of Africa made it an anachronism. It was out of keeping with the full meaning of our independence:

it symbolized an hierarchical pinnacle that no longer had reality in the Ghana-Britain relationship. It injected a falsity into our relationship with the states on our continent. We are committed to the pursuance of an African Union. We are obliged in our affiliations to consider their effects upon our progress towards this cardinal goal. Numbers of our people, moreover, believe it to be the height of incongruity for the inhabitants of the Ghanaian town of Tamale, for instance, to find the Head of their State living in Buckingham Palace, London. The Head of the West African State of Ghana should be a Ghanaian having his residence in Ghana.

It seemed tendentious, therefore, to find myself dubbed a dictator by some and an *enfant terrible* by others when rumours of my intention began to appear in the British press. A disinterested consideration of the facts would have produced a more sober reaction. However, as I mentioned earlier, people in other countries tend to interpret the actions of foreigners in terms of their own experience. Hence the irresistible temptation of Britishers to say that what is good for Britain is good for Ghana.

But how could a Queen resident abroad, or her representative who was a national of a foreign State, seek to symbolize the people of Ghana? They were such obvious strangers to our country, to our way of life, to the spirit of our people. The very presence of a Governor-General in the official position which he occupied was an affront to the sovereignty which we had fought for and achieved. It would have been equally an affront had the Governor-General been an African.

It is no discourtesy to Queen Elizabeth II if I and my people harbour the same conscientious objection to taking an oath to her as we would to swearing allegiance to the President of the United States, or the President of the Soviet Union.

Nor should anything I have said be taken as reflecting the slightest disrespect to our two Governors-General. It was largely due to their tact and understanding allied to their broad liberal views that our relationship was so free from friction.

The President, according to our Republican Constitution, is not only the Head of State but also the chief executive and head of government. This formula was not reached by us without keen examination and comparative study of the many different republican systems of the world. We pondered for many months whether we should establish the system followed in such countries as India and the Soviet Union, whereby the titular Head of State is the holder of an honorary position without power; or whether to combine the Premiership with the Presidency and give the highest position in the land to the effective leader of the nation, as in the United States. We decided upon the latter formula, making our necessary adaptations.

Our decision took account of what seemed to us the most logical, the most democratic and the most straightforward formula. In a democracy, the real leader of the country is the man who has been democratically elected as leader of the party which commands a majority in Parliament, which has been democratically elected by the people. He is in fact the people's choice. Why, then, should he not combine the governmental powers with the ceremonials attaching to the headship of the State? In our present environment and circumstances our people associate primacy with power. The position of a titular President, merely signing acts of Parliament upon which he makes no impact, would not have been easy for them to grasp. It is not easy indeed for the student of democracy to grasp, for it is a meaningless fiction, without content.

It is our hope that the system we have adopted, which combines the Premiership with the Presidency, will give stability and resolute leadership in the building of our country. In our opinion, it responds to the mood of our people and meets the exigencies of our actual situation. The reservation of certain powers to the President was felt to be necessary in order to allow opportunity for decisive action in pushing forward our development.

Ghana has established a democratic structure employing the normal paraphernalia associated with such a governmental form, which is really ahead of our pre-industrial status. To have effective control over the rate of our development, we had to hold something in reserve. We had to trim our political coat to suit our social and economic cloth.

The increased authority given to the President is to enable him to exercise the positive leadership that is so vital to a country seeking to pull itself up by its bootstraps. If I may change the metaphor, it is in some ways the work of Sisyphus, except that instead of a stone our task is to roll a whole people uphill. There are some jobs in the world that can be best done by a committee, others need a managing director.

I will not hide the fact that I am impatient when it comes to building Ghana. We have to get on with the job resolutely. Each minister must regard himself as a managing director and get his particular job done in the allotted time, and properly done. He must know that inexplicable failure can result in his giving place to another to prove his capacities. Real difficulties leading to legitimate delay always receive understanding consideration. But the driving urge to succeed must permeate every branch of government, stemming from the ministerial fountain-head, who must combine a high sense of responsibility with a high sense of urgency. Each minister must show himself an example to the people by his devotion to his work, by simple living, by leading in service. Ghana faces immense difficulties in her tasks of reconstruction. It is by no means a simple business to raise educational levels, to train skilled workers and to impart a sense of responsibility speedily, especially in circumstances of restricted availability of local qualified personnel and material resources. Nevertheless, there is much that can be done quickly if everyone puts every ounce of ability and strength into the building of the nation. It is a prime task of leadership in Ghana to make the people aware of the compelling need to put forth their most intense effort on behalf of the progress of the country and of themselves.

Within a society poising itself for the leap from pre-industrial retardation to modern development, there are traditional forces that can impede progress. Some of these must be firmly cut at their roots, others can be retained and adapted to the changing need. The place of chiefs is so interwoven with Ghanaian society that their forcible eradication would tear gaps in the social fabric which might prove as painful as the retention of other more unadaptable traditions. The constitution takes careful account of these factors, and the Declaration of Fundamental Principles states that 'the office of Chiefs in Ghana, as existing by customary law and usage, should be guaranteed'. I am fully aware of the body of opinion that regards chieftaincy as an anachronism, but when it is possible for the Asantehene to advise the chiefs within the Kumasi State Council 'to change according to the times', I think we are fully justified in our decision to maintain the tradition. Addressing the Council on 24 May 1960, the Asantehene was reported to have said that

> it was impossible at this stage of the country's development to forecast that the former privileges, coupled with a large number of attendants, would ever be enjoyed by any modern Ghanaian chief. The Asantehene observed that with the increased number of new schools in every hamlet of Ghana, chiefs would not find it easy to have attendants such as umbrella bearers.[1]

In Ghana, a chief without his umbrella bearer is an unthinkable phenomenon. For the most powerful paramount chief in this country to warn that chiefs will, by reason of wider educational facilities, in due course be denied one of the main symbols of their office, is tantamount to warning of the natural attenuation of chieftaincy under the impact of social progress. If, in the interregnum, chieftaincy can be used to encourage popular effort, there would seem to be little sense in arousing the antagonism which its legal dissolution would stimulate. The adaptation of our chiefs to what must, for them, be distressing exigencies created by the changing relations in the national polity, has been remarkable. We could wish that other forces with vested interests might have proved as adaptable.

More obstructive than chieftaincy were the entrenched clauses in our independence constitution concerning the appointment, promotion, transfer and termination of appointment of civil servants. Disagreeable to us in the extreme, they had the effect of surrounding each civil servant with a barricade which the government was allowed to scale only with the greatest difficulty.

The new constitution retains the status and financial provisions of the earlier one. Powers of appointment and dismissal, however, have been transferred to the President, who exercises them through a Civil Service Commission. Only those who are disloyal or incompetent need fear this change, all the rest will be strengthened by it. For promotion, which formerly came from

[1] *Daily Graphic*, Accra, 25 May 1960.

time-serving, will now be the reward of merit. The new constitution contains a high challenge to our civil servants. Their
response will be recorded in the accelerated rate of our national
development.

The changes in our constitution which I have so far described
and explained, have been designed to create an environment in
which Ghana can proceed more positively with national reconstruction. But even as I have always been concerned with the
independence and development of Ghana as part of the total
liberation and reconstruction of Africa, and have made this a
guiding principle in the foreign policy of my government, so I
felt that our constitution should make a positive demonstration
of Ghana's willingness to surrender her individual sovereignty
to the total sovereignty of Africa, if this should ever be required.
Our relations with the rest of Africa did indeed have more than
a little bearing on our decision to sever the link with the British
Crown and transform our state into a republic. But we considered that some more revolutionary illustration of our attachment to the cause of African Union should be embedded in the
instrument that governs the country's policy. Hence, in the pre-
amble to our new constitution, there is to be found the statement
that:

> We the people of Ghana . . . in the hope that we may by our
> actions this day help to further the development of a Union of
> African States . . . do hereby enact and give to ourselves this
> constitution. . . .

While the Declaration of Fundamental Principles includes these
specific conditions:

> That the Union of Africa should be striven for by every lawful
> means, and, when attained, should be faithfully preserved; and
>
> That the independence of Ghana should not be surrendered
> or diminished on any grounds *other than the furtherance of African
> Unity*.

This, I believe, is the first time that an independent, sovereign
state has voluntarily offered to surrender its sovereignty for the

sake of unity.[1] It is our contribution, made freely, openly and sincerely by the government and people of Ghana, towards the linking together of neighbouring brother states as the best means of promoting the welfare of the people throughout the whole continent. It is our fervent hope that other states in Africa will follow suit, and that we need not wait until the entire continent has seen the light of brotherhood. A start can be made with as little as two, three or four states willing to submit themselves to a sovereign union.

Ghana, Guinea, Mali and some other newly emergent African states have made a start by inscribing this ideal in their constitutions. It is for others to water this seed of destiny until it flourishes into a glorious tree of union and brotherhood among the peoples of Africa.

[1] The constitutions of Guinea, Tunisia, Mali and U.A.R. also contain a similar provision.

CHAPTER ELEVEN

THE ADMINISTRATIVE INSTRUMENT

A NEW SOCIAL structure does not automatically follow the attainment of political freedom. That, like the battle for independence, has to be fought for and won by an army of stalwarts as determined in purpose as those who waged the struggle for freedom.

This second stage of the revolutionary process, when reviewed soberly, appears if anything, harder than the first. More than once, during the pre-independence days, I was assailed by doubts whether we would have the forces to carry it through. There was my party, the Convention People's Party, and the overwhelming mass support behind us. These, however, did not sit in the seat of administration from where policies for achieving our second important objective of raising ourselves out of our socio-economic backwardness are put into action. They were, in reality, an extra-administrative army, on whose co-operation we could rely for the carrying out of our programmes at the more intimate level of village, hamlet and township. But there would have to be a fully manned force at the central point of administration capable of carrying through from top to bottom the necessary directives for fulfilling the government's policies.

For all the protestations of the British that the aim of their colonial policy was to prepare the people of the subject territories for self-government, it was only when the nationalist movements took the reins that any real move was made to implement its When we took over, our civil service was definitely and absolutely British in substance and nature; it was certainly not African. It was the realization of this fact that caused me, sometimes with dismay, to recognize that when we did take firmly into our hands the reins of government, there would be the danger of finding ourselves in possession of an administrative

machine that had a general staff and other ranks but was devoid
of officers.

My cabinet, my general staff, would come from among the
Party, and down below was the rank and file of our army – the
people. These were our own. But what of the group in between,
the officers and the N.C.O.s, who would be responsible for the
execution of policy laid down from above? Where were our tried
and loyal African commanders? Where were the African
directors of our campaign for clearing away the debris of
colonialism and erecting our own Ghanaian edifice more in keeping with our wider, progressive perspective? The finest plans we
could conceive for our country would never leave the blue-print
stage unless we had first-class civil servants whose outlook was
attuned to our African aspirations and upon whose loyalty we
could depend unquestioningly.

The civil service, being the administrative arm of government,
is the instrument for putting into effect the economic and social
programme of the government. It is through its machinery that
the political platform of the party in power is given effective
implementation. Our civil service, the one which we inherited
during our spell of internal self-government between 1951 and
March 1957, was the machine that had been formed by the
imperial power to carry out its colonial policy. Though we had
joint control, it was as a junior partner. We were, it is true, the
ruling party, but the imperial government still reigned supreme,
and we were subordinate to its colonial pro-consul, the Governor.

Two courses of action lay open to me and my party. We could
boycott the existing colonial government machinery, the civil
service, the police, the judiciary. Or we could co-operate with it,
meanwhile strengthening the position of myself and my colleagues in the cabinet and so advance the date for full independence.

In choosing the second, we did not forget, but tried to bury,
past differences and sought co-operation with the existing executive machinery of government. Two major aims impelled
this decision: the speeding up of Africanization, and the prevention of a breakdown in administration through a wholesale
exodus of British officials. There was no regret for the departure
of those officials who were so opposed to our aims as to render

them quite unfit and unreliable co-workers. We felt equally well rid of those who were likely to resent taking orders from an African. My keenest anxiety was to avoid any dislocation of government. We had at all costs to hold off any possibility of a situation of instability which would enable Britain and other colonial powers to point at us the finger of scorn and gloat over the disastrous effects of handing over self-government 'prematurely' to Africans.

It was of prime importance to us, therefore, and the freedom movements in other parts of Africa, that we should be able to effect a smooth and gradual take-over of power, free from serious administrative shocks. Therefore, we decided in favour of maintaining the services of those British officials who were civil servants in the best sense of the word, non-partisan in the fulfilment of their duties and prepared to carry out orders given by an African. It called for what I termed at the time 'tactical action', but what an American friend jokingly suggested might be more appropriately named 'tactful' action.

In countries like Britain, where the civil service does not change with a change in the governing party, as it does, for instance, in the United States, the administration is expected to remain as loyal to the new government as it had been to the ousted one. Here you get the insistence upon the fiction that civil servants are non-political. This fiction, if carried to its logical conclusion, would in fact deprive the civil servant of his basic democratic right to vote. For in casting his vote, he exercises a choice in favour of one political party and thereby demonstrates a bias.

That his vote is secret does not alter the fact of selection. In order to make a selection he must have his personal views, whether private or openly expressed, upon the alternative programmes or objectives of the parties contending for power. As a good civil servant, however, he is required, should the party returned to power not be the one of his choice, nonetheless to give it his absolute loyalty and unswerving integrity. This in most instances he does, for he has been trained to understand that it is only his patriotic duty to serve faithfully the existing government of his country. It is in the rare, extreme cases, where the servants of government find the pull between government policy in certain respects and their conscience too great, that they abandon their loyalty in submission to their conscience.

In the case of our civil service, we were reliant not upon our own nationals but almost entirely upon nationals of a power which had been ruling us and who had been trained to conduct the policy of that power. Bound to the interests of their own country for so long, it could hardly be expected, apart from a few exceptional cases, that they would change their attitude towards us overnight. What we needed was our own African civil service.

If the colonial power had been sincere in its claim of preparing the Gold Coast for self-government, one of its primary contributions would have been to speed up Africanization of the civil service and to offer access to the top posts to Africans. An excuse frequently offered for the putting off of self-government was that the country did not have a sufficiency of administrators and personnel trained in other respects for the hard responsibilities of running a state. But nothing was done to make good the deficiency. At no time throughout the period of British administration was any African allowed to fill the highest posts of the civil service. Africans who were employed were allowed into the junior grades and denied the prospect of rising to the higher ranks. The British justification for holding them down was that they lacked the appropriate academic qualifications and the necessary administrative experience. The sophistry of imperialist reasoning is studded with these truths of the vicious circle. Educational facilities were inadequate to provide academic standards for Africans, and experience can only be gained by experience. The logic of the British argument and its laggard approach to the problem would have kept us waiting a hundred years and more before we had a trained civil service to implement self-government.

We were not prepared to wait, and I turned my attention to the problems as soon as I became Leader of Government Business in 1951. Eighty per cent of the Gold Coast senior civil servants were British. The twenty per cent African government employees were mainly in the lower ranks of the senior service. Hence I had to retain the most essential of the eighty per cent, move up the best of the twenty per cent to take over from the British who would leave, and introduce more Africans into the senior grades of the service. This would ensure an ample nucleus of African civil servants ready to take over the highest positions of trust when we gained full independence.

This programme would, I knew, have the effect of reducing the incentive of British officials to stay. I made no secret about my ultimate intentions and aims, and they knew that their days were numbered. In the subsequent bargaining I would have had, if I had not already been sceptical of the claim, to revise the self-asserted claim that British civil servants entered the colonial service from a sense of altruistic concern for the betterment of the 'backward, primitive peoples'. John Stuart Mill's description of the colonial civil service as 'a form of outdoor relief for the sons of the British middle class' is more apposite.

For their point of view I had full understanding. I knew they had careers to consider and had joined the colonial service under certain conditions of security. They would be unable in the new régime of independence to retain the status they had enjoyed under the old colonial régime. They had the choice of leaving or of surrendering their existing terms of appointment and joining the Gold Coast service under full local control. I therefore offered inducement in the form of a compensation programme for loss of career. There was a good deal of haggling and I was rather saddened at the open explosion of the myth of the British colonial civil servant's disinterestedness in financial rewards, his missionary purpose of carrying 'the white man's burden'. One hundred and forty decided to leave immediately and another eighty-three left shortly after. The Africanization programme therefore had to be stepped up. On the surface, some of the British officials appeared to adjust themselves to the new conditions and seemed to adapt their minds to working under, or side by side with, their African colleagues.

After 1957, when Ghana achieved independence, the position of our civil service became better than it had been in 1951. But it was still far from satisfactory. For though the British had ceased to rule, they had hedged us in with the detailed safeguards, set out in the constitution, of the position, salary, pension rights and tenure of office of the civil servant. Reading these, one might be forgiven for imagining that this charter had been specially framed to guarantee the security of the civil servant rather than to afford the opportunity for the free, democratic evolution of a whole society. Insistence on the insertion of these clauses by the British delegation to the negotiations on the constitution stemmed from two purposes: to safeguard the interest of the British expatriate who would be continuing his service with the Ghana government; to give the Ghanaian civil servant the same status and security enjoyed by the British colonial civil servant.

The first purpose we considered unnecessary. All along it had been made clear by us that there was room in the new Ghana for experienced service from men and women who worked here in the Gold Coast civil service and desired to help the new state. I expressed our willingness to welcome the continued stay of those who were prepared to be loyal to the new government and faithfully carry out the policies initiated by their political chiefs. I guaranteed their salaries and pension rights and compensation for loss of Colonial Office career. I considered it an imposition, however, for the Ghana Government to be forced to retain the services of those who had elected to stay and were later found to be incompetent, obstructive or disloyal. Let me say at this point that many expatriates have given excellent service to Ghana and have discharged their duties faithfully. Others have proved less than competent and have failed to pull their weight. Some, we know, continued in the service with the set purpose either of hindering our efforts or of holding a watching brief for British interests. It is certainly not just that the rights of such civil service members should be safeguarded by clauses entrenched in the constitution. As an independent government, the power to appoint and dismiss civil servants must surely rest with the government of the state, and this should hold whether the civil servant is a British expatriate or a Ghanaian. For they play a delicate, sometimes a key, part in carrying out government policy.

The second British purpose is understandable: the desire to bequeath to Ghana the pattern of civil service obtaining in Great Britain. The purpose, however, is dictatorial and unrealistic, and ignores the totally different needs of a less developed state. I agree that the British civil service enjoys a high reputation for integrity, for probity, for loyalty to whatever government comes to power, for abstention from political interference. It also has the reputation of being cautious, conservative, staid, static, often corollaries of personal security. These are decidedly not the qualities required by a new state about to launch its people on a vast new programme of dynamic development.

Government and civil service are inter-related. Government determines policy, the body of civil servants carries it out. The finest programmes will get bogged down if the civil servants who direct their practical execution are incompetent and without dedication. Our desired rate of development must not be impeded because we are obliged to carry white-collar government employees who will put in a standard stint of office hours and then forget all about the job; who will never put a foot wrong but who will never have an original idea; who will think the task performed with the writing of a competent letter; who will be more concerned with status and prestige than with helping the public; whose fear of responsibility will always prompt the passing on of decisions and action; who will model themselves on the Homburg-hatted umbrella-carrying civil servant of an established state rather than on the pioneer worker of a new and developing country.

Security of employment is a fine principle and one which I endorse, but I do not think a civil servant in Ghana today has greater right to security than the fisherman, the cocoa-grower, the driver, the port worker, the teacher, the road labourer or market woman. I am averse to our civil servants being lodged in the State apparatus like a nail without a head: once you drive it in, you cannot pull it out. Government must retain the right of dismissal, and the civil servant must be made to realize that he can be dismissed if he does not perform the job required of him. He must be grappling with his work all the time, thinking twenty-four hours a day how best he can serve his country by his performance for the ministry in which he works. The Ghanaian civil servant must be utterly devoted and dedicated to the ideal of reconstructing our country. He must show leadership, he must, like his Minister, set an example to the people he serves. He must be a pioneer.

These are the demands which we make of our civil service. They are high, for the task of the civil servant in the building up

of Ghana is crucial. Our best laid plans will go awry if they are
not handled with heart as well as head.

At the moment of independence, we had several first-class
African officials who could assume the highest positions of trust
in several ministries, but there still remained many ministries
whose permanent secretary was an expatriate. Expatriates also
continued to fill many of the high-grade key positions in the
execution of policy. Nor can I say that every African civil servant
was suited to his job. Some were good and experienced. Some
were good, but lacked training. Some were second-rate. When-
ever I and my cabinet colleagues sat down to formulate policy,
we always had to keep in mind the capability limits of our civil
service in the implementation of our programmes in the time
we had set.

I have come to appreciate, however, that even some of the
African staff who, to put it conservatively, were lukewarm in
their support of my government and its programme, given
responsibility, have risen to the demands made upon them. My
ministerial colleagues and I work a very full day and the pace
we set is quite gruelling. It has warmed me to see how many
members of my staff, accustomed as they were to the meander-
ing methods of the colonial administration, have stiffened their
rate of work to meet the new and urgent demands made upon
them.

Innumerable exasperations and difficulties remain, and the
more I think about this problem of the civil service in less
developed countries planning for development, the more I feel
that the leaders of freedom movements and of emergent states
must pay added attention to the need to start early in the selection and training of their future executive officers. Some countries, like India, Pakistan and Ceylon, were able to send their
sons to overseas universities to train for future leadership, and
were given the opportunity of introducing them into certain
branches of their colonial administration. They too experienced
difficulties, in spite of having a core of civil servants of their own
nationals. Other countries, like Israel, spent the immediate years
before they achieved independence in training up a corps of
high-level officials who never actually worked in the British
administration but who studied the problems of organization

and administration, and were ready to take over the duties of government the moment the British departed.

For most countries emerging into independence, this has not been done. Nor have they been able, as Ghana was not able, to speed the Africanization of their civil service at the necessary rate. We know colonialism and we know that we cannot look to the colonial power for help in this matter. It is something we Africans have to do ourselves. Our chief difficulty during the revolutionary struggle is that our main activity is political and not administrative. Because of this, our best men and women cannot be spared for civil service training, as they are needed to advance the political battle. With independence they become ministers, members of parliament, regional party leaders, regional officers, ambassadors. Yet top civil servants, gifted with administrative skill and imbued with the fervour of independence and the hope of development, are vital to the reconstruction of a state. To rely on expatriates is to endanger the revolution. For the men and women who carry out our policy must be as devoted and dedicated to the idea of freedom and national growth as the leaders of the country. They must be free of patriotic and intellectual attachments to outside forces. With our own nationals of integrity we get a civil service concerned only with the public welfare. Theirs is a twenty-four hours a day job, just like that of their political leaders. Upon them, to a large extent, depends the quality of the country's development and the speed with which it can be fulfilled.

In 1952 there was only one Ghanaian head of department. By 1957 the figure had risen to twenty-two. Now all the permanent and pensionable posts are held by Ghanaians.

An Institute of Public Administration has been established, where post-graduate students take a year's diploma course in the theory and practice of public administration. There are also special short courses and seminars for senior civil servants: and research is being carried out to find new techniques in public administration specially appropriate for Africa. Degree courses in administration are being offered.

The country needs expert civil servants, aware of, and integrated into, the society around them, and with interests directed particularly towards the problems of Africa. Hitherto, many civil servants entered the service with little or no training. A knowledge of minute writing, the Civil Service Act, and office routine, was about all the practical training they had experienced.

We have now achieved our aim of building up a Ghanaian civil service able to administer the country efficiently, and I would like my brothers in the emerging states of this continent to know that Ghana stands ready to help them in their initial stages of self-government. Our civil service is at their disposal. We can lend them top officials to start their ministries, we can send them instructors to train their own indigenous civil service. It is a problem whose complexity they will discover only with the departure of the colonial power. It would indeed be a boon to all the new African states if those of us who have enjoyed a somewhat longer period of independence were to make available some of our officials to form a kind of African civil service pool, standing at the service of emerging African states and ready to serve the new Union of African States.

CHAPTER TWELVE

RECONSTRUCTION AND DEVELOPMENT

STATES EMERGING from colonialism face the gigantic problem of transforming their almost purely trading and raw-material producing economies into productive units capable of bearing a superstructure of modern agriculture and industry. We have, all of us, a similar dearth of capital, trained labour and technically-skilled personnel to assist forward our development at the pace which our objectives demand. Our late start, and the speed at which we must work if we are to modernize our countries, are bound in some degree to sharpen the stresses and strains which have accompanied industrialization everywhere in the world.

Every advance in methods of production made by the foremost industrialized countries increases the gap between them and us. There is a theory that the countries which appear last upon the industrial scene can automatically start at the latest point of development reached by the most advanced. This theory can only be applicable where the accumulation of capital is great enough to make an effective take-off possible. Even in those circumstances, there must also be available a literate population able to provide a sufficient body of trained labour, and managers to head and man the evolving industrial machine.

These circumstances do not exist in Ghana. They do not exist in any of the colonialized territories, where subsistence farming, mono-crop production and extractive industries have dominated the economy under the influence of financial and commercial monopolies.

In Ghana, we have had to obtain technical knowledge and staff from better equipped sources, and this process will continue until we are able to produce a sufficient number of our own experts. We are getting help from international bodies like

U.S.O.M., U.N.T.A.B., F.A.O., W.H.O., but since we are
having to compete with so many other bidders, we have had to
apply also to private quarters. Even there, the demands are too
heavy to leave an ample supply of best quality people. In order
to secure even the minimum of well-qualified technicians we are
having to offer terms of service which make development for us
disproportionately costly. Money which we could otherwise
spend on more basic requirements has to go, for example, into
housing and other amenities for foreign personnel. These would
be matters for private provision if we were able to recruit the
same people locally. They are, moreover, requirements which
create precedents that our own people demand when they come
to take over posts formerly held by expatriates. We are trying to
establish more realistic standards of service for our local people
in government employ, though we have met a certain amount of
resistance.

I do appreciate that in a market where many are competing,
we have to make our terms of service to expatriates as inviting as
we can, even though they place an additional strain upon our
far from unlimited resources. Yet I feel a strong sense of injustice
in that we lately-colonial countries are forced to bear such additional burdens through the fact of that very backwardness in
which we were kept by the countries which have made their
industrial progress to a large extent out of us. It is these same
imperialist powers who are reaping another harvest today by
providing the machinery, equipment, management, consultants
and personnel which are the requisites of our reconstruction.

Capital investment, too, we have to seek abroad. There has
not been developed in Africa even that bourgeois accumulation
of wealth based upon landholding, trade, commerce and industry which has arisen to some extent in some unadvanced
countries in Asia, let alone the accumulation out of which Europe
financed its industrial revolution. This I think can be attributed
in a measure to the fact that the British banking firms which
operated here were essentially banks of exchange and looked
unfavourably upon the dispensing of credit to African entrepreneurs. This attitude was upheld by the fact that our system of
land tenure does not encompass individual ownership of freehold.
When it came to the question of the provision of collateral against

loans, our people were at a disadvantage, since even the ownership of buildings could be brought into dispute where the right to the land on which they were erected might well be disputed.

Lands in Ghana in theory belong to the 'Stools', headed by the chiefs. But when Europeans arrived in our midst, bringing enticements of money and goods, many chiefs signed away concessions; and some, in complete disregard of custom, made outright sales. What is worse, parcels of land were sold by families in possession of them, to different purchasers, and this started a whole series of law suits which, until my government came into office, was the chief source of income to our lawyers, many of whom made fortunes out of persuading parties to land quarrels to resort to the extended machinery of native law over tracts of land frequently not worth £100. The whole question of land tenure in Ghana is one which requires examination and careful overhaul. It becomes increasingly clear that the system is too cumbersome and complex to adjust to the needs and pace of our development.

My government has made efforts to put some order into the administration of Stool lands, which has now been brought under the control of local authorities. This measure was adopted as a means of stopping the misappropriation of funds from land administration, which was beginning to assume alarming proportions. We have also made laws which enable the government to acquire lands suitable for development purposes.

Certain changes in our land tenure system seem to me inevitable if we are to pursue our development plans, but these will have to be very carefully worked out. They must avoid the creation of rifts in the body politic, and will accordingly have to take into account customs and fundamental traditions. One of the blessings of our land tenure system is that it has not turned ours into a nation where land hunger would have forced us to break up vast holdings for redistribution among a destitute peasantry. Our customs, moreover, had erected a kind of social security adapted to our subsistence economy. Some of our farmers, it is true, have fallen victims to the rapacity of money-lenders. My government is trying to meet this problem of peasant indebtedness by way of credit and other facilities. We are also stimulating the growth of the co-operative movement and encouraging farmers to join the United Ghana Farmers' Council, the farmers' representative council in Ghana, which assists the sale of their produce and makes monetary advances to them at the beginning of the crop seasons.

Thrift has not been a characteristic of our people, largely because they have not enjoyed enough income to make the question anything but academic. How to instil a need to spend and save wisely among them has become a major preoccupation now that they are beginning to enjoy higher incomes and the taste for amenities. Our family system actually discourages family heads from saving, for the system, in effect, penalizes the man with initiative in favour of the lazy and the weak. The indigent members of the family live upon the more fortunate ones. A praiseworthy and useful practice in our past, more or less stagnant society based on subsistence farming, it acts today as a break upon ambition and drive. At the present time, the man who makes a reasonable living finds his money eaten up by his relatives (and this includes the most extended members reaching to the nth degree of relationship), so that he simply cannot meet his personal obligations, let alone save anything.

But save we must, if we are to build up the hard reserves of capital necessary for our development. Side by side with the family hindrance to saving, there has been a real and developing increase in expenditure upon a vast miscellany of imported goods. The danger inherent in trying to 'keep up with the Joneses' which results in the rising cost in personal expenditure is something upon which we are trying to put a brake, not merely because this kind of spending encourages inflation, but because it produces false standards and illusory ideas of wealth in an economy which has not yet got off to a real start on the road of reconstruction and development. It is for these several reasons that we have introduced compulsory savings and curtailed the importation of what we regard as inessential goods. We have also established a national lottery, extended post office savings facilities, and set up a savings branch in our national bank. We are looking into the means of encouraging investment in new businesses and industrial undertakings, which will encourage enterprise and initiative and help in building up managerial skill.

Investment capital is our great need. Our colonial status prevented us from accumulating as individuals the reserves of capital necessary to establish on a private basis those major enterprises which will lay the foundations of a sound industrialized economy and expand and diversify our agriculture.

Only the government, in fact, has resources large enough to make a realistic approach to the problem of reconstruction and development. And even government, because of low national production, is obliged to seek investment from abroad. But while wanting to attract capital, we are continually on the alert to ensure that this does not endanger our independence by making us subordinate to a new form of imperialism. The kind of investment assistance we prefer is that which will enter into a partnership arrangement with the government, or any of our statutory institutions, under which our own citizens will be trained to take over management, direction and technical posts at all levels. We are already receiving assistance of this kind, and more is on the way.

I must say that we are rather chary of the fortune hunters who come to our shores in shoals, seeking to make use of what they regard as our innocence and naïveté in these matters; or of that army of business people, who have followed in one delegation after another, more intent upon taking money from us in the form of commodity sales which would enhance their own national revenues, than upon contributing to our economic expansion. There are circumstances in which the import of foreign capital is of benefit to the importing country, especially in the case of the emerging developing country where large-scale sources of capital accumulation are small and not so easy to mobilize. Foreign capital is thus useful and helpful if it takes the form of a loan or credit to enable the borrowing country to buy what it needs from whatever sources it likes, and at the same time to retain control of the assets to be developed.

One of the worst things that can happen to less developed and emerging countries is to receive foreign aid with political and economic strings attached. These aids are very often wrapped up in financial terms that are not easily discernible.

Foreign investment made in an emerging and developing country by a foreign company in order that such company can make a profit, has nothing to do with *aid*. This does not mean that a developing country may not find it advantageous to make a contract with a foreign company for the setting up of, say, a factory or an industry.

Real aid is something quite different. It consists of direct gifts or loans that are given on favourable terms and without strings attached.

In other words, the problem is how to obtain capital-investment and still keep it under sufficient control to prevent undue exploitation; and how to preserve integrity and sovereignty without crippling economic or political ties to *any* country, bloc or system.

We have had enough of European monopoly domination of our economy. We have emancipated ourselves politically, and we have now to shake off the economic monopoly that was the objective of foreign political control. This is the crux of our economic policy, and the essential heart of our endeavours. For unless we attain economic freedom, our struggle for independence will have been in vain, and our plans for social and cultural advancement frustrated. Hence we are extremely vigilant in scenting out the subtle and insidious infiltrations of neo-colonialism and the sabotage of foreigners enjoying our hospitality and the privilege of building economic enterprises in our midst. In furtherance of our goal of unshackling ourselves from foreign economic domination, we are creating agencies which will assist in breaking through this alien monopoly and stimulate capital accumulation for re-employment in wider development.

A country's capital is, of course, also to be found in its body of technical, scientific and managerial knowledge, as well as in its productive capacity. In these fields we have to acknowledge deficiencies which we know it will take time to wipe out. Moreover, the low rate of productivity makes our labour, in spite of the relatively small wages it receives, quite expensive. At the present time, low nutrition, a deficient sense of responsibility, the fear of being out of work, govern the rate at which work is performed. These factors are the environmental effects of historical circumstances. Tribal controls and taboos followed by the autocratic paternalism of colonialism have held in leash the sense of initiative and responsibility which develops in a freer society. As living conditions grow better under the improvements which the government is pledged to effect, and indeed has already made to some extent, as unemployment lessens and the momentum of development gathers speed, a quickening of productive output throughout the economy must follow. Productive increase will also respond to encouraging incentives, which need not always be of a financial nature. For a productivity increase which is completely eaten up through expanded consumption will defeat the development programme, whose investment capital must come from surpluses. Some austerity is imperative and our new controls are aimed at this. At the same time, we are trying to eliminate, by party discipline and other means, wide gaps between the lower and higher income groups. We are setting our hands as firmly as we can against the growth of a privileged section.

There must also be guards against the danger of spiralling inflation, which too often attends a constructing economy, such as ours is rapidly becoming. Careful planning can and must keep inflation within limits so that the advantages of economic development shall not be dissipated in an ever-soaring cost of living and building.

But the building of a new state requires more than the preparation of programmes, the design of plans and the issue of instructions for their implementation. It requires the whole-hearted support and self-identification of the people, and the widest possible response to the call for voluntary service. A war on illiteracy has to be waged; and a country-wide self-help programme of community development arranged, to promote the building of schools, roads, drains, clinics, post offices, houses and community centres.

The effects of self-help schemes, valuable in themselves and the incentive they give to initiative, are, however, local in compass and limited in purpose. Rapid development on a national scale and the attainment of economic independence demand a more intensive and wider application of ability and inventiveness, the speedy acquisition of technical knowledge and skills, a vast acceleration of productivity as a prerequisite to accumulation of savings for re-investment in industrial expansion. In a less developed society there are several impediments to industrialization, quite apart from the lack of requisite capital accumulations, technical skills, scientific knowledge and industrial enterprise, which, unless they are eliminated, will stultify our efforts at advancement. For they have their cumulative effect precisely in the lack of these requisite reserves.

Customs which extol the virtues of extended family allegiance sustain nepotic practices, and regard the giving and taking of 'presents' as implicit and noble, because they promote the family welfare. They encourage indolence and bribery, they act as a brake upon ability, they discourage that deeper sense of individual responsibility which must be ready in a period of active reconstruction to accept obligation and fulfil trust. Above all, they retard productivity and oppose savings, the crucial factors in the rate of development. Polygamy donates its quota to these retarding influences, while our laws of succession and inheritance stifle the creative and inventive urge.

It is certainly not accidental that the industrial revolution came first to England, where the law of primogeniture entailed the inheritance of estates to the eldest son and made it necessary for the younger ones to follow pursuits which increased capital wealth. The historian, G. M. Trevelyan writes:

A distinguishing feature of the English gentry, which astonished foreign visitors as early as the reign of Henry VII, was their habit of turning their younger sons out of the manor-house to seek their fortunes elsewhere, usually as apprentices to thriving merchants and craftsmen in the towns. Foreigners ascribed the custom to English want of family affection. But it was also, perhaps, a wise instinct of 'what was best for the boy,' as well as a shrewd calculation of what was best for the family fortunes. The habit of leaving all the land and most of the money to the eldest son built up the great estates, which by steady accumulation down the years, became by Hanoverian times so marked a feature of English rural economy.

The younger son of the Tudor gentleman was not permitted to hang idle about the manor-house, a drain on the family income like the impoverished nobles of the Continent who were too proud to work. He was away making money in trade or in law. He often ended life a richer and more powerful man than his elder brother left in the old home.[1]

Another incentive was Puritanism which encouraged frugality and frowned upon wastefulness and ostentatious expenditure. As far as the national economy in an under-developed country is concerned, savings converted into ornaments and squandered in celebrating religious festivals, in extravagant wedding and funeral expenses, are as much lost as though they were thrown into the sea. Tribal society, counting little but sunrise, sunset and the moon's apogee, welcomed these festive breaks in the monotony of passing days, and has carried over the customs into the present, where another, more stirring philosophy needs to induce industriousness and thrift.

The legend of the medieval church that 'to labour is to pray' encouraged tillage of the soil. It was improved upon by the exhortations of Protestantism to work hard and be thrifty, which raised to a cardinal virtue the saving of money and its investment in profitable enterprise. Our less energetic society must be goaded into the acceptance of the stimuli necessary to rapid economic development by alterations in our social relationships and habits, if necessary by law. Japan, for instance, since the end of the Second World War, has legislated for a curtailed family unit which comprises husband and wife and their children. Legally, the husband has no responsibility for any other members of the family outside this close unit. Moreover, children are being taught not to look to their parents to will them an inheritance but to fend for themselves. The initiative, energy and drive thus released are being turned to the expansion of Japan's national economy.

A sense of devotion and sacrifice helps to instil acceptance of narrower standards for the present in the interest of wider ones in the future. A certain amount of belt-tightening is essential.

The Welfare State is the climax of a highly developed industrialism. To assure its benefits in a less developed country is to promise merely a division of poverty. Undoubtedly there must be an investment of a proportion of the capital reserves in the establishment of minimum wage levels to assure

[1] G. M. Trevelyan: *English Social History* (Longmans 1946), p. 125.

proper diet, as well as minimum health and housing facilities. But poverty is progressively reduced only as productivity increases and industrialization progresses and part of its surplus can be made available in increased wages, better housing and generally improved social conditions.

CHAPTER THIRTEEN

TOWARDS ECONOMIC INDEPENDENCE

WHERE INDEPENDENCE has been preceded by a struggle, there remains a residue of enthusiasm to start off the new national existence, which, if properly harnessed and directed, provides a spur in dealing with the tasks of state building. However, there is an accompanying lessening of tension, a sense of pressure eased, a pause for breath after battle. There is a feeling that, having made the supreme and sustained effort called for in ridding the country of colonial rule, a well-earned rest can now be taken.

The government has to make it clear that a new and greater effort is demanded to consolidate the nationalist victory. The people have to be fully re-animated so that they will drive forward with zest and courage to a more formidable battle in which they will be faced with different obstacles and hardships as the new state develops.

In Ghana, the Convention People's Party had the task of rousing the spirit of devotion and sacrifice necessary for the programme of development which it was given a mandate to discharge. The pre-independence slogan of 'Self-Government Now' was replaced with that of SERVE GHANA NOW. We held out no glowing hopes of wealth without labour. On the contrary, we stressed the need for everyone to work doubly hard now that we were labouring for ourselves and our children, and not for the enrichment of the former colonial power. The rewards would be national and individual dignity, the satisfaction which comes from creation and a raised standard of life. Foremost of all would be economic independence, without which our political independence would be valueless.

Under colonial rule, a country has very restricted economic

links with other countries. Its natural resources are developed only in so far as they serve the interests of the colonial power. However, once political independence has been achieved, the country's full potentialities can, and must, be explored. The domestic economy must be planned to promote the interests of its own nationals; and new and wider economic links must be created with other countries. Otherwise, the newly-independent country may fall victim to the highly dangerous forces of economic imperialism, and find that it has merely substituted one kind of colonialism for another.

In the past, all Ghana's economic links were with the West, mainly the United Kingdom. Since independence, we have forged new links with countries such as Russia, China, Poland, Czechoslovakia and Yugoslavia. The *Report of the United Kingdom Trade and Industrial Mission to Ghana*, published in 1959, showed that 85 per cent of all Ghana's import trade was in the hands of European firms (mainly British), 10 per cent in the hands of Asians (Indians, Syrians and Lebanese), and only 5 per cent in Ghanaian hands. Now, many Ghanaians are participating fully in the import and export business of the country. This was at one time the privilege of the few, because the market was limited to the sterling area only, and many of the popular brands of merchandise were monopolized by the few principal firms with foreign capital. In 1960, Ghana bought goods to the value of £G129,617,497 from the outside world and sold goods worth £G115,982,854.

In planning national development, the constant, fundamental guide is the need for economic independence. This involves a stock-taking of the national resources, both actual and potential, human as well as material, and the need to develop them by means of careful priorities and skilful integration so as to produce a strong, healthy and balanced economy. An important essential is to reduce our colonial-produced economic vulnerability by lessening the dependence on mono-crop farming.

Although cocoa still remains our main export, we have succeeded to some extent in diversifying our agriculture. We plan to relate our agricultural production primarily to the needs of the domestic market and to provide raw materials for secondary industries. We have begun to export bananas, coconuts, copra, palm kernels, and palm oil, kola and other nuts, plantains, rubber, coffee, spices, and tobacco. Several of these products, such as palm oil, tobacco, coffee and rubber, we shall use in increasing amounts in our own industries.

The government has provided grants for the regional development of water resources, for soil conservation and improvement projects, for financing experimental plantations of new crops, and for the application of new techniques to old crops. Our farmers are getting practical advice on how to use their land to the best advantage and to produce greater yields. They are being assisted by hire purchase and co-operative schemes to acquire modern agricultural machinery and processing equipment. More rational marketing procedures are being steadily introduced. Ghana has begun to export agricultural products which have never been grown here before, and improved methods of growing established crops have led to substantial increases in yield.

Diversity of agriculture has been accepted as a shibboleth, but if the development is simply towards the end of exportation, this can defeat the aim, since the fact that so many countries are now concentrating upon similar objectives can produce an over-extension of the sellers' market with subsequent depression of world prices. The fall in world prices of raw materials since the end of the Second World War has deprived the less developed countries of the staggering sum of £574,000 million, an amount greater than all the so-called aid which these countries have received from the advanced nations. This in itself represents a denial of tremendous capital for much-wanted development that would not have happened had we newly emergent states been united and strong enough to make our bargaining on the international commodity markets effective.

The major advantage which our independence has bestowed upon us is the liberty to arrange our national life according to the interests of our people, and along with it, the freedom, in conjunction with other countries, to interfere with the play of forces in the world commodity markets. 'Under-developed countries, utilising their newly won independent status, can by purposive policy interferences manage to alter considerably the direction of the market processes under the impact of which they have hitherto remained backward,' maintains Gunnar Myrdal.[1] This is a reality which we recognize, and we are using the international organizations and other media to exert pressures in our favour. Nevertheless, the richer countries are still in a position to limit the returns we obtain for our primary products, and we would seem to be more strategically placed as the major producer of a single raw material, either agricultural or extractive, for which there is a heavy world demand. Our cocoa production has hitherto given us such a commanding position but, with other comers tending to equalize the field, we are discovering that a satisfactory price level can be held only by agreement with the other large producers, such as Brazil, Nigeria, and others. With judicious use of our joint bargaining power, we may continue to use our exports of primary products to assist our industrialization.

Fluctuations in primary product prices are one of the insecurities in planning for less developed countries. Yet this cannot invalidate planning, which is the prime medium by which development can be undertaken in the given conditions. The government has to take the place of the adventurous entrepreneurs who created the capital basis of industrialization in the advanced countries.

The fishing industry has also benefited from government planning. A local building yard is turning out high-standard, powered fishing vessels to increase the scope of our fishing fleets. Complementing it, is a partnership association with overseas interests in a storage and refrigeration plant to take vegetables and other perishable goods as well as fish. A fishing harbour has been built at Elmina near Cape Coast, at one time a thriving Portuguese slaving and trading fort. A far larger fishing harbour has been constructed at our new coastal town of Tema. We hope that these two harbours, with adequate refrigeration facilities, will not only provide an adequate supply of high protein food for our people but enough fish to give work to a canning factory, the output from which will swell our exports.

In the industrial sphere, our aim has been to encourage the

[1] Gunner Myrdal: *Economic Theory and Under-Developed Regions*, Gerald Duckworth & Co. Ltd, p. 66.

establishment of plants where we have a natural advantage in local resources and labour or where we can produce essential commodities required for development or for domestic consumption. During 1961, over sixty new factories were opened. Among them was a distillery, a coconut oil factory, a brewery, a milk processing plant, and a lorry and bicycle assembly plant. In addition, agreements were signed for the establishment of a large, modern oil refinery, an iron and steel works, a flour mill, and sugar, textile and cement factories.

In forestry, we have introduced a programme for conservation and disease control, which will both safeguard our forest reserves and permit an advance in timber production. For Ghanaian lumber continues to be greatly prized in overseas markets and has a high place on our export list. Production in our local timber and cork factories has been expanded, and a marked improvement has taken place in the output of our mining of gold, diamonds, manganese and bauxite.

Our First Development Plan, launched in 1951, concentrated on communications, public works, education and general services. It prepared the way for our industrialization drive.

This was the keynote of our Second Development Plan which will provide for the establishment of many factories, of varying size, to produce a range of hundreds of different products. Financial provision is being made to ensure that adequate facilities will be available to prospective investors in industrial development.

Capital projects, such as the Volta River scheme and Tema harbour and its extension, will provide opportunities for our people to develop skills at all levels. An essential element in our industrial development must be the building up of our store of technical and managerial knowledge. We are encouraging foreign investment, but to accept it merely for the purpose of widening our industrial base without strengthening our own skills and techniques will leave us as economically impoverished as we were under colonialism. Unless our own nationals are given the opportunity of learning the job on the spot, side by side with foreign 'experts', we shall be as ignorantly backward as ever.

There is an argument that contends that young nations

emerging from colonialism are indulging in wasteful expenditure by duplicating industries and ventures which have already been perfected by the older industrialized nations of the world, whose products are available at lower cost than that for which they can be manufactured by us. It may be true in some instances that our local products cost more, though by no means all of them, and then only in the initial period. But even if it were substantially the fact, it is not an argument that we can accept. It is precisely because we were, under colonialism, made the dumping ground of other countries' manufactures and the providers merely of primary materials, that we remained backward; and if we were to refrain from building, for example, a soap factory simply because we might have to raise the price of soap to the community, we should be doing a disservice to the country.

Every time we import goods that we could manufacture if all the conditions were available, we are continuing our economic dependence and delaying our industrial growth. It is just these conditions that we are planning to provide, so as to make ourselves independent of the importation of goods and foodstuffs that we can produce ourselves. These are the conditions which will assist to build up our body of knowledge, techniques and skills, to make us more self-confident and self-sufficient, to push towards our economic independence. Another no less important aspect is that the exchange thus saved can be used to finance capital machinery for our own industries, which alone can give value to our industrialization.

Under colonial administration, postal, telegraphic and rail communications, broadcasting, such electricity and water services as existed, were all publicly owned and administered. Since independence we have added an airline, a shipping line, and a national bank. We have met with active resistance from vested interests in our efforts to establish our own mercantile fleet.

In connection with the founding of Ghana Airways, it was maintained that there were enough international airlines to serve our needs, and that the formation of a new one was an unnecessary multiplication, which would only serve to satisfy our national pride. Even if this were true, which it is not, it was an argument which did not appeal to us. Naturally, it increases our self-confidence to observe our own people helping to control the intricate mechanisms involved in the functioning of our own airways services, and we certainly experience a glow of pride in seeing our flag flying on planes and ships travelling to other countries. But again, we must encourage every kind of project that will add to our technical skills and national experience, and the operation of our own airlines and shipping makes a valuable contribution to this end.

We are at present planning to chart routes which will connect up the more important cities and towns of Africa. One of the factors making contact between Africans difficult is the absence of proper and plentiful means of communication. At the present time, Africa's communications look outward and not inward. They connect us rather with countries overseas than with ourselves. Shipping is not planned to go all the way round the coast, connecting roads criss-crossing the continent are non-existent, and the established routings operated by the existing international airlines are planned to serve travellers from Europe rather than Africans wishing to go from one part of this continent to another.

The routings of the European airlines frequently make it necessary for us to go, for instance, from North or East to West Africa by way of Europe. The absurdity of this is too obvious to need stressing. Almost every country in Europe has its own airline and the routes over the European continent are many and well-served, and no one thinks it at all strange that B.E.A., for example, duplicates some of Sabena's services. Therefore, the contention that we young nations on other continents should refrain from entering this vital field of communications smacks to us of the old imperialist attitude. Africa is a considerably larger continent than Europe, and there is more than enough reason for us African nations to develop communications between ourselves as a means of bringing us closer together and making our common intercourse easier and more fruitful.

The difficulties in getting our Black Star shipping line started have been successfully overcome and we are now enlarging it with a number of vessels whose keels have been laid in Germany, England, Holland and other countries. An efficient and adequate shipping fleet of our own will establish a powerful instrument to break the hold which the monopoly interests, including foreign shippers, have upon our trade. The revenue that goes abroad every year merely in the shipment of our cocoa runs into several millions sterling. Without shipping of our own, we are placed at the mercy of the foreign shipping lines, who could hold us to ransom, as they have in the past, at any time they wished. With our own shipping we shall become independent of external maritime agencies. We shall bring revenue to our own coffers, and once more make a fine addition to our skills and experience.

In connection with our communication projects, we have organized a nautical training school and a flying school which are designed to supply us with sufficient trained personnel to man and officer our ships and aircraft. Training is planned to proceed in stages so as to afford an annual output of men for immediate absorption into the shipping and flying services.

All industries of any major economic significance require, as a basic facility, a large and reliable source of power. In fact, the industrialization of Britain, America, Canada, Russia, and other countries too, emerged as a result of the discovery of new sources of energy. Newer nations, like our own, which are determined to catch up, must have a plentiful supply of electricity if they are to achieve any large-scale industrial advance. This, basically, was the justification for the Volta River Project.

This project, and the extension of the port and harbour at Tema, will have a massive effect on our national economy and enlarge its development. The Volta River scheme involves the production of hydro-electrical power by damming the river and applying the great volume of resultant cheap power to convert our bauxite resources into aluminium and to provide electrification for the nation's other industries. The Volta is our largest river, and we have enough bauxite to feed an aluminium smelter with a capacity of 200,000 tons. As originally conceived, the project called for raising the level of the water through the erection of a single high dam with a power station below to harness the energy released by the drop and convert it into electricity. Almost its whole output was to be devoted to the working of a smelter for rolling bauxite into aluminium sheets. This and the estimated cost of £300 million sterling dimmed the attractiveness of the project.

Nevertheless, I put it up to the colonial administration, who could see no prospect of raising the capital. It was obvious that the project would have to wait for independence and that I would have to take upon myself the task of enlisting financial help from overseas. With independence, we would be in a position to give government guarantees to outside investors. As soon as we became free, I started pushing the project, but quickly came up against a blank wall – the leading manufacturers of aluminium. They were organized into a consortium controlling the bulk of the world's output, and were not interested in a new competitor, still less in a new source of cheap aluminium. They expressed polite interest; one even sent a study mission to make an on-the-spot investigation and then turned the project down.

In the middle of 1958, I accepted an official invitation from President Eisenhower to visit the United States. During the talk I had with him I told him of the Volta River scheme. This led to a meeting with members of the Henry J. Kaiser Company, one of the large independent aluminium producers. They promised to send a team of experts to reassess engineering aspects of the original scheme. The team made their investigations and were favourably impressed. Their reassessment report recommended the construction of the dam at a different point from that originally proposed, and the extension of the scheme by the provision of two other hydro-electrical stations which would supply the more northerly part of the country with much-needed water and power.

The original Volta River project was designed to channel the bulk of the electricity produced by the dam to an aluminium smelter, and a comparatively small proportion only would have been made available for domestic consumption. The reassessment report recommended the installation of a national electricity grid covering the major part of Southern Ghana, from the harbour and industrial town of Tema, through Accra, Takoradi, Tarkwa, Dunkwa, Kumasi, Koforidua and back to the dam site at Akosombo. By the addition of the two smaller stations at Bui and Kpong, at higher points on the Volta, the national grid will extend into the territory on the other side of the river. At selected points on the grid there will be outlets from which electricity will be distributed for domestic and industrial users over an extended area. The routing of the grid will also provide outlets for power supplies to many of the larger mines. If transmission lines could be installed economically, there would be sufficient electricity to provide power for the whole country, and even to have some to sell to our neighbours.

This scheme was accepted in principle by the government, not only because it provided for reasonably economic operation in the early years by selling power to a smelter, but because it also provided for the production of a large and reliable source of electrical power, for many years to come, for Ghana's development. The main hydro-electrical project at Akosombo is being financed by Ghana, Britain, the United States and the International Bank, while an agreement has been reached with the Soviet Union for the design and construction of the power dam station at Bui.

One of the incidental results of the project will be the formation of an inland lake, which will cover 3,275 square miles and will be the largest man-made lake in the world. The lake will, it is estimated, eventually produce up to 10,000 tons of fresh fish a year, much of it readily accessible to areas of Ghana too far from the sea for our sea-water catches to be readily transported there. The lake fishing industry may well become very important, and it is proposed to develop this as soon as the lake has filled, and the fish have had time to multiply. A further advantage is that about six hundred square miles of land around the shores of the new lake will be flooded each season at high water, and should be suitable for the intensive cultivation of crops such as rice.

A private company has been formed by some of the world's greatest producers of aluminium, to establish the smelter at an estimated cost of £100 million. This company, known as Valco (Volta Aluminium Company Limited), will employ about 1,500 people. Once its pioneer company relief period is over, it will pay taxes to the Ghana Government, and also pay the Volta River Authority nearly £2½ million yearly for electricity.

The construction of the port and harbour at Tema was an integral part of the Volta River scheme. Some two thousand workers were employed to build thousands of housing units, planned with modern shopping areas in each suburb, a good network of roads, and sites for the aluminium plant and subsidiary factories. These will serve, and be served by, the large port area with its main, lee and south breakwaters. The quays have provision for extension, spacious sheds and warehouses, and railway links to each point of need.

The port started to operate in 1961, and already the town boasts almost 30,000 inhabitants. The ultimate population will be about 250,000. A whole fishing village has been moved from the condemned slums in which it was housed to a new one providing modern amenities.

Tema is Ghana's first planned city. To see its construction, and to remember the quiet palm-fringed cove which it replaces is to feel a sense of creation and development. More important, to see our men at work and to recall their pre-independence lounging under the palms, is to refresh our faith in our capacity to build our country.

The harbour, one of the largest in Africa, took over seven years to build. At peak periods during its construction, more than 3,500 men worked on it, some of them in the hills twenty miles away, where they quarried over ten million tons of rock for the main breakwaters. The harbour is nearly half as large again as the one at Takoradi, 160 miles to the west, and it encloses about 400 acres of water. It has a fishing harbour, and will eventually have five quays and fifteen berths.

Some two weeks before I opened the harbour at Tema, I officially launched the Volta River scheme by pressing a button to dynamite a slice out of the hillside at Akosombo. Hundreds of people danced, cheered, sang and fired guns into the air as the local chief poured libation and offered a sheep in sacrifice. One of my greatest dreams was coming true. In a few years there will be sufficient power to serve the needs of our industrial growth for a long time ahead.

CHAPTER FOURTEEN

BUILDING SOCIALISM IN GHANA

WHEN I SAT down with my party colleagues after independence to examine our urgent priorities, we framed a short list. We must abolish poverty, ignorance, illiteracy and improve our health services. These were direct and simple objectives not exactly amenable to legislation. In our situation they were formidable long-term objectives involving the elimination of social ills which have troubled the world since the beginning of history and still, in varying degrees, plague all the countries of the globe.

Delegations, official and semi-official, travel abroad from time to time, examining what other countries have to offer us in the way of experience and knowledge that can be applied to our circumstances. I maintain that there is no universal pattern for industrialization that can serve as an absolute model for new nations emerging out of colonialism. Looking around, we find no examples that are identical. European countries stretched their industrialization over a much longer period and in a different economic, scientific and social epoch. The United States cleared virgin land and used slave labour to amass its primary wealth. It has a geographic span that gave it special opportunities for a rapid industrial expansion and large-scale manufacture. The Soviet Union, starting from practically nothing, covering a vast land mass with manifold resources, swept away the former bureaucracy, and employed an authoritarian dictatorship to achieve its purpose.

Frequently, the nearest models are those countries, like Japan, or China, or India, that have made or are making their industrial revolution against conditions more nearly approximating to our own and in a time cycle closer to ours. India and China cover huge stretches of land and have excessive populations. Japan, though much smaller, has also created a population that gives her one of the highest densities in the world. These are factors which bear directly upon the planning for industrial development and economic independence. They provide both causes and solutions in the drawing up of programmes, and the degree of adjustment that is made to the problems which they also raise will depend upon the economic course that is taken.

In Ghana, we have embarked on the socialist path to progress. We want to see full employment, good housing and equal opportunity for education and cultural advancement for all the people up to the highest level possible. This means that:

- prices of goods must not exceed wages;
- house rentals must be within the means of all groups;
- social welfare services must be open to all;
- educational and cultural amenities must be available to everyone.

It means, in short, that the real income and standard of life of all farmers and workers must rise appreciably.

I have already made it clear that colonial rule precluded that accumulation of capital among our citizens which would have assisted thorough-going private investment in industrial construction. It has, therefore, been left to government, as the holder of the means, to play the role of main entrepreneur in laying the basis of the national economic and social advancement. If we turned over to private interests the going concerns capitalized out of national funds and national effort, as some of our critics would like to see us do, we should be betraying the trust of the great masses of our people for the greedy interests of a small coterie of individuals, probably in alliance with foreign capitalists. Production for private profit deprives a large section of the people of the goods and services produced. If, therefore, we are to fulfil our pledge to the people and achieve the programme set out above, socialism is our only alternative. For socialism assumes the public ownership of the means of production, the land and its resources, and the use of those means in fulfilment of the people's needs.

Socialism, above all, is predicated upon the ability to satisfy those needs. It is obvious, therefore, that Ghana at this time is not possessed of the socialist means. Indeed, we have still to lay the actual foundations on which they can be built, the modernization of our agriculture and the industrialization of our country. We have to transfer to the hands of the people the major means of production and distribution.

Our rate of development will be governed by the surpluses that will be made available out of heightened productivity, which includes, besides the greater output from labour and increased agricultural yields, the more efficient employment of investment and the resulting increased productivity. Government interference in all matters affecting economic growth in less developed countries is today a universally accepted principle, and interests, domestic or foreign, enjoying the opportunities of profitable gain, cannot object to some control of the reinvestment of part of that gain in the national development of the country in which it is reaped. Today, not even in the advanced countries dedicated to private enterprise is the principle of *laissez faire* allowed absolutely free play. Restrictions of all kinds interfere with the uninhibited movement of capital. The government of Ghana, while making investment in our development as attractive as possible, cannot, however, place that development and our ultimate economic independence in jeopardy by surrendering their intrinsic prior requirements.

These requirements are at the central heart of our planning, and in the context of our national independence and advancement and the greater objective of Pan-African unity they must govern our policies.

The road of reconstruction on which Ghana has embarked is a new road, parts of whose topography are only hazily sensed, other parts still unknown. A certain amount of trial and error in following the road is inevitable. Mistakes we are bound to make, and some undoubtedly we have already made. They are our own and we learn from them. That is the value of being free and independent, of acquiring our experience out of the consequence of our own decisions, out of the achievements of our own efforts.

Our planning will be geared to our policy of increasing government participation in the nation's economic activities, and all enterprises are expected to accept this policy and to operate within the framework of our national laws. Our aim is the building of a society in which the principles of social justice will be paramount. But there are many roads to socialism, and in the circumstances of our present retardedness, we must employ all the forces at our disposal while we fashion others which will accelerate our progress towards our goal.

Ghana's economy may be divided into five sectors. These are: (1) State enterprises; (2) enterprises owned by foreign private interests; (3) enterprises jointly owned by State and foreign private interests; (4) co-operatives; and (5) small-scale Ghanaian private enterprise. The government has given recognition to the activities of these different sectors, and has decided that in no sector of the economy will exclusive rights of operation in respect of any commodity be conferred on any single person. Private small-scale personal enterprise, however, is reserved to Ghanaians, in order to encourage and utilize personal initiative and skill among our own people.

Naturally the operations of these different sectors have to be taken into account in our calculations for planning our basic economic reconstruction. We have to create in the quickest possible time, without a hasty improvisation that will ultimately defeat our objective, a diversified, many-sided economy able to supply a growing population with the basic commodities that will lessen the burden now imposed on the country by the need to import so many of its requirements. In order to increase our material resources, we have, as a major priority, to raise significantly agricultural productivity. This is a pre-condition for our industrial growth, as all our plans can founder on a countryside that does not contribute a rising quota of production. There must be a transformation of our subsistence farms into commodity producing farms, so that they may provide enough food for our steadily rising population, give raw materials to feed secondary industries and cash crops to help pay for our necessary imports. Priority will be given to those investments which will quickly promote capital formation; will save imports or increase exports; and reduce the differences between the different regions of the country created by colonialism.

Our over-all plan will take account of our population and their requirements, taking into consideration the yearly increase, which is estimated at about three per cent. It will count our man-power and our actual and potential reservoir of skills, and will set annual targets of achievement. These targets will embrace not only output and the absorption of planned numbers of workers in the different categories and at different levels, but will arrange for the training of skilled workers, and of managers and executives qualified and able to see that the planned projects are carried out efficiently, economically and to schedule.

Within the general planning are included our educational, social welfare and health programmes. They are devised in relation to the needs of our healthy development and the improvement of the lives of the people. Apart from the humanitarian principles by which the government is guided, an educated, healthy population represents the human investment in our development, and anything that can be spared from our surpluses will be added to the already planned allocations for the purpose.

Our planning will stretch out into the regions beyond the main centres. At the present time there are big differences in the degree of economic and social development between the various regions of the country, and our population density is extremely uneven. Regional planning will contribute to reducing the differences by providing a more even distribution of economic activity between the various regions, by utilizing the natural potentialities of each region. It will also aim at controlling and reducing unnecessary migration, with its attendant problems. Our over-all planning, in short, will be designed to unify and discipline economic activity. It will expand the creative spirit of the people by the tasks of responsibility that will be given them in management, supervision and invention.

Control from the top must ensure that individual executives and administrators do not misinterpret policy and instructions and break out of the co-ordinated pattern with the introduction of improvised schemes. As we proceed, it may be found that certain priorities may have to give way to others which may present themselves as more urgent in relation to the needs of capital formation or strategic development. Thus, while there must be the strictest control to safeguard against unrelated over-spreading on any project, there must be a certain elasticity to allow for emendation or adjustment without upsetting the general plan and our budgeting.

Our present budgetary and fiscal systems have been taken over from the colonial régime and call for adjustment to the socialized objective of our planning. These are being overhauled and adapted to our development needs and the planned growth of our diversified agricultural and industrial base. Our fiscal policy must be so framed as to release the maximum initiative and husband our national financial resources for efficient and effective investment in our development. It would simply defeat our whole objective of economic independence, for instance, to encourage foreign investment in our development and see the flight of capital from Ghana exceed or even approximate the totality of such investment.

Under the new policy, surpluses must be pressed out of rising production to finance development. As the state sector widens, development finance will come less and less from taxes and dues, though private enterprise, both foreign and domestic, will continue to provide its quota through these avenues. Our real wealth will come from increased productivity. This does not mean that every advance in productivity will lead to an immediate rise in the standard of living. This is especially the case in the early stages of industrialization, when the need to plough back capital for further development is of paramount importance. Wages, however, must be set at a level which will provide proper diet and maintain working energy, while the increased productivity is used to give effective balance between the desirability of capital development and secondary industries at any given time.

The socialist objective implies the universal good of the nation, and in the interests of that socialist objective it will be necessary for all of us to forgo some immediate personal desire for a greater benefit a bit later on. Speedier development out of surpluses or social services in the interest of the community confer more advantages upon a greater number of people than would increased wages for certain groups of workers.

But as productivity rises appreciably and the socialist base of the economy extends through increasing public ownership of the means of production, the government will not only be able to mobilize a greater surplus for use in the interests of the country, but will be in a position to reward labour for its greater exertions by increased wages.

If our new economic and industrial policy is to succeed, there must be a change of outlook among some of those who are responsible for running our affairs. They must acquire a socialist perspective and a socialist drive keyed to the national needs and demands. The executives of our public and statutory organizations must achieve a new attitude to their jobs, which they owe to the struggles of the people and the labours of our farmers and workers. No economy, least of all a young one like ours struggling to find a stable base, can afford to drain its resources in subsidizing unproductive ventures from which only well-paid executives profit. Moreover, it cannot afford to waste resources in men and materials, but must use them wisely in pursuit of the socialist objective.

The spirit of service to the nation must permeate throughout our society. In a dawn broadcast on 8 April 1961, I spoke of the dangers arising from Ghanaian public men attempting to combine business with political life, and warned that those who could not give entirely disinterested service should leave politics or be thrown out. Legislation has since limited the amount of property our public men may own.

Our profound need at the present time is for tolerably proficient technicians, capable of manning, supervising and managing our agricultural and industrial developments. Necessarily, there must be a nucleus of more advanced graduates to take over teaching jobs in these spheres and to provide us with a corps of scientific knowledge which can sustain invention and apply its learning to our extended development. For the moment, however, while we require advanced engineers, physicists, scientists, bio-chemists, and others, the emphasis cannot lie in this direction.

We are having to devise an educational system that will provide in the shortest possible time a body of skilled personnel able to serve the country's needs at all levels. The University of Ghana has been reformed so that too much emphasis will not be placed, as under the colonial administration, on purely literary and academic subjects. While we appreciate that these are necessary and desirable, they are at this juncture in our national life rather in the nature of luxuries which we cannot afford to indulge in as much as we should like.

In accord with our needs, the government has introduced free and compulsory primary and middle school education, with the view to the total literacy of the country by the time we celebrate the tenth anniversary of our Republic. We have, unfortunately, a shortage of teachers. To meet this shortage, emergency training centres have been established where volunteers can obtain the appropriate certificates; while the problem of inadequate accommodation is being coped with by the adoption of a shift system in many schools.

The study of science has been made compulsory for all school curricula, and primary technical schools are to be established. These schools will be manned by graduates and will operate alongside the general primary schools. They will give concurrent training to boys and girls, so that by the time the pupil leaves primary school, the technical training gained will give sufficient proficiency for semi-skilled work. The bright scholar can continue his technical training together with his general studies at secondary school to prepare him to complete a short technical course at one of our technological institutes.

The University of Ghana at Legon and the Kwame Nkrumah University of Technology at Kumasi and many other colleges and institutes in various parts of the country cater for higher education and research. The Ghana Academy of Sciences carries out research in the sciences, history, languages, sociology, medicine, and so on. The work of these institutions is planned and co-ordinated by the National Council for Higher Education. The annual meeting and report of the Ghana Academy of Sciences are matters of national importance, for they record progress and outline plans for the future. We attach considerable importance and pride to the title of 'Academician', which is to be recognized as one of the highest national awards.

There are many problems for the solution of which we must look to our scientific institutions. For instance, with more and more cocoa coming to glut the market, the Cocoa Research Institute will turn its attention to setting up, without any loss of time, a department for dealing with cocoa derivatives and their uses. We have, too, many species of timber that are not being utilized. This is a complete waste and the Timber Utilization Research Unit is being turned into an institute, adequately

staffed so that it can cope with the problem and give effective
results. We are faced with the task of producing crops for
conversion into commodities, and must depend upon our
research institutes to assist us with the problems involved. The
demands that will be made upon our scientific institutions as we
proceed will grow more varied and extensive, and we shall have
to strengthen them.

One of our problems at the present time is that of unemployment, particularly among school-leavers whose education has
not gone very far. To meet this problem, we have formed a
Workers Brigade, which has absorbed about 12,000 young men
and women, who are being trained in discipline, responsibility
and citizenship. They are being given the elements of skill which
will enable them to find employment in agriculture and industry
as our development gathers momentum. Their training is meanwhile being supplemented by valuable experience in work on
community projects and in co-operative agriculture. The Volta
River project will require 15,000 workers over a period of five
years and our official employment exchanges are now placing
almost 2,000 workers in all kinds of jobs every month.

With the changes brought by the new social and economic
policy, there has been a re-examination of the role of our trade
unions. The public and semi-public sectors of the economy have
been widening out, so that the government is now the largest
employer of labour in the country, while its regulations are
placing an increasing obligation upon private enterprise not only
to respect the rights of labour but to make its contribution to the
investment in our national development. The workers understand that they are working for a state which is directed by a
government of their own choosing, whose programme they have
helped to formulate through party membership, and which they
actively endorse and support. Hence the aspirations of the people
and the economic and social objectives of the government are
synonymous.

The role of the trade unions, therefore, in our circumstances, is
entirely different from that in a capitalist society where the
motivating force is the accumulation of private profit. The aims
of our trade unions, being identified with those of the government, weds them to active participation in the carrying out of the

government's programme. Within the capitalist states, the trade unions play the role of watchdogs for labour against the employers. Even so, they are by no means 'free'. Their leaders are bought off by the sweets of office and often have their secret arrangements with employers. More than that, they have for the most part accepted the ideology of their capitalist class and, through its exposition throughout their extensive forums and the witch-hunting of those who do not conform, have openly identified themselves with that ideology.

In such circumstances there cannot be any talk of freedom. In Ghana, the trade unions are openly associated with the Convention People's Party as one of its wings. They have no need to hide this association behind hypocritical sophistries. They are, in fact, drawing the workers into the implementation of government plans by setting up works councils inside the public enterprises to give effective expression to their national consciousness.

For it is only through the consent of the people in action that our target for national reconstruction can be achieved. In cooperation with the Trades Union Congress, we are devising a programme of productivity and waste-avoidance incentives which will include promotions, decorations, cash bonuses and publicity for individuals who have done exemplary work.

By the industry and example of the Ghana labour movement, we hope to inspire other Africans still fighting colonialism. Our cruel colonial past and the present-day intrigues of neo-colonialism have hammered home the conviction that Africa can no longer trust in anybody but herself and her resources. Imperialism, having been forced out through the door by African nationalism, is attempting to return by other, back-door means. African workers, as the likeliest victims of these infiltrations, must be on their guard. There is a constant endeavour to use the African trade union movement as a protagonist in the cold war conflict, and some of the leaders, through flattery and the acceptance of financial assistance for their unions, have allowed themselves to be suborned. This is a dangerous situation as it can drag Africa into active participation in cold war politics and deprive us of our safeguarding weapon of independent non-alignment. Unfortunately, there are also some leaders of the African independent states who cannot see this danger. Moreover, because of their alliances with European powers, they are obliged at times to act against the interests of their workers and their trade unions in support of the alien interests in their countries. The African trade union movement must promote the independence and welfare of the African worker; it cannot run the risk of subordinating the safety of African independence and the needs of African development to other, non-African influences.

I see in the All-African Trade Union Federation, because of its independent African orientation, a dynamic and positive instrument for drawing together the peoples of the African countries. It can act as a rallying pivot for all the African trade union movements on the continent; it can become an immediate practical union, bringing together the labour movements existing in the independent African states and leaving room for others to join as they become free. We in Africa must learn to band together to promote African interests or fall victims to imperialist manœuvres to re-colonize us.

The development of a united African trade union movement will give our working classes a new African consciousness and the right to express themselves in the councils of world labour unfettered by any foreign view and uncoerced by external force. The International Confederation of Free Trade Unions and the World Federation of Trade Unions are organizations committed to the ideological policies of West and East. The All-African Trade Union Federation will give the world a new force independent of both of them, and loyal not only to the needs of the new Africa and the new African, but also to the international working class.

The growth of this new African trade unionism is linked up with the future of Africa. Such a dynamic force, allied to political action, is the surest means of routing out of our continent the last remnants of colonialism and exploitation, since it will stimulate the effectiveness of the nationalist movements.

Just as political independence could not have been attained without the leadership of a strong, disciplined party, so Ghana's economic independence and the objective of socialism cannot be achieved without decisive party leadership. I am convinced that the Convention People's Party, based as it is on the support of the overwhelming majority of the people, is best able to carry through our economic plans and build a socialist state. The structure of the C.P.P. has been built up out of our own experiences, conditions and environment. It is entirely Ghanaian in content and African in outlook, though imbued with Marxist socialist philosophy.

At all stages, we seek the fullest co-operation of the people and their organizations, and in this way, and through public control of the means of production, we hope to evolve the truest kind of democracy within the Aristotelian meaning. By mass consultation we shall associate the people with the running of the nation's affairs, which must then operate in the interests of the people. Moreover, since control of the modern state is linked up with the control of the means of production and distribution, true democracy can only be said to exist when these have passed into the hands of the people. For then the people exercise control of the State through their will as expressed in the direct consultation between government and them. This must surely provide the most concrete and clearest operation of true democracy.

To attain this democratic, socialist control, we have from time to time to make a review of the administrative apparatus at our disposal, remembering that it was originally bequeathed to us by a colonial régime committed to a very different purpose. Even though this apparatus has already been subjected to considerable change, it still carries vestiges of inherited attitudes and ways of thought which have been transmitted even to some of our newer institutions. In our adaptations, because we are embarking upon an uncharted path, we may have to proceed pragmatically. Changes which are made today may themselves call for further change tomorrow. But when we are endeavouring to establish a new kind of life within a new kind of society, based upon up-to-date modes of production, we must acknowledge the fact that we are in a period of flux and cannot afford to be hidebound in our decisions and attitudes. We must accommodate our minds and attitudes to the need for constant adaptation, never losing sight of principle and our expressed social objective.

With this new approach to our economic and industrial development, every avenue of education and information must be used to stir and nourish the political consciousness of the people and make and keep them aware of the welfare objectives of the government's planning. We must at all times ensure their fullest support, without which our plans for their enhanced well-being can fail. They must be refreshed by the *élan* which swept them into the battle for political emancipation in order to carry through the more exacting battle for economic freedom and advanced social progress.

Socialism needs socialists to build it. Accordingly, we are taking positive steps to ensure that the party and the country produce the men and women who can handle our socialist programme.

Those members who are to be in the forefront of the educational drive take refresher courses in party political teaching. The youth of the country are organized in the Young Pioneers Movement, which is designed to give them training in citizenship within a society which will be rooted in co-operation and not acquisitive competition. For this end Africa needs a new type of citizen, a dedicated, modest, honest and informed man. A man who submerges self in service to the nation and mankind. A man who abhors greed and detests vanity. A new type of man whose humility is his strength and whose integrity is his greatness.

Members of the Young Pioneers take part in educational and cultural activities. They learn about the history of Ghana and Africa, and about the present political scene in Africa. They have their choral and dramatic groups, and attend classes in many practical subjects. Through manual work and self-help schemes they are instilled with the idea of service. Physical training, too, plays an important part in the movement, to teach the virtues of team work and the need to build healthy bodies and minds. Teachers and instructors are recruited directly from schools and teacher training colleges for part-time work; others are prepared at the Party's training centre, the Kwame Nkrumah Institute at Winneba, which is responsible for the Party's general political education.

All, from members of the Central Committee, Ministers and high party officials to the lowest propagandist in the field, pass through a course at the Institute. Farmers, factory workers, and others from all walks of life meet at Winneba, where they have the opportunity to broaden their political knowledge and ideological understanding. They strengthen their qualities of loyalty and discipline, thereby increasing the total discipline of the party and the loyalty of the general membership.

The Institute does not cater for Ghana alone. Its doors are open to all from Africa and the world who seek knowledge to fit themselves for the great freedom fight against imperialism, old or new.

Party study groups exist all over the country, in factories, workshops, government departments and offices, in fact, in every nook and cranny of Ghana, for the study of African life and culture, party ideology, decisions and programmes, and for explaining government policies and actions. For we have a tremendous, herculean task before us. It calls for all our attention, all our brains. Our party, through all its members, must show its merits in this our greatest mission yet, the building of a socialist Ghana, and the laying of the foundations for the political and economic unification of Africa.

CHAPTER FIFTEEN

TOWARDS AFRICAN UNITY

THERE ARE those who maintain that Africa cannot unite because we lack the three necessary ingredients for unity, a common race, culture and language. It is true that we have for centuries been divided. The territorial boundaries dividing us were fixed long ago, often quite arbitrarily, by the colonial powers. Some of us are Moslems, some Christians; many believe in traditional, tribal gods. Some of us speak French, some English, some Portuguese, not to mention the millions who speak only one of the hundreds of different African languages. We have acquired cultural differences which affect our outlook and condition our political development.

All this is inevitable, due to our historical background. Yet in spite of this I am convinced that the forces making for unity far outweigh those which divide us. In meeting fellow Africans from all parts of the continent I am constantly impressed by how much we have in common. It is not just our colonial past, or the fact that we have aims in common, it is something which goes far deeper. I can best describe it as a sense of one-ness in that we are *Africans*.

In practical terms, this deep-rooted unity has shown itself in the development of Pan-Africanism, and, more recently, in the projection of what has been called the African Personality in world affairs.

The expression 'Pan-Africanism' did not come into use until the beginning of the twentieth century when Henry Sylvester-Williams of Trinidad, and William Edward Burghardt DuBois of the United States of America, both of African descent, used it at several Pan-African Congresses which were mainly attended by scholars of African descent of the New World.

A notable contribution to African nationalism and Pan-Africanism was the 'Back to Africa' movement of Marcus Garvey.

The First Pan-African Congress was held in Paris in 1919 while the peace conference was in session. The French Prime Minister, Clemenceau, when asked what he thought of the holding of a Pan-African Congress, remarked: 'Don't advertise it, but go ahead.' His reaction was fairly typical among Europeans at the time. The very idea of Pan-Africanism was so strange that it seemed unreal and yet at the same time perhaps potentially dangerous. Fifty-seven representatives from various African colonies and from the United States of America and the West Indies attended. They drafted various proposals, though nothing much came of them. For example, they proposed that the allied and associated powers should establish a code of law 'for international protection of the natives of Africa'.

The Second Pan-African Congress was held in London in 1921. The British Government, if not sympathetic, was tolerant, and 113 delegates attended. This Congress, though far from being truly representative of African opinion, nevertheless went some way towards putting the African case to the world. In a *Declaration to the World*, drafted at the closing session, it was stated that 'the absolute equality of races, physical, political and social, is the founding stone of world and human advancement'. They were more concerned in those days with social than with political improvement, not yet recognizing the pre-emption of the latter in order to engage the former.

Two years later, in 1923, a Third Pan-African Congress was held in London. Among the resolutions passed was one which asked for a voice for Africans in their own governments; and another which asked for the right of access to land and its resources. The political aspect of social justice was beginning to be understood. But in spite of the work of DuBois and others, progress was slow. The movement lacked funds and membership was limited. The delegates were idealists rather than men of action. However, a certain amount of publicity was achieved, and Africans and men of African descent for the first time gained valuable experience in working together.

A Fourth Pan-African Congress was held in New York in

1927, which 208 delegates attended, but after that the movement seemed to fade out for a time.

A non-party organization, the International African Service
Bureau, was set up in 1937, and this was the forerunner of the
Pan-African Federation, the British section of the Pan-African
Congress movement. Its aim was 'to promote the well-being and
unity of African peoples and peoples of African descent throughout the world', and also 'to strive to co-operate between African
peoples and others who share our aspirations'.

Pan-Africanism and African nationalism really took concrete
expression when the Fifth Pan-African Congress met in Manchester in 1945. For the first time the necessity for well-organized,
firmly-knit movements as a primary condition for the success of
the national liberation struggle in Africa was stressed.

The Congress was attended by more than two hundred delegates from all over the world. George Padmore and I had been
joint secretaries of the organizational committee which planned
the Congress and we were delighted with the results of our work.
Among the declarations addressed to the imperialist powers
asserting the determination of the colonial people to be free
was the following:

> The Fifth Pan-African Congress calls on intellectuals and pro-
> fessional classes of the Colonies to awaken to their responsi-
> bilities. The long, long night is over. By fighting for trade union
> rights, the right to form co-operatives, freedom of the press,
> assembly, demonstration and strike, freedom to print and read
> the literature which is necessary for the education of the masses,
> you will be using the only means by which your liberties will be
> won and maintained. Today there is only one road to effective
> action – the organization of the masses.[1]

A definite programme of action was agreed upon. Basically,
the programme centred round the demand for constitutional
change, providing for universal suffrage. The methods to be
employed were based on the Gandhist technique of non-violent
non-co-operation, in other words, the withholding of labour,

[1] *Declaration to the Colonial Peoples of the World* (by the present author),
approved and adopted by the Pan-African Congress held in Manchester,
England, 15–21 October 1945.

civil disobedience and economic boycott. There were to be variations of emphasis from territory to territory according to the differing circumstances. The fundamental purpose was identical: national independence leading to African unity. The limited objective was combined with the wider perspective.

Instead of a rather nebulous movement, concerned vaguely with black nationalism, the Pan-African movement had become an expression of African nationalism. Unlike the first four Congresses, which had been supported mainly by middle-class intellectuals and bourgeois reformists, the Fifth Pan-African Congress was attended by workers, trade unionists, farmers and students, most of whom came from Africa.

When the Congress ended, having agreed on the programme for Pan-African nationalism, a working committee was set up with DuBois as chairman and myself as general secretary. The Congress headquarters were moved to London, where shortly afterwards the West African National Secretariat was also established. Its purpose was to put into action, in West Africa, the policies agreed upon in Manchester. I was offered, and accepted, the secretaryship.

We published a monthly paper called *The New African*, and called two West African Conferences in London. By this time the political conscience of African students was thoroughly aroused, and they talked of little else but the colonial liberation movement. The more enthusiastic among us formed a kind of inner group which we called *The Circle*. Only those working genuinely for West African freedom and unity were admitted, and we began to prepare ourselves actively for revolutionary work in any part of the African continent.

It was at this point that I was asked to return to the Gold Coast to become general secretary of the United Gold Coast Convention. I accepted with some hesitation. There was my work for the West African National Secretariat to consider, and also the preparations which were being made for the calling of a West African National Conference in Lagos in October 1948.

I called at Freetown and Monrovia on the way home, and spoke with African nationalists there, telling them of the conference plans and urging them to attend. The political contacts I made in both Sierra Leone and Liberia were to prove significant later, though the conference in Lagos never, in fact, took place.

When I returned to West Africa in 1947, it was with the intention of using the Gold Coast as a starting-off point for African independence and unity. With the mass movement I was able to build up in the Convention People's Party, the Gold Coast secured its freedom and emerged as the sovereign state of Ghana in 1957. I at once made it clear that there would be no meaning to the national independence of Ghana unless it was linked with the total liberation of the African continent. While our independence celebrations were actually taking place, I called for a conference of all the sovereign states of Africa, to discuss plans for the future of our continent.

The first Conference of Independent African States met in Accra in April 1958. There were then only eight, namely, Egypt, Ghana, Sudan, Libya, Tunisia, Liberia, Morocco and Ethiopia. Our purpose was to exchange views on matters of common interest; to explore ways and means of consolidating and safe-guarding our independence; to strengthen the economic and cultural ties between our countries; to decide on workable arrangements for helping fellow Africans still subject to colonial rule; and to examine the central world problem of how to secure peace.

When, on 15 April 1958, I welcomed the representatives to the conference, I felt that at last Pan-Africanism had moved to the African continent where it really belonged. It was an historic occasion. Free Africans were actually meeting together, *in Africa*, to examine and consider African affairs. Here was a signal departure from established custom, a jar to the arrogant assumption of non-African nations that African affairs were solely the concern of states outside our continent. The African personality was making itself known.

Because many of the speeches made at the conference were similar in content, it was alleged in some quarters that there had been previous collaboration. I am able to state categorically that all of us who spoke had prepared our speeches independently. If they showed identity of thought and belief, it was because our attitudes in Africa were assuming an identity of vision and purpose.

The Accra Conference resulted, as indeed I hoped it would, in a great upsurge of interest in the cause of African freedom and unity. But matters did not rest there. Some weeks after the conference ended some of my colleagues and I set out on a tour of the countries which took part in the conference. Our purpose was to convey to the heads of states and governments, many of whom were unable to attend the conference personally, the good wishes of the government and people of Ghana.

Everywhere we went we were enthusiastically received, and were able to discuss ways and means of strengthening further the ties of friendship between our respective countries. Plans to improve cultural and economic relations were the subject of a series of communiqués. Our common background and basic common interests drew us together.

The year 1958 was memorable not only for the first conference of independent African states, but also for the opening of the All-African People's Conference in Accra in December 1958. Delegates from 62 African nationalist organizations attended the conference.

The will to unity which the conference expressed was at least equal to the determination to carry forward the process of independence throughout Africa. The enthusiasm generated among the delegates returning to their own countries profoundly influenced subsequent developments. The Belgian Congo, Uganda, Tanganyika, Nyasaland, Kenya, the Rhodesias, South Africa, all were affected by the coming together in Accra of representatives of the various freedom movements of the continent. The total liberation and the unity of the continent at which we aimed were evolving and gaining reality in the experience of our international gatherings.

In November 1959, representatives of trade unions all over Africa met in Accra to organize an All-African Trade Union Federation. The African labour movement has always been closely associated with the struggle for political freedom, as well as with economic and social development.

A further step forward in the direction of all-African co-operation took place a few months later when the conference to discuss Positive Action and Security in Africa opened in Accra in April 1960. It was called by the government of Ghana, in

consultation with other independent African states, to consider
the situation in Algeria and in South Africa, and also to discuss
and plan future action to prevent Africa being used as a testing
ground for nuclear weapons. Equally important matters to be
considered were the total liberation of Africa, and the necessity
to guard against neo-colonialism and balkanization, both of
which would impede unity.

In mid-1960 a further conference of Independent African
states, twelve in number, was held in Addis Ababa, and yet
another all-African conference met in Accra. The latter, a conference of African women to discuss common problems, opened
on 18 July. The delegates spoke of freedom and unity, and of the
urgent need for social and economic progress.

While their conference was taking place, events in the newly-
independent Congo were causing one international crisis after
another. The province of Katanga was attempting to secede
from the Republic of Congo, and Patrice Lumumba, the
Congolese Prime Minister, had asked for United Nations aid.

Some of the dangers of neo-colonialism and balkanization,
which we had foreseen, now became realities. Foreign business
interests, as well as policies connected with the cold war, began
to dominate the Congo political scene and prevented early action
by the United Nations which, if it had been used to effect the
purpose for which it had been called in, could well have been
decisive in maintaining the sovereignty of Lumumba's government.

If at that time, July 1960, the independent states of Africa had
been united, or had at least a joint military high command and a
common foreign policy, an African solution might have been
found for the Congo; and the Congo might have been able to
work out its own destiny, unhindered by any non-African
interference.

As it was, the position in the Congo steadily worsened, and all
the unrest and dangers of disunity became fully apparent. The
only people to score from the situation were the neo-colonialists
and their allies in South Africa and the Rhodesias, who used
the struggle in the Congo as an argument to demonstrate the
inability of Africans to manage their own affairs.

In a last minute attempt to save the situation, and to show

some kind of African solidarity, a conference of independent African states met in Leopoldville from 25–30 August, at the invitation of Patrice Lumumba. At the conference, which was at Foreign Ministers' level, delegates aired their views on the Congo crisis. Although the conference did not achieve its purpose, it was significant in that it enabled the delegates to see for themselves what was really going on in the Congo and to report on this personally to their governments. A valuable object lesson, however, on the imperative need for unity in defence of the independence of Africa had been demonstrated.

Against a background of continuing struggle in the Congo, and of trouble in South Africa, Algeria, and other parts of the continent, an All-African People's Conference met in Cairo early in 1961. About two hundred delegates attended. The conference warned independent African states to beware of neo-colonialism, which was associated with the United Kingdom, the United States of America, France, Western Germany, Israel, Belgium, the Netherlands, and South Africa. It also warned states to be on their guard against imperialist agents in the guise of religious or philanthropic organizations. Resolutions included a call to the 'anti-imperialist' bloc to help in the development of African economies by granting long-term loans at low interest rates to be paid in local currencies. They demanded the expulsion of South Africa from the United Nations Organization; the dismissal of Mr Hammarskjöld; the immediate release of Jomo Kenyatta; the immediate independence of the Rhodesias and the dissolution of the Central African Federation. The conference also called for a trade boycott of the Rhodesias; criticized policies in Angola, Cameroon and the Congo, and affirmed that M. Gizenga's régime in Stanleyville was the legitimate Congo government.

As the years go by, further All-African People's Conferences will take place, and their resolutions and declarations will become increasingly significant as they gain more power. Other all-African gatherings will continue to make their impression, whether they are held to discuss political, social or economic problems. Hardly a week goes by without news of some gathering together of Africans from different parts of the continent. As the whole of Africa becomes free, these gatherings will gain in membership, strength and effectiveness. But it is only when full political unity has been achieved that we will be able to declare the triumphant end of the Pan-African struggle and the African liberation movements.

CHAPTER SIXTEEN

SOME ATTEMPTS AT UNIFICATION

THE FIRST step towards African political union was taken on 23 November 1958, when Ghana and the Republic of Guinea united to form a nucleus for a Union of African States. We established a system of exchange of resident ministers, who were recognized as members of both the government of Ghana and the government of Guinea.

The following year, in July 1959, the Presidents of Liberia and Guinea, and I, met at Sanniquellie to discuss the whole question of African emancipation and unity. At the end of our talks we issued a Declaration of Principles, in which we stated that the name of our organization would be the Community of Independent African States. Members of the Community would maintain their own national identity and constitutional structure; and each member of the Community would agree not to interfere in the internal affairs of any other member. The general policy of the Community would be to build up a free and prosperous African Community for the benefit of its peoples, and the peoples of the world. The policy would be founded on the maintenance of diplomatic, economic and cultural relations, on a basis of equality and reciprocity, with all the states of the world which adopted positions compatible with African interests. One of its main objectives would be to help African territories not yet free to gain their independence.

Membership of the Community was declared open to all independent African states and federations, and any non-independent country of Africa was given the right to join the Community on attainment of independence. The motto adopted for the Community was INDEPENDENCE AND UNITY.

On 24 December 1960 I met President Sekou Touré of Guinea and President Modibo Keita of Mali at Conakry, with the result that a special committee met in Accra from 13 to 18 January 1960 to formulate proposals for a Ghana-Guinea-Mali Union. The three of us had a further series of meetings in Accra from 27 to 29 April 1961, and agreed upon a Charter.

Our Union was named The Union of African States (U.A.S.) and was to form the nucleus of the United States of Africa. It was declared open to every state or federation of African states which accepted its aims and objectives. Articles 3 and 4 of the Charter contained the aims and activities of the Union, and I quote them below in full:

Article 3. The aims of the Union of African States (U.A.S.) are as follows:

to strengthen and develop ties of friendship and fraternal co-operation between the Member States politically, diplomatically, economically and culturally;

to pool their resources in order to consolidate their independence and safeguard their territorial integrity; to work jointly to achieve the complete liquidation of imperialism, colonialism and neo-colonialism in Africa and the building up of African Unity;

to harmonize the domestic and foreign policy of its Members, so that their activities may prove more effective and contribute more worthily to safeguarding the peace of the world.

Article 4. The Union's activities shall be exercised mainly in the following fields:

a. *Domestic Policy.* The working out of a common orientation of the States.

b. *Foreign Policy.* The strict observance of a concerted diplomacy, calculated to achieve closer co-operation.

c. *Defence.* The organization of a system of joint defence, which will make it possible to mobilize all the means of defence at the disposal of the State, in favour of any State of the Union which may become a victim of aggression.

d. *Economy.* Defining a common set of directives relating to economic planning, aiming at the complete decolonization of the set-ups inherited from the colonial system, and organizing the development of the wealth of their countries in the interest of their peoples.

e. *Culture.* The rehabilitation and development of African culture, and frequent and diversified cultural exchange.

The Charter also provides for regular conferences between the Heads of State of the Union. In fact the supreme executive organ of the Union is the Conference, which meets once a quarter in Accra, Bamako and Conakry, respectively, and is presided over by the Head of State of the host country. At these conferences we exchange views on African and world problems, and see how we can best strengthen and widen our Union.

After the second summit conference of U.A.S. held at Bamako on 26 June 1961, we issued a joint communiqué in which we reaffirmed our determination to continue to support the African peoples in their struggle for national liberation, particularly in Algeria, the Congo, and Angola. On the problem of the European Common Market we agreed on a common policy, and decided to take joint action in order to establish an African Common Market.

Our conferences have been characterized by an identity of view on most of the problems examined and an atmosphere of perfect understanding. They have been followed by meetings of official representatives from our different countries to examine ways and means for giving effective realization to our decisions, out of which recommendations are being made and action endorsed. This shows clearly the workability of union between African states. It is my great hope that the U.A.S. may prove to be the successful pilot scheme which will lead eventually to full continental unity.

The ultimate goal of a United States of Africa must be kept constantly in sight amidst all the perplexities, pressures and cajoleries with which we shall find ourselves confronted, so that we do not permit ourselves to be distracted or discouraged by the difficulties and pitfalls which undoubtedly lie ahead.

During 1961 sharp differences appeared between the so-called Casablanca and Monrovia groups of states. The Casablanca states, comprising Ghana, Guinea, Mali, Libya, Egypt, Morocco and the Algerian F.L.N. met from 3 to 7 January 1961 in the Moroccan capital. The delegations of Ghana, Guinea, Mali and Egypt were led by their Heads of State, the Algerian Provisional Government by Ferhat Abbas, and Libya by her Foreign Minister. Ceylon sent their ambassador in Cairo, Mr A. C. Pereira, as an observer. The conference was convened by the late King Mohammed V of Morocco, who was chairman, and the then Crown Prince led the Moroccan delegation.

The central theme of the conference was the situation in the Congo, and the failure of the United Nations to deal with it by effectively enforcing its own resolutions. It was agreed that the states should withdraw their troops from the Congo unless the U.N. command acted immediately to support the central government; Mobutu's army should be disarmed; all Belgians and others not under U.N. command should be expelled; and the Congo Parliament reconvened.

Among other important decisions reached were those concerned with Algeria, the French testing of atomic bombs in the Sahara, and the whole question of *apartheid*. In general, the conference reaffirmed, and undertook to implement, the decisions taken at the Bandung, Accra, Monrovia and Addis Ababa conferences, when it was agreed to impose transport bans and boycotts on South Africa.

But perhaps the most far-reaching result of the Casablanca Conference was the publication of the 'African Charter of Casablanca'. This established a permanent African Consultative Assembly, and three permanent functional committees: the first, political, comprising Heads of State; the second, economic, comprising Ministers of Economic Affairs; and the third, cultural, consisting of Ministers of Education. A joint African High Command, composed of the Chiefs of Staff of the independent African nations, was also provided for in the Charter. They were to meet periodically 'with a view to ensuring the common defence of Africa in case of aggression against any part of the continent, and with a view to safeguarding the independence of African states'.

The Charter ended:

> We, the Heads of African States, convened in Casablanca from the 3rd January to the 7th January, 1961, reaffirm our faith in the Conference of Independent African States, held in Accra in 1958, and in Addis Ababa in 1960, and appeal to all Independent African States to associate themselves with our common action for the consolidation of liberty in Africa and the building up of its unity and security. We solemnly reaffirm our unshakeable adherence to the United Nations Charter and to the

Declaration of the Afro-Asian Conference held in Bandung, with the aim of promoting co-operation among all the people of the world, and of consolidating international peace.

In my speech at the closing session of the conference, I warned against the dangers of delay in achieving unity:

> I can see no security for African states unless African leaders, like ourselves, have realized beyond all doubt that salvation for Africa lies in unity . . . for in unity lies strength, and as I see it, African states must unite or sell themselves out to imperialist and colonialist exploiters for a mess of pottage, or disintegrate individually.

Certain sections of the foreign press gave great publicity to the Casablanca conference. Some saw in it a step forward on the way to unity; others seemed to take great delight in pointing out that only a handful of African states attended, and it could therefore not be regarded as truly representative of African opinion.

Nigeria, Tunisia, Ethiopia, Liberia, Sudan, Togoland, Somalia, India and Indonesia were all, in fact, invited to the conference. French Community states, which coalesced round the meetings in Abidjan and Brazzaville at the end of 1960, were not asked. There seemed, therefore, some justification for the view that three different 'blocs' were emerging in Africa.

This view received added support when the Monrovia Conference took place in May 1961. The sponsors of the conference were Cameroon, Liberia, Nigeria, and Togoland. Out of the twenty-seven independent African states twenty sent delegations, and fifteen of them were led by Presidents and Prime Ministers. The President of Liberia was elected chairman.

The seven absentees were Ghana, Guinea, Mali, Morocco, Egypt, Sudan and the Congo. The Congo had not been invited, because of the lack of settled government there.

Four main topics were discussed, namely, ways and means to achieve better understanding and co-operation and ways of promoting unity in Africa; threats to peace and stability in Africa; the establishment of special machinery to which African states might refer in case of disputes amongst themselves; and the possible contribution of African states to world peace. It was agreed that a technical commission should meet at Dakar to draw up plans for co-operation in research, communications, and so on; and principles for a permanent association were agreed. These included the principle of non-interference in the domestic affairs of other independent states; the political equality of all independent African states; freedom to accept or reject political unions, and respect for the territorial integrity of all states.

In more detailed resolutions the conference condemned South Africa, supported independence for Algeria, pledged loyalty to the United Nations, offered assistance to the Angolan nationalists, and condemned all nuclear tests.

Both the Casablanca and Monrovia conferences resulted in meetings of experts to consider detailed plans for economic co-operation among the respective members. Experts of the Casablanca countries, meeting in Conakry, recommended the ending of customs barriers over five years from 1 January 1962, and the ending of quota systems and preferential treatment from the same date. They also proposed the creation of a 'Council of African Economic Unity' (C.U.E.A.) and an African development bank; and suggested the formation of joint air and shipping lines.

Experts of the Monrovia group, meeting at Dakar, also discussed the setting up of an African development bank. They recommended the promotion of trade between African countries by regional customs unions, and the progressive establishment of common external tariffs. Among other suggestions were the harmonization of development policies, including investment codes and conventions, an investment and guarantee fund, the exchange of economic information, and the co-ordination of research programmes. It was agreed that a network of roads and railways should be built to link the countries together, and joint shipping and air-lines formed. They agreed, also, to co-operate in educational schemes and to adopt common standards.

The fundamental similarity of aims between those who met at Casablanca and Conakry and those who met at Monrovia and Dakar are apparent from a study of the resolutions passed and recommendations adopted. Both aim ultimately at some kind of unity. The Casablanca powers are convinced that political unity should come first, as the necessary prelude to the creation of the extended field for which integrated plans for development in the economic and social spheres can be worked out. Their belief in the importance of putting political aims first is strengthened by experience in their own countries, where political independence had to be achieved before economic reconstruction could be taken in hand.

There may be some significance in the fact that Monrovia, which has given its name to the group that attaches priority to economic associations, is the capital of the one country on the African continent which has not had to fight a battle for its political sovereignty. Nevertheless, Liberia has had ruggedly to hold its national integrity and viability against the territorial and economic encroachments of outside powers throughout its somewhat chequered history, and must many times have wished for the help that its colonialized neighbours were then unable to give.

In spite of the very real difference of approach between the two groups to the vital issue of unity, it cannot be said that there is a rigid division between us. On the contrary, every opportunity and means are used for cordial intercourse and useful discussion. For example, the Prime Minister of Nigeria enjoyed a very friendly visit to Guinea in December 1961. At about the same time, we welcomed to Ghana the President of Mauritania, a country which our Casablanca colleague, Morocco, did not then recognize.

In December 1960 His Imperial Majesty Haile Selassie I, Emperor of Ethiopia, visited Ghana. In the communiqué issued at the end of the visit it was declared that the Heads of State of Ghana and Ethiopia agreed: 'That a Union of the African States is a necessity which should be pursued energetically in the interests of African solidarity and security.'

President Abdulla Osman of Somalia expressed similar views on unity during his official visit to Ghana in October 1961. In a joint communiqué we reaffirmed our faith and belief in African unity as the most reliable safeguard against neo-colonialism and the balkanization of the African continent.

In a world divided into hostile camps and warring factions, Africa cannot stand divided without going to the wall. Patrice

Lumumba, who had seen and suffered from the evils of disunity in the Congo, held this view very strongly when he came to Accra in August 1960. It may not be generally known that he agreed then to work in the closest possible association with other independent African states for the establishment of a Union of African States.

There are bound to be differences between the independent states of Africa. We have frontier troubles, and a host of other inter-territorial problems which can only be resolved within the context of African unity.

At the Lagos conference of independent states, held in January 1962, North Africa was not represented at all. This was because the Algerian provisional government was not invited. The Casablanca powers, and the Sudan, also declined to go to Lagos for this reason. Nevertheless, with the Congo and Tanganyika taking the place of Tunisia and Libya, the Lagos attendance was as large as that at Monrovia, 20 of Africa's 28 independent states being represented.

The conference agreed upon a whole new complex machinery for inter-African co-operation. It included a semi-permanent council of ministers, a biennial representative assembly, and a permanent secretariat of the African and Malagasy states. Among resolutions passed were those calling for a development bank, a private investment guarantee fund, an organization for health, labour and social affairs, an educational and cultural council, and certain other commissions to deal with various practical matters.

In the early flush of independence, some of the new African states are jealous of their sovereignty and tend to exaggerate their separatism in a historical period that demands Africa's unity in order that their independence may be safeguarded. I cannot envisage an African union in which all the members, large or small, heavily or thinly populated, do not enjoy legal equality under a constitution to which all have laid their hand. But the insistence on not wanting to cede certain functions to a central unifying political authority in which all the members will have an equal voice is unrealistic and unfounded. On the other hand, an association of a confederate or even looser nature, which does not give effective powers to a central authority and

determine those to be left to the sovereign states, can leave the
way open for the domination of the smaller and weaker members
by larger and stronger ones.

Ghana has declared her stand in no uncertain terms. We have
provided in our republican constitution for the surrender of our
sovereignty, in whole or in part, in the wider interests of African
unity. Guinea has made the same provision. So have Mali,
Tunisia and the United Arab Republic. Every African must
judge for himself which view is the more progressive and
realistic; which is dedicated fully to the practical needs and
interests of Africa, unrestrained by fear of external pressures;
and which reflects the true voice of Africa.

CHAPTER SEVENTEEN

ECONOMIC AND POLITICAL
INTEGRATION: AFRICA'S NEED

AFRICA, it is frequently maintained, is poor. Yet it is widely acknowledged that its potentials provide tremendous possibilities for the wealthy growth of the continent, already known to contain vast mineral and power resources. The economic weakness of the new African states has been inherited from the colonial background, which subordinated their development to the needs of the colonial powers. To reverse the position and bring Africa into the realm of highly productive modern nations, calls for a gigantic self-help programme. Such a programme can only be produced and implemented by integrated planning within an over-all policy decided by a continental authority.

The superstructure of colonial particularism upon Africa's subsistence economies, has resulted in a highly uneven regional development of the continent. On the whole, the coastal areas, the mining regions, and the highland areas where soil and climate are good, have been exploited within the limitations of colonial requirements for raw materials. Areas requiring more pre-exploitation study and comparatively higher capital investments were left more or less untouched. Hence there are in Africa huge areas of practically virgin land which, for these reasons and from geographical considerations, it has up till now been thought useless to try to develop. Within the confinement of these limitations Africa has, however, managed to produce from its agriculture the following percentages of the world supplies, according to the 1954 figures:[1]

66% cocoa; 58% sisal; 65% palm oil; 26% groundnuts; 14% coffee; 11% olive oil.

[1] *Economic Development in Africa* 1954–5. U.N. & F.A.O. Report.

Considerable amounts of barley, wool, cotton, maize, tea, rubber, tobacco, wheat, pyrethrum, cloves and rice are also produced.

In mineral production, our continent provided, according to United Nations Organization findings for 1956[1], the following proportions of the world's output:

96% of gem diamonds (excluding U.S.S.R.); 69% cobalt; 63% gold; 48% antimony; 37% manganese; 34% chromite; 32% phosphate rock; 24% copper; 19% asbestos; 15% tin; 4% iron ore; 4% bauxite.

Nigeria produces 85% of the world's supply of columbite. Ghana is the second largest manganese producer in the world.

In addition, Africa possesses some of the world's greatest known reserves of uranium ore, and this may make possible the relatively early introduction of nuclear-electrical plants. As well as the known deposits at Shinkolobwe in the Congo, reserves of fissionable raw materials have been found in Ghana, Nigeria, Rhodesia, Nyasaland, Mozambique, Madagascar, various parts of the former French tropical territories, and in Ethiopia.

Power resources are no less impressive. Africa has the greatest water power potential in the world. Most of it lies within the tropical area, the Congo having 21.6% of the world total. Actual installed capacity, however, is only about 1% of the world total. Ghana has made a start on the Volta River project. There are new projects on the Konkoure in Guinea, on the Kouilou in former French Equatorial Africa, and a dam is envisaged at the Inga falls in the lower Congo. Hydro-electrical development has taken place on the Sanaga at Edea in Cameroon, at Boali near Nabui, and on the Djoué near Brazzaville. In the Congo, there are hydro-electrical developments on the Lufira and Lualaba rivers, and on the Inkisi. Mention must also be made of the projects on the Dande, Catumbela and Cunene rivers in Angola; and on the Revue river in Mozambique. In East and Central Africa there are the Owen falls dam and the Kariba dam.

Coal and iron ore are necessary for industrialization. Africa

[1] *Economic Survey of Africa since* 1950. Published 1959.

has coal reserves estimated at 4,500 million tons. Coal of coking
quality is mined at Wankie in Southern Rhodesia and low grade
coal is mined in Nigeria, the Congo and Mozambique. In
addition, coal is known to exist in Tanganyika, Northern
Rhodesia, Madagascar and Nyasaland. Iron ore is mined in
Southern Rhodesia, Liberia, Guinea and Sierra Leone. When
a full geological survey is carried out, further deposits may be
found. New oil deposits are also suspected. Meanwhile, oil has
been discovered in the Sahara, Nigeria, the Gabon basin and
near Luanda in Angola. The French Government certainly
seemed to be impressed with the Sahara potentialities, to judge
from the importance attached to them in negotiating the Algerian
peace settlement. Oil prospecting has been going on in Ghana,
Somalia, Ethiopia, Zanzibar, Tanganyika, Mozambique, and
Madagascar. In recent years a methane gas deposit with a heat-
producing potential equal to 50 million metric tons of coal was
reported beneath Lake Kivu.

All these are known resources, and they are by no means inconsiderable. What economic possibilities will be opened up as
our whole continent is surveyed and its economic exploitation
tackled on a total basis, there is no telling. From our experience
in Ghana, where we have already discovered many new resources, we can anticipate that the economic potentialities of
Africa must be immense.

On the agricultural plane, too, Africa is estimated to have a
vast unused potential. Crop, animal-breeding and pest-control
experiments are being carried out which will undoubtedly result
in higher and more varied output. In the timber industry, trials
are being made which should lead to a big expansion. Africa
contains about 27% of the total world forest area, and not enough
profitable use has so far been made of it. Some thirty species of
trees are now being regularly accepted in the world markets and
successful tests have been carried out in the pulping of mixed
tropical woods. A pilot pulp and paper mill has been established
near Abidjan, and there are expectations of the increased use of
tropical woods for plywood and presswood.

So much was neglected under colonialism that would even
have benefited the imperialist interests, if their concern had not
been limited to developing the best land, the most lucrative

mines, the harbours and towns connected with their economic engagements. They wanted quick and easy returns, and would not occupy themselves with what appeared to be less promising areas of exploitation.

Our African view is different. There is no single part of the African continent which is not precious to us and our development. And with the technological resources available today, what would formerly have been regarded as miraculous can now be done with the help of scientific aids, provided the means are there. Nowadays even climate is not regarded as an impossible impediment to economic progress, and certainly not drought. About two-fifths of tropical Africa is steppe or desert; at least one-third is savannah country with a seasonal rainfall. At first sight, this may seem unpromising, but the problems presented can be overcome to some extent by large-scale irrigation and suitable afforestation.

Soil, of course, presents special problems. Much of the soil in rain forest and savannah areas is poor. But a lot can be done to improve it. Artificial manures, composting, litter-farming, green manuring, can be employed. The growth of mixed farming has been held up by the tsetse fly. Full control of the tsetse can only be achieved, like that of the anopholes mosquito (the bearer of malaria), on a continental scale, since insect pests are no respecters of territorial boundaries. With the elimination of the tsetse, mixed farming could go ahead, and animals could then supply the restorative manures to our soil.

There is indeed a vast horizon of improvement waiting upon development in Africa. The Niger river inland delta scheme and the Gezira scheme in the Sudan, for example, might be greatly extended. Irrigation work could be carried out along the Gambia, Senegal, Rufiji, Tana, and Zambesi rivers, and in the Lake Chad basin. Immense advances could be made in the way of controlling the flow of smaller streams, the digging of shallow surface reservoirs, and the bunding of flat areas to reduce run-off and increase soak-in during the rainy seasons. Swamp areas such as the Bahr el Ghazal region in the Upper Nile, the Bangweulu swamp in Northern Rhodesia and the Okovanggo swamp in Bechuanaland, could be thoroughly explored to see if, with suitable treatment, they cannot be turned into useful agricultural areas. In Northern Rhodesia alone, the six largest swamps total 13,754 square miles, or six per cent of the total area. In rain forest regions, mechanical trench diggers might be made more use of, to improve drainage. Mango trees could be cut out, and fields bunded and sown with rice. Efforts in this direction are being made in Sierra Leone. Experience gained there could be profitably put at the disposal of other African countries with similar problems.

An essential part of what is today termed the infrastructure of development is communications. Lord Lugard, a pioneer carrier of the 'white man's burden', said that 'the material development of Africa may be summed up in one word – transport.'[1] Although this is obviously an over-simplification, the development of transport on a continental basis is vital to African intercourse and economic advancement. What Africa really requires is a fully integrated transport system for the continent, properly planned by a central organization, which will examine the relative potentials and economics of road, rail, river, air and sea systems in correlation with an over-all plan for inter-African trade and progressive economic and social development. At the present time, commerce and the exchange of goods between African countries is small. Colonialism interrupted the interchange that existed before its incursion and subsequently all forms of communication – roads, railways, harbours – were pointed outwards, the necessary auxiliary arms for transporting raw materials from their African sources to their European convertors overseas. These communications are now proving inadequate to meet the increasing demands being made upon them by the expanding traffic that independence has brought. All over Africa, harbours, railways, roads and airports have become greatly overburdened in recent years.

When we talk about these communications looking outward, more is meant than that they point towards the coasts and overseas. Railways were deliberately constructed for taking goods to ports planned and equipped for on-board ship-loading rather than for both loading and unloading. Thus most of our existing railways still consist of single track routes with a few branch and connecting lines. They were designed by the colonial powers to

1 Lord Lugard: *The Dual Mandate in Tropical Africa*, Blackwood 1922, p. 5.

link mining areas or to carry cash crops and raw materials from collection points to the ports for export. Farmers had to find their own means of getting crops to the collecting centres. Ghana and Nigeria are better served with railways than most parts of Africa, each having main eastern and western lines which are linked together. Ghanaian railways handle some two million tons a year, more than the combined lines of former French West Africa, but less than 1 per cent of the tonnage carried in the United Kingdom. Roads, too, are quite inadequate to meet the growing needs of emergent Africa. The cost of making them is high, and the building of a continent-wide system would have to be centrally planned and financed.

The climate and geography of Africa present special problems for the construction and maintenance of both roads and railways. But these difficulties could be surmounted within the framework of a plan for over-all African development, which would set aside reserves of funds and materials for the purpose. Such a vast scheme would, naturally, take time to complete and priorities would certainly be necessary to secure speedier fulfilment at points of development vital to the corporate progress of the continent. But with the will to attack and overcome the many problems and their involvements, the real 'opening up' of Africa will begin. And this time it will be by the Africans for the Africans.

This contention is supported by the example of the United States. America's real expansion began with her union, which assisted the building up of a vast network of railways and roads, so that D. W. Brogan, an accepted authority on American political history, after remarking that in America, 'regions as unlike as Norway and Andalusia are united under one government, speak a common language, regard themselves as part of one nation', is able to assert: 'This unity is reinforced by the most elaborate transportation system in the world, a system the elaboration of which has been made possible by the political unity.'[1]

Ports and waterways are no less important than good roads and railways. Africa has the shortest coastline in relation to its

[1] D. W. Brogan: *U.S.A.: An Outline of the Country, its People and Institutions*, Oxford University Press, p. 9.

size of any continent but it is not so fortunate with its natural harbours. We do have a few excellent artificial ports, and facilities exist for more. Notable among them are those at Monrovia and Tema. Older ports include Dakar, Freetown, Lagos, Dar-es-Salaam, Mombasa, Beira, Matadi, Port Harcourt, and Alexandria, to name only some. Among ports which have recently been greatly improved is Conakry in Guinea. There is need for the building of new ports and the improvement of old ones.

In the case of inland waterways the problem is also important even though navigable waterways have only limited importance in most areas. There are exceptions. In West Africa, the River Niger plays a significant part in the bulk shipment of palm oil, timber, peanuts, and imported petroleum products. On the Senegal river, small ships operate all the year round on the 177 miles from St Louis to Podor; and for a limited time on to Kayes. It is estimated that there are about 9,000 miles of navigable rivers in the Congo, and the system is reckoned to be the most important inland waterway of tropical Africa. Rivers like the Zambesi, Rufiji and Tana, which flow into the Indian Ocean, are navigable for short stretches. Considerable use, on the other hand, is made of the Middle Nile in the Sudan. Then there are the East African lakes. Shipping on Lake Victoria totalled some 215,000 tons in 1956.

Coastal lagoons and tidal creeks must also be taken into account. A canal in the Ivory Coast allows movement by lagoon across half the coast, and permits the collection and dispersal of goods to Abidjan at reduced costs. Porto Novo in Dahomey is linked by lagoons to Lagos. When the Volta river project is completed, low-cost water transport will be provided from the artificial lake area to the Northern region. Waterways of all kinds can be improved or extended if we pool our resources.

Air transport, both for passengers and freight, probably has the greatest future. Many large international airlines operate services in Africa, but most of them have planned their routes to serve the needs of passengers travelling to and from countries outside Africa. Most of the best routes run from North to South. Air links between, for example, East and West African countries are generally poor and few and far between. So far, the demand for internal air services has been limited, but this is something which is changing with the growing need for inter-continental communication and trade.

The necessary capital for all these developments can only be accumulated by the employment of our resources on a continental extension. This calls for a central organization to formulate a comprehensive economic policy for Africa which will embrace the scientific, methodical and economic planning of our ascent from present poverty into industrial greatness.

Internal customs barriers can be eliminated; differences in domestic structures accommodated. Currency difficulties must disappear before a common currency. None of our problems is insuperable unless we are set against their solution. In July 1961 customs barriers between Ghana and Upper Volta were removed. An African Development Institute is to be set up at Dakar to train economists, to provide experts who can be sent on request to African States, to carry out research, and to co-ordinate policies. This Institute, when it is operating, will, it is hoped, go some way towards counteracting the excessive duplication of experimental work that now goes on in Africa because we have no central economic planning organization for directing research and pooling knowledge and experience.

There are some who refute the requirement of continental unity as the essential prerequisite to full industrialization. Others refer to economic confederations like the Zollverein of nineteenth-century Germany as likely patterns upon which we might model our African co-operation for industrial fulfilment. This ignores the historical fact that the Zollverein proved unequal to the task of creating the capital formations Germany needed to carry forward her industrialism, which only got fully under way when the states surrendered their sovereignty to the German Empire. It was the unification of Germany which provided the stimulus to expanding capitalism and gave a suitable population basis for the absorption of manufactured goods, particularly as population growth in Germany was high and quickly reached forty-one millions. At that period of scientific invention, this was a large enough consumption group to enable Germany to progress from a mainly agricultural country in 1871 to the industrial achievements that led her into the scramble for colonies before the middle 'eighties. In the first decade of the twentieth century, German capitalism attained the stage of commercial and financial monopoly whose expansionist needs impelled her into the 1914 war.

The German example illustrates the advantages of uniting parts into a more effective whole. This German development took place within the typical national exclusivism of the nineteenth century, which reached its apotheosis under the Wilsonian doctrine of self-determination after the end of the First World War, when the countries of the Austro-Hungarian Empire assumed sovereignty behind boundaries whose internecine possibilities were subsequently exploited by the great powers. Motivated by the ambitions of rising bourgeoisies for political control as the means to capitalist development, the leaders of the European nationalist movements, once they assumed power, discovered that they were too weak to stand by themselves. But instead of coalescing into a wider fraternity of nations which would have strengthened their economies and provided a defence against big-power encroachments, they hugged their exclusivism and made pacts with the stronger states, which in the end undermined their self-confidence and failed to save them from imperialist expansion.

Today, the major European powers, confronted with the deepening competitiveness of acquisitive production, intensified by the new scientific inventions, shrinking empires and the enlargement of the socialist conclave of nations, are forming their associations of strength, both economic, political and military. It seems, then, curiously paradoxical that in this period when national exclusivism in Europe is making concessions to supernational organizations, many of the new African states should cling to their new-found sovereignty as something more precious than the total well-being of Africa and seek alliances with the states that are combining to balkanize our continent in neo-colonialist interests.

Some of these states are aligning themselves with the European associations in the mistaken belief that they will profit sufficiently to prosper their economies. It is true that the overseas members of the European Common Market are enjoying at the present time certain benefits from the European Development Fund.

But in the face of the enormous requirements of industrial development, these are infinitesimal in size and restricted in character. Out of the applications submitted, the projects so far approved ignore the requests for the establishment of industries and concentrate on social projects and the building of roads, railways and ports. These, it is true, are necessary to fuller development and the raising of welfare, and undoubtedly are welcome additions to the economic and social base. But it is wishful thinking not to recognize them as the bribes they are, and to suppose that the European Common Market, which is devised to increase the welfare of the European member countries, should conscientiously promote industrialization in the raw material producing countries of Africa. It is equally romantic to think that the Development Fund could ever be big enough to provide anything like the investment capital the African states require for substantial development. As is only to be expected, emphasis is placed upon modernization and improvement schemes that will increase European economic strength,[1] and widen still more the productivity gap between Europe and Africa.

The enticement of aid which the European Common Market holds out demands close examination and it is particularly curious that Mr Leopold Senghor, President of the Republic of Senegal, should lend himself to a subtle appeal to the English-speaking countries to enter. In an interview appended to an article in *International Affairs* for April 1962, President Senghor expresses his pleasure about it,

> above all for Africa, because we ourselves, a French-speaking state, are associated with the Common Market, and I think that, if Britain joins in, the English-speaking countries of Africa will wish to do so too. From a purely selfish point of view that might not be entirely to our advantage, for the greater number of participants, the smaller the individual share in the European fund. But I think there is a more important side to it: what we lose on the level of material aid, we gain on the level of cohesion and co-operation. We shall then be able to harmonize our technical

---

[1] Stuart de la Mahotière: *The Common Market*, Hodder & Stoughton 1961, pp. 30–48. This book offers a comprehensive survey of the subject from a European supporter.

and economic co-operation between Africans, both French-speaking and English-speaking.[1]

This argument, despite the gratuitous magnanimity expressed, is a special plea for collective colonialism of a new order. For if technical and economic co-operation between Africans (whom he is careful to divide linguistically) is a feasibility, as President Senghor's inference allows, then where is the need to tie it in with the European Common Market, which is a European organization promoted to further European interests? The overseas associated members have gone in as providers of raw materials, not as equals dealing with equals. What reasons have they to assume that cohesion and co-operation will be fashioned by those controlling the instrumentalities of the Market for the good of Africa's common development? All the evidence, both past and present, surely points in the other direction; that the design is to maintain the historical relationship of European industrial convertor and African supplier of primary products.

Notwithstanding the outward signs of change that have taken place at many points of the continent, the nature of African economy has remained practically unaltered since the first European adventurers came to its coasts in the fifteenth century. It is purely and simply a trading economy. Our trade, however, is not between ourselves. It is turned towards Europe and embraces us as providers of low-priced primary materials in exchange for the more expensive finished goods we import. Except where we have associated and formed a common selling policy, we come into a competition that acts to force down the prices we receive to the profit of the overseas buyers. It is because of the effects of this colonial relationship in limiting their economies, that some of the African states have joined the European Common Market. They have the hope that by this means they will inject new life into their economies. But this is an illusion, because the benefits received by way of aid will do nothing to change the fundamental nature of these economies, and they can, therefore, never thrive in the way that most advanced countries do. They may well regress, because, while inter-

[1] Leopold Senghor: *Some Thoughts on Africa in International Affairs*, April 1962.

national trade between highly industrialized countries may be mutually beneficial, 'a quite normal result of unhampered trade between two countries, of which one is industrialised and the other less developed, is the initiation of a cumulative process towards the impoverishment and stagnation of the latter.'[1]

The tariff arrangements of the European Common Market must deepen the divisions between the overseas members and the non-members on the African continent on account of the increased competitiveness that must result between them. Quota restrictions and depressed prices can be the only outcome. In his 'comprehensive guide' to *The Common Market*, Stuart de la Mahotière forecasts the extension of industrial monopolies to deal with the keen competition which will develop between the European members of the Market, and declares that 'the keynote to success will undoubtedly be in the first instance the ability to keep costs down and prices competitive.'[2] Raw materials and labour costs are the two major items in production costing, so it is quite obvious where the 'keynote to success' must lead. The development aid which the associated African members may receive from the European Fund will be outbalanced by a gradual decline in the national revenues from primary products. Even united African arrangements for the maintenance of a common selling policy for certain raw materials such as cocoa, cannot be upheld if one or more of the parties to the arrangements adheres to the European organization. The prices which will be fixed by the European members will apply to all the overseas members supplying the Common Market, and the Common Market states within the African alliance will have to conform to the fixed prices if they are to enjoy the aid for which they joined it. African loyalty will be split between the European attachment and the African association, and the obligation to the former will nullify fidelity to the African interest.

This is the neo-colonialism of the European Common Market, which holds out to the undeveloped African states the threat of discriminatory tariffs for those who do not come in, and the promise of aid for those who do. It is a 'heads I win, tails you

[1] Gunnar Myrdal: *Economic Theory and Under-Developed Regions*, p. 99.
[2] Stuart de la Mahotière: *The Common Market*, p. 110.

lose' policy, which aims to create a bitter schism among the independent African states or else to cajole them all into the fold of the European market, in the same old imperialist relationship of the European rider on the African horse. Any of the states that enter deprive themselves of the possibility of independent action. They will have lost their freedom to trade wherever it is most advantageous or to secure capital from the most convenient sources. They will, moreover, have surrendered their policy of non-alignment by attaching themselves to the European economic organization which is linked with the North Atlantic Treaty Organization (N.A.T.O.). Even worse, they will be compelled to betray the cause of African freedom, by the support they will be obliged to give to the imperialist suppression of the emancipation struggle in Africa. In short, they will have sold their African birthright for a mess of neo-colonialist pottage.

Nor could there be any idea of solid industrialized advancement for these African states in the interests of their people. For, having returned themselves to the imperialist fold, this time of their own 'free' will and not by territorial conquest, the same forces which kept them tagging behind the industrialized countries of the West will continue to operate. The African countries will once more be wide open to imperialist exploitation. Political independence will be a sham and will have gained nothing except the aggrandizement of certain opportunist groups within the national societies and the enrichment of the neo-colonialist interest. Economic independence will be farther away than ever and the conflicts within these African societies will be more severe, because the class divisions will crystallize sharply under the more ruthless demands of neo-colonialist monopoly to feed its greedier and greedier economic and military machines.

An African Common Market, devoted uniquely to African interests, would more efficaciously promote the true requirements of the African states. Such an African Market presupposes a common policy for overseas trade as well as for inter-African trade, and must preserve our right to trade freely anywhere. If it is a good thing for the European buyers to regulate their affairs with their overseas suppliers by combination, then it must be equally good for Africans to do likewise in offering their wares.

Besides, an African Common Market that does not concert its policy in regard to its exports seriously reduces its effectiveness, since the mutuality of interest might well be violated by individual actions in regard to the sale of crops common to several of the members. One of the principal objectives of our African Common Market must be to eliminate the competition that presently exists between us, and must continue to do so while any one of us mistakenly shelters under the umbrella of the European Common Market. The cash crops that we produce must be pooled, so that our combined totals will give us a commanding position and, through a united selling policy, enable us to extract better prices. For instance, Ghana and Nigeria between them produce about 50 per cent of the world's cocoa. So far we have been selling against each other, but in uniting our policy, we can beat the undercutting tactics of the buyers who set us one against the other.

The surpluses thus derived from increased revenues resulting from a common selling policy could be placed to realistic development (rejected by the European Development Fund), and give a spurt to fundamental industrialism. The trade now beginning to be developed between us would be stimulated, while a common currency would eliminate the difficulties of exchange as well as the illegitimate dealings which at present rob us of part of our wealth. A common currency, free of links with outside currency zones, would enable us to reserve the foreign exchange made from our export trade for essential imports.

In the same way, the pooled sum of our present individual investments in our similar national projects, if used within an integrated plan, would give greater benefit in mutual development. Indeed, the total integration of the African economy on a continental scale is the only way in which the African states can achieve anything like the levels of the industrialized countries. The idea of African union is not just a sentimental one, emanating from a common experience of colonialism and a desire for young, untried states to come together in the effervescence of their new freedom, though sentiment undoubtedly has its part. The unity of the countries of Africa is an indispensable precondition for the speediest and fullest development, not only of the totality of the continent but of the individual countries linked together in the union.

Advancing science, the new technologies, the constant improvements in modes of production and techniques of management, the economic realities of this second half of the twentieth century demand large expanses of land, with their variegated natural resources, and massive populations, to obtain the greatest benefits from them and thereby sustain their profitability. To-day, those powers embracing large aggregates of population and earth surface are more capable of full industrialization.

Unfortunately, in the present-day conflict of political ideologies, these are the powers that make claims to 'greatness'. The others are virtual satellites oscillating between their orbits. The current impact of the cold war on world affairs governs the external policy, and influences in many ways the internal policies of most of the rest of the world. Only China, with its huge population and massive land extent, combined with its non-competitive, centrally planned system of production and distribution, has a rate of productivity that is making her a potential challenger of the only two powers whose weight counts in our present world. That is the root reason why the United States refuses to admit China into the United Nations and why the Soviet Union is respectful of her attitudes. China's rate of productivity puts her ahead of the declining imperial powers whose industrial extension, limited by their shrinking empires, has led them into the European Common Market, in the hope that the increased productivity and expanded market offered by 170 million people will provide a more effective challenge to America's industrial – and hence political – mastery of the capitalist world. Industrial output in China increased 276 per cent in the years between 1950 and 1957, and it is estimated that if the relative rates of development persist, she will outstrip Japan and Britain in the not too distant future.

Only the Soviet Union, China, and perhaps Indonesia among the under-developed countries possess the material and population base sufficient for successful (socialist) economies. The individual territories of Africa and South America, to say nothing of the territorial boundaries of such countries as South

Korea, Formosa, Pakistan, South Vietnam, Laos, Cambodia, Jordan, Libya, Morocco, Tunisia, Greece, Turkey, and the West Indies, are too limited. . . . As a consequence, there is an implicit movement in the world today towards regionalism – not the regionalism of the various pacts inspired by the capitalist world, although some of these may unwillingly foster the movement. But a regionalism based upon economic and cultural identification and co-operation.[1]

The greatest single lesson that can be drawn from the history of industrial development in the world today is the uncounted advantages which planning has in the first place over the *laissez faire* go-as-you-please policies of the early pioneers of industrialism; and secondly, how immensely superior planning on a continental scale, allied to a socialized objective, has proved for the giant latecomers into the realm of modern statehood over the fragmented discordant attempts of disunited entities, as on the South American continent. The rates of growth of the Soviet Union and China are much higher even than that of the other continental giant, the United States of America, whose economic evolution stretched over a longer period of time and whose capital accumulations, as a result of large-scale plantation farming by slave labour, and the conversion of its products into manufactured goods, were already considerable before her large-scale industrialization got under way in earnest, after the war to maintain the union. America is the most vocal proponent of free enterprise, unfettered by central planning. Her society shows the most glaring social inequalities, from the Negro sharecropper living close to or below the subsistence line and financial tycoons amassing astronomical fortunes, with all possible gradations of wealth and poverty in between. Sixteen million people still remain unintegrated with the body politic.

Soviet embarkment upon planned industrialization occurred on the edge of the nineteen-thirties, after a really critical approach had been made to the intricate problems involved in making the 'take off' with a paucity of reserves and resources rather greater than our own at the present time. There were the

[1] Prof. Oliver C. Cox of Lincoln University, U.S.A., in a paper entitled *Factors in Development of Under-Developed Countries*, delivered in Accra, June 1959.

conditions created by the aftermath of revolution and civil war, including the destruction of such industrial plant as had existed under the Czarist empire or its alienation to the states that had seceded. There was a population scattered unevenly over a sixth of the earth's surface, in varying stages of development, from nomadic tribes on the steppes and wastelands to a cultured intelligentsia in Leningrad and Moscow and a relatively small proletariat working in the main cities and towns. The internecine strife and hatreds among these people was proverbial, and the multiplicity of languages and religions not much less than in present-day Africa. Over and above all this, the Soviet Union had to make its way in a state of isolation forced upon her by her exclusion from the world comity of nations on account of the social ideology she had adopted as her guide. Furthermore, she was surrounded by a *cordon sanitaire* of satellite states, which were used as the threatening outposts of the great powers.

Against all the disadvantages, the open enmity and contrivance aimed at her success, and the appalling devastation and material and human losses resulting from the Second World War, the Soviet Union, in a little over thirty years, has built up an industrial machine so strong and advanced as to be able to launch the Sputnik and follow it up by being the first to send a man into space. There must be something to be said for a system of continental organization allied to clearly defined socialized objectives that made this remarkable achievement, and I pose it as an example of what an integrated economic programme could do for Africa. I am aware of the deep social disturbances that were created and the harshness of the repressive machinery used against critics, dissenters and others in the course of attainment. In recognizing the achievement I can only regret the excesses, though I may, out of our own experience, understand some of the causes that produced them.

Nor would I suggest that we in Africa should slavishly pattern our course on the Soviet model. I merely present it as an example of what can be done through planning an integrated economic course on a united continental plane. I have frequently said that there is no universal pattern of development that is applicable to African conditions, environment and particular economic circumstances. The economic theories that have emanated from

Europe have been erected out of the experience there. They were not evolved as guides in advance of economic development, but were the result of analysis of that development after the event. Even Lenin's theory of imperialism issued from his study of the growth of capitalism and its monopolistic expansion. And when he came to lead the emergent Soviet state into rehabilitation on socialist foundations, he had no blue-print which he could use as a guide.

We are more fortunate, and we are not isolated. We may have enemies, but we have friends, too. We have the examples of the United States, of the Soviet Union, of China, of India. They are all operating their economies on a continental scale and offer us a choice of means and methods which we can adapt to the African scene. But one thing is certain, unless we plan to lift Africa up out of her poverty, she will remain poor. For there is a vicious circle which keeps the poor in their rut of impoverishment, unless an energetic effort is made to interrupt the circular causations of poverty. Once this has been done, and the essential industrial machine has been set in motion, there is a 'snow-balling' effect which increases the momentum of change. But the essential industrial machine, which alone can break the vicious circle of Africa's poverty, can only be built on a wide enough basis to make the take-off realistic if it is planned on a continental scale.

At the moment, we call our conferences and meetings, which, while obviously useful, must remain ineffective unless supported by joint action. The African economy has shown little improvement since the establishment of the Economic Commission for Africa (E.C.A.) in 1958. During the spring 1962 session of the Commission, it was pointed out that the population of Africa had probably increased by some 8 per cent since 1958, with the result that there were nearly 20 million more people to feed. Yet advances in agriculture and industry had not kept pace with the rising population. In fact, figures showed that the African balance of trade had actually deteriorated.

It is clear that radical changes in economic planning in Africa are urgently needed, and this can only be achieved quickly and effectively if we are united politically. At the 1962 meeting of the E.C.A. to which reference has just been made, speakers found it difficult to separate economic and political issues. This is because they are, for us, inseparable at this time in our history. For the radical changes that are urgently needed in economic planning can only be brought about quickly and effectually if we are united politically. Conversely, our national independence can only be given full meaning if a vast pool of economic and industrial resources can be created to provide the various African states with a strong enough base to support the welfare of their peoples.

In the isolation of purely national planning, our rate of progress can only be halting, our individual developments doomed to slowness, no matter how intensive our efforts or how careful our projects. Expansion of extractive industries, extension and diversification of agriculture, establishment of secondary industries, some infra-structure, the building of a few key industries – this is what we may expect within the confines of our national planning, and even this is not assured. Certainly not without the most careful trimming and austerity, and an uneven struggle at all times against coercive pressures, both external and domestic.

Each of us alone cannot hope to secure the highest benefits of modern technology, which demands vast capital investment and can only justify its economics in serving an extensive population. A continental merging of our land areas, our populations and our resources, will alone give full substance to our aspirations to advance from our pre-industrial state to that stage of development that can provide for all the people the high standard of living and welfare amenities of the most advanced industrial states.

It may, of course, be argued that any economic integration at this time would be like a pooling of poverty. But this ignores the essential core of integration: that it will co-ordinate all the existing resources, economic, agricultural, mineral, financial, and employ them methodically so as to improve the over-all surplus, to assist a wider capital development. Further, a co-ordinated survey of the continental resources, actual and potential, human and material, will permit planning to eliminate the present imbalance in identical forms of primary trading economies and provide for the erection of a complementary pattern of development which will give the fullest opportunity for progressive capital formations. We would still need to exchange primary products for capital goods, and I have explained how an African Common Market and common currency would facilitate the accumulation of reserves from our pooled production and common selling policy. Moreover, within the unity of integrated economic planning, we should be better placed to extract the most advantageous aid agreements free of clauses that would jeopardize our independence of action. The larger potentials of greater land area and numbers would offer greater attraction to outside investment capital because of their anticipated higher profitability ratio. Another advantage for outside investment capital would be the soundness of the guarantees that unified continental development could offer. No single individual could undertake such investment, so that it would have to be done by corporate or public investment. In fact, the trend today is towards public investment, because public guarantees are demanded. Foreign countries will not loan to a private individual in another country but will only lend to a private institution or a public institution with a guarantee from the government. As a rule, it will not come without this guarantee, and often enough the investment will not be allowed to come to the borrowing country without the approval of the government of the lender. That kind of investment is the more solid kind of investment that Africa needs from abroad, and both international and public capital would find it much less complex to deal with and secure guarantees from an all-African administration than from the several governments they now have to deal with. It would make for easier co-operation all round.

Separatism, indeed, cuts us off from a multitude of advantages which we would enjoy from union. Though Ghana is bearing the cost of erecting the Volta dam, we would be more than willing to share its benefits with our immediate neighbours within a common economic framework. The Inga dam, a blueprint dream for the Congo, may not get beyond that stage without the co-operation of other African states, for no single state could afford to build it. Yet if it were built, the dam would provide 25 million kilowatts of electricity, which is estimated to be four-and-a-half times the output expected from the largest hydro-electrical plant in the Soviet Union: the Bratsk Dam.

The Inga project could go a long way towards electrifying the whole of the African continent.

If the independent states had a united, integrated economic policy, the building of the Inga dam could be carefully planned to support an extended industrial growth, catering for a far larger population. Its cost would, therefore, be economically spread. This is only a single illustration of what African integrated economic planning might do. Extend it to all sectors of our economies, and its possibilities are infinite.

I have often been accused of pursuing 'a policy of the impossible'. But I cannot believe in the impossibility of achieving African union any more than I could ever have thought of the impossibility of attaining African freedom. When I came back to Ghana in 1947 to take a leading part in the anti-colonial struggle, I was dubbed an 'irresponsible agitator'. Independence at that time looked a long way off. None of us really imagined that by 1962 most of the African countries would have thrown off political domination and embarked upon their own national existence as sovereign states. But that did not stop us from going forward with our efforts, buoyed by the certainty of ultimate victory. And it has come, as I said, much sooner than anticipated.

That is how I feel about African union. Just as I was convinced that political freedom was the essential forerunner of our economic growth and that it must come, so I am equally convinced that African union will come and provide that united, integrated base upon which our fullest development can be secured. There is no doubt that the task before us is a challenging one. No easy road to the achievement of modern industrialization has so far been discovered. The most we can hope is to learn from the more glaring mistakes of those who have preceded us on the road what we should obviously avoid, and what will most assist us in pushing forward to the goal as speedily as possible without sustaining too many bitter shocks to the body politic.

But there is absolutely no doubt that the key to significant industrialization of this continent of ours lies in a union of African states, planning its development centrally and scientifically through a pattern of economic integration. Such central planning can create units of industrialism related to the unit resources, correlating food and raw materials production with the establishment of secondary manufactures and the erection of those vital basic industries which will sustain large-scale capital development. The national components will each perform their essential role in the practical implementation of the total plan and feel secure in the co-operative task of eliminating the economic unevenness that now exists between the different regions. The individual character of population groups might properly be expressed in special kinds of development within the universal plan, particularly in the fields of specialized production, whether in agriculture or industry, of handicrafts and culture. This would infuse energy into the realization of the planned development, as the people would be given every opportunity to expand their individual genius.

Because of the enormously greater energy, both human and material, that would be released through continentally integrated planning, productivity increase would be incomparably higher than the sum of the individual growths which we may anticipate within the individual countries under separatism. The cumulative surpluses that must result would achieve continuing capital formations for increasing the African investment in expanding development. It is quite obvious that integrated continental planning cannot find a substitute in the kind of tinkering that limits us to inter-territorial associations within customs unions, trade agreements, inter-communications services, and the like. While these will naturally increase our common intercourse and provide for certain inter-action, they can only be partially beneficial in their effects. For such tinkering does not create the decisive conditions for resolute development, since it ignores the crucial requirement of continental integration as the essential prerequisite for the most bountiful economic progress, which must be based in the widest possible extension of land and population. The planned industrialization, moreover, must be geared to the social objective of the highest upliftment of the masses of the people, and presupposes the elimination of those acquisitive tendencies which lead to sectional conflicts within society. By these means alone can Africa maintain the popular support without which the planned programme cannot succeed, and arrive at that economic freedom which is the intertwined goal of political independence.

In the face of the forces that are combining to reinforce neo-colonialism in Africa, it is imperative that the leaders should begin now to seek the best and quickest means by which we can collectivize our economic resources and produce an integrated plan for their careful deployment for our mutual benefit. If we can do this, we shall raise in Africa a great industrial, economic and financial power comparable to any that the world has seen in our time.

Such effective economic links, however, are impossible to establish without sound political direction to give them force and purpose. Therefore, we must come to grips first with the major and basic issue of African unity, which alone can clear the way for the united effort in erecting the powerful industrial and economic structure which will give substance and reality to our dream of a strong African continent, absolutely freed from political and economic colonialism.

CHAPTER EIGHTEEN

NEO-COLONIALISM IN AFRICA

THE GREATEST danger at present facing Africa is neo-colonialism and its major instrument, balkanization. The latter term is particularly appropriate to describe the breaking up of Africa into small, weak states, since it arose from the action of the great powers when they divided up the European part of the old Turkish Empire, and created a number of dependent and competing states in the Balkan peninsula. The effect was to produce a political tinderbox which any spark could set alight. In fact, the explosion came in 1914 when an Austrian archduke was murdered at Sarajevo. Because the Balkan countries were so closely tied up with the great powers and their rivalries, the murder resulted in the First World War, the greatest war which had been fought up to that time.

In the same way as alliances by the Balkan states with rival powers outside the Balkans resulted in world war, so a world war could easily originate on our continent if African states make political, economic and military alliances with rival powers outside Africa. Already political commentators have referred to Africa as a vast new battleground for the cold war.

As the nationalist struggle deepens in the colonial territories and independence appears on the horizon, the imperialist powers, fishing in the muddy waters of communalism, tribalism and sectional interests, endeavour to create fissions in the national front, in order to achieve fragmentation. Ireland is the classic example, India another. The French dismembered the Federation of West Africa and that of Equatorial Africa. Nigeria was broken into regions and is anticipating further partitions. Ruanda-Urundi has been fragmented with independence. Because we in Ghana survived pre-independence attempts to split us, the British foisted on us a constitution that aimed at disintegrating our national unity. The Congo, hastily invested with independence, with malice aforethought, immediately became the battleground of imperialist-fomented division.

These are all part of the policy of intentional balkanization of Africa for manipulation by neo-colonialism, which in effectiveness can be more dangerous to our legitimate aspirations of freedom and economic independence than outright political control. For instance, Lenin maintained that:

> A form of financial and diplomatic dependence, accompanied by political independence, is presented by Portugal. Portugal is an independent, sovereign state, but actually, for more than two hundred years, since the war of the Spanish Succession (1701–14), it has been a British protectorate. Great Britain has protected Portugal and its colonies in order to fortify her own positions in the fight against her rivals, Spain and France. In return, Great Britain has received commercial privileges, preferential conditions for importing goods and especially capital into Portugal and the Portuguese colonies, the right to use the ports and islands of Portugal, its telegraph cables, etc., etc.[1]

The form taken by neo-colonialism in Africa today has some of these features. It acts covertly, manœuvring men and governments, free of the stigma attached to political rule. It creates client states, independent in name but in point of fact pawns of the very colonial power which is supposed to have given them independence. This is one of the 'diverse forms of dependent countries which, politically, are formally independent, but in fact, are enmeshed in the net of financial and diplomatic dependence'.[2] The European power forces the conclusion of pacts with the balkanized states which give control of their foreign policy to the former. Often, too, they provide for military bases and standing armies of the alien power on the territories of the new states. The independence of those states is in name only, for their liberty of action is gone.

France never subscribed to the thesis of ultimate independence for her colonial territories. She had always maintained her

---

[1] Lenin: *Imperialism, The Highest Stage of Capitalism*, pp. 137–8.
[2] *ibid*, pp. 136–7.

colonies as tightly closed preserves. When it became obvious that national sovereignty could no longer be withheld, the ground was prepared for maintaining the emerging independent nations within the French orbit. They were to remain suppliers of cheap raw materials and tropical foodstuffs while continuing to serve as closed markets for French products.

Soon after the Second World War, France set up two financial organizations for the purpose of 'aiding economic development' in her overseas territories. These were F.I.D.E.S. (*Fonds d'Investissement et Développement Economique et Social*) and the C.C.O.M. (*Caisse Centrale de la France d'Outre-mer.*)

Subventions from C.C.O.M. went to the budgets of the former French colonial territories to help meet the cost of public administration and the maintenance of French forces in the territories. Investment in the social and economic development of France's overseas territories was largely an euphemism for the siphoning of funds through F.I.D.E.S. into these former French colonies and back again to France. It has been estimated that as much as 80 per cent of such so-called investment returned to France in the form of payments for materials, services, commissions, bank charges and salaries of French staffs and agents. Projects undertaken were mainly in the sphere of public services and agriculture. They were woefully inadequate and improperly planned, with little or no regard for local conditions or needs. No attempt was made to lay the foundations for industrial growth or a diversification of agriculture which would assist true development. F.I.D.E.S. and C.C.O.M. have given place to the F.A.C. (*Fonds d'Aide et de Coopération*) and C.C.C.E. (*Caisse Centrale de Coopération Economique*). The newly named agencies, however, perform the same functions as the old ones on exactly the same terms. Investment continues to support the production of exportable community crops and the trading enterprises of French commercial houses and contracting firms who secure their supplies from French factories and industrial centres. French bankers and financial concerns linked with some of the biggest raw material converters are being encouraged to extend the exploitation of minerals in the former colonial territories for exportation in their primary form.

Thus, even though independent in name, these countries

G

continue the classical relationship of a colonial economy to its metropolitan patron, i.e. providers of primary products and exclusive markets for the latter's goods. Only now the relationship is covered up under the guise of aid and protective solicitude, one of the more subtle forms of neo-colonialism.

Since France sees her continued growth and development in the maintenance of the present neo-colonialist relationship with the less developed nations within her orbit, this can only mean the widening of the gap between herself and them. If the gap is ever to be narrowed, not to say closed, it can only be done by a complete break with the present patron-client relationship.

When neo-colonialism can make such effective penetrations by other means, there seems a certain illogicality, viewed from their standpoint, in clinging bitterly to political control of the remaining territories in Africa. Unless, of course, it is to use time to increase the differences and deepen the schisms, and to allow South Africa to build up her military forces, to use, in alliance with the Rhodesias and Portugal, against the fighters for freedom and the new African independence. It is in this context that the former insistence on the inviolability of the Central African Federation in the teeth of African opposition must be understood and met. There is discernible a curious variance of purpose when one compares the British concurrence to the demand for regionalism in Nigeria and their refusal for so long to concede to African clamour for the dissolution of the Central African Federation. It was claimed for the continuance of Central African Federation that it made for economic cohesion and progress. If a larger aggregate is good for one part of Africa, the settler-controlled part, then surely it must contain the same beneficent seed for the independent parts.

The conversion of Africa into a series of small states is leaving some of them with neither the resources nor the manpower to provide for their own integrity and viability. Without the means to establish their own economic growth, they are compelled to continue within the old colonial trading framework. Hence they are seeking alliances in Europe, which deprive them of an independent foreign policy and perpetuate their economic dependency. But this is a solution that can only lead backwards, not forwards. The forward solution is for the African states to stand together politically, to have a united foreign policy, a common defence plan, and a fully integrated economic programme for the development of the whole continent. Only then can the dangers of neo-colonialism and its handmaiden balkanization be overcome. When that has been accomplished, our relations with Europe can enter upon a new phase.

Although the end of European rule in Africa is in sight, European economic interests are ascendant and its political and cultural influences strong. In a number of territories, 'mother country' ideology and cultural identity have strongly affected certain political leaders. Paul-Marc Henry, designated French 'official expert' on African affairs, has argued that the story of nationalism in French Africa is basically different from that in British territories. He says:

> African deputies and senators have learned their politics not in the narrow confines of territorial problems, but in the strange and stimulating world of the French parliament. . . . One could argue that the world as seen from Paris is rather distorted. French deputies themselves were not always aware of the real factors in power politics. The continuous presence of friendly and able African colleagues led them to believe that there was no such thing as African nationalism in French areas, that the idea was a foreign import and, in some cases, one of those notorious plots against Franco-African community and its spiritual achievements. On the other hand, there was no better school for intellectual and political sophistication than that of the French Parliament of the Fourth Republic.[1]

Henry's remarks serve to underline the myopia which seems to have become endemic to the French ruling class since the days of the Bourbons. The transmission of the affliction to Africans whose attitudes have been conditioned by sophisticated flatteries away from an African orientation towards a 'Franco-African community' can only be regarded as sinister and inimical to African interests. Mesmerized by the 'strange and stimulating world of the French parliament', issues as seen at

[1] Paul-Marc Henry: Article entitled 'Pan-Africanism – A Dream Come True' in *Foreign Affairs*, April 1959.

Abidjan can be quite as distorted for African politicians as they can for French deputies in Paris.

Viewed thus, it is small wonder that General de Gaulle's referendum of 28 September 1958, on the constitution of the French Community, should have triumphed with the single dissentient vote of Guinea. The weight of the General's promise of largess for those who remembered the intertwined destiny and common cultural heritage of the Community and the threat of excommunication for those who rejected this destiny, and forswore their noble inheritance, was irresistible. While the long-standing politicians of the rest of French Africa were dismayed at the prospect of a future severed from the embracing arms of France, Sekou Touré rallied his countrymen round him for a 'No' vote, and Guinea was rudely ejected from the Community.

The French Community was evolved by General de Gaulle to replace the French Union, devised by the statesmen of the Fourth Republic within *la loi cadre*, the outline law. The French Union was an attempt to contain the rising tide of African consciousness by the cover of a spurious autonomy in certain departments of administration. Events in Ghana and our steady progress to full independence revealed the counterfeit character of the French Union, and with the near civil war precipitated by the attempted military seizure of power in Algeria, General de Gaulle, ensconced in power in Paris, formulated the French Community to replace the sham pretensions of the Union. When promulgated, the provisions of the constitution of the Community in respect of the powers they allotted to the African territories were seen to fall short of those regarded as too constricted under the Union. The breaking down into separate entities before the referendum of the Federation of West Africa and that of Equatorial Africa was the key to the new political policy of France. It was balkanization in practice. It reinforced the ambitions of political personalities and deepened schisms which were on the way to being closed. A new rift was opened in African politics between Republicans and Federalists, that is, between those who felt they would advance their careers within the strict limits of autonomy and those who, responding to popular clamour, sought association with other units. This popular pressure in the African lands has achieved several modifications in the working of the Community constitution and has even succeeded in making some of the clauses inoperative.

The coming together of Senegal and Sudan in the Mali Federation secured them a joint independence within the Community, subject to the French retention of a military base. The Mali Federation, because of the difference in the political attitudes of the leaders, Mr Leopold Senghor and Mr Modibo Keita, has since divided once more into its national parts, Senegal and Mali. Houphouet-Boigny followed by demanding independence for the countries of the Conseil de l'Entente,[1] Ivory Coast, Upper Volta, Niger and Dahomey, without preceding agreements. Sovereignty has since been conferred on Togo, the Congo Republic (Brazzaville), Chad, Gabon, Cameroon, the Central African Republic (formerly Ubangui Shari), and Madagascar. And at last, Algeria has wrested independence after seven years of bitter fighting.

Now that African freedom is accepted by all except the diehard racialists as an inescapable fact, there are efforts in certain quarters to make arrangements whereby the local populations are given a token freedom while cords attaching them to the 'mother country' remain as firm as ever. This arrangement gives the appearance of nationhood to the African territory but leaves the substance of sovereignty with the metropolitan power. A certain token aid is pumped in by the colonialist power in order to mislead the people and give the impression that something is being done for them. It is meant to divert the nascent demand for a change of government involving more positive independence and a programme envisaging popular welfare. The intention is to use the new African states, so circumscribed, as puppets through whom influence can be extended over states which maintain an independence in keeping with their sovereignty. The creation of several weak and unstable states of this kind in Africa, it is hoped, will ensure the continued dependence on the former colonial powers for economic aid, and impede African unity. This policy of balkanization is the new imperialism, the new danger to Africa.

Its mechanics are simple. In the dynamics of national revolution there are usually two local elements: the moderates

[1] Council of Understanding.

of the professional and 'aristocratic' class and the so-called extremists of the mass movement. The moderates would like some share in their government but are afraid of immediate responsibility because they lack experience and skill. They are prepared to leave the main areas of sovereignty to the colonial power, in return for a promise of economic aid. The so-called extremists are men who do not necessarily believe in violence but who demand immediate self-government and complete independence. They are men who are concerned with the interests of their people and who know that those interests can be served only by their own local leaders and not by the colonial power. They know that the tasks of independence are onerous and that without colonialist help they may make mistakes. But they prefer to make their own mistakes in freedom rather than to be denied the opportunity of responsibility, in the belief that even good government is no substitute for self-government.

Having learned from experience that the greater and more bitter their resistance to 'extremist' demands for independence the more extreme and more powerful they become, certain colonial powers began to respond more positively to signs of nationalist stirrings in some of their territories. The understanding dawned that in the absence of a bitter struggle, there is a chance of treating with the moderate leaders, who may be tempted to show their followers that the masters are 'being reasonable' and are open to persuasion, that quiet and peaceful negotiation can produce an advance towards freedom. The colonial power, experienced in the ways of diplomacy, seeks to curb the efforts of the extremists by ostentatiously polishing the silver platter on which they promise to hand over independence. Underneath the shining surface is the dross. Only the outward form will have changed, the intrinsic relationship is maintained. Foreign imports are still protected, local development clamped down, fiscal policy controlled from the metropolitan capital.

The impact of such semi-independent states on the liberation of Africa has been unfortunate, even dangerous. Bound up as these countries are with the policies of their sponsors, they try to shun the issues involving colonialists and the still enslaved peoples on the African continent, where they do not directly align themselves on the colonialist side. Some of their leaders, it must be confessed, do not see the struggle of their brother Africans as part of their struggle. Even if they did, they would not be free to express their solidarity. The imperialists can thus sit back and regard with sly satisfaction the rift between Africans. The results can only be to retard the independence of countries not yet free and to cause friction and disunion among the peoples of Africa. Here is a phenomenon against which all African freedom fighters must be on their guard and resist to the utmost.

In Africa today there are several apparently independent states who, consciously or not, accept this pattern and serve the interests of the new imperialism, which seeks to salvage something from the wreck of the old imperialism. The European Common Market is an outstanding example. The new threat this organization offers to African unity is no less ominous for being unobtrusive.

As far as Ghana is concerned, we do not oppose any arrangement which the nations of Europe may wish to make among themselves to seek greater freedom of trade within Europe; but we are most decidedly and strongly opposed to any arrangement which uses the unification of Western Europe as a cloak for perpetuating colonial privileges in Africa. We therefore naturally protest against any economic or political grouping of European powers which seeks to exert political and economic pressures upon the newly emergent countries of Africa, or which discriminates against the trade of those countries which are not willing to participate in these exclusive and unfair arrangements. The operation of the European Economic Community, as at present conceived, will not only discriminate against Ghana and other independent states of Africa economically, but what is more important, it will perpetuate by economic means the many artificial barriers which were imposed on Africa by the European colonial powers.

Any form of economic union negotiated singly between the fully industrialized states of Europe and the newly emergent countries of Africa is bound to retard the industrialization, and therefore, the prosperity and the general economic and cultural development, of these countries. For it will mean that those African states which may be inveigled into joining this union will continue to serve as protected overseas markets for the manufactured goods of their industrialized partners, and sources of cheap raw materials. The subsidy which they will receive in return for assuming these obligations will be small compared with the losses which they will suffer from perpetuating their colonial status, losses which are to be measured not only in terms of their own retarded economic, technical and cultural development, but in the harm which they do the peoples of Africa as a whole. The question must be raised as to where this subsidy comes from. It is difficult to believe that it is a purely altruistic contribution made by the European members of the Market to the cause of African well-being. Such subsidy must, in fact, come out of the trading profits made from forcing down the prices of primary products bought from the African countries and raising the cost of the finished goods they are obliged to take in exchange. It is also included in the cost of the projects which constitute the subsidy, a good part of which returns to the European contributors in the form of payments for materials, services, salaries, and banking commissions and interest.

It is true that by joining they obtain a preferential market for their cash crops and minerals in the territories of European economic union. But the advantages of this are largely illusory since most of the commodities which they export are goods which the European partners would in any case have to buy from them. On the other hand, they deprive themselves of the advantages of meeting their own requirements in the world market and will be bound to have to pay considerably more for everything they buy, quite apart from the hindrances which the Common Market is bound to impose on their own internal industrial development. Admittedly, the Rome Treaty introduces explicit safeguards concerning tariff protection by the overseas territories of the European Economic Union. But in the circumstances, I am by no means confident that these safeguards will prove effective. The ex-French colonies of Africa have plenty of direct experience of the difficulties they have encountered in setting up manufacturing industries in those cases where these safeguards operate to the disadvantage of industries in France.

It is true, of course, that the producers of primary materials are always at a disadvantage in bargaining with powerful manufacturers in industrial countries. This naturally follows from their economic weakness, a weakness which can be corrected through unity of action between the different raw material producing countries, and not through exclusive trading arrangements between the strong and the weak. The case of Daniel and the lions may occasionally come out right, but it is not a safe basis for economic planning.

The pattern of imperialist aid to Africa is set not only to draw the unwary back into the neo-colonialist relationship but to tie them into cold-war politics. This has been amply explained by Mr Walt Whitman Rostow, Counsellor and Chairman of the Policy Planning Council of the U.S. State Department, in an interview given to the weekly journal, *U.S. News and World Report*.[1] Asked what America is doing about the underdeveloped areas, Mr Rostow refers to the 'gradual creation of a pattern to succeed the colonial period. We helped pioneer this pattern in our relationship with the Philippines'. After commenting upon the new relationships established with their former colonies by Britain, France and Belgium, who 'is making an important continuing contribution to the Congo,' he states that: 'As the residual problems are solved we look, as I say, to a new partnership based on the common interests of the northern and southern parts of the free world.' This Mr Rostow admits is a long-term process. 'In playing the game in the underdeveloped areas you must be prepared to play for a long time,' and hence, in some of the underdeveloped countries, 'as in most of Africa, we have to start from a very low level – *with specific projects, not national plans of a sophisticated kind.*'[2] For, says Mr Rostow, using the examples of Italy and Greece in the Marshall Plan period, 'we are buying time to protect crucial pieces of real estate – and the possibility of human freedom for those who lived there. And in the end we sweated it out and won. . . . Buying time is one of the most expensive and thankless things we do with our money – as in South Korea.'

This is perhaps one of the most cynical but clear-cut summings up that has ever appeared in print of the approach of a rich power to the needs and hopes of the new nations of the world.

[1] Dated 7 May 1962. This journal is published in Washington by the United States News Publishing Corporation.
[2] Italics added.

There is no need to underscore the intention it so blatantly exposes in 'playing the game' of 'buying time'. It should be an object lesson for all those African statesmen who think that associations with non-African powers will foster their true interests and give them the opportunity to prosper their nations within continuing independence of action. This objective can only be achieved by close economic association between the African states themselves, which in turn presupposes close political co-operation between them. It is on account of its retrograde consequences for the cause of African unity and economic independence that the government of Ghana is so completely opposed to the European Community in its present form.

That many of the leaders of the new African states find themselves in a perplexing position, there is no doubt. They are strongly dependent on foreign contributions simply to maintain the machinery of their governments. Many of them have deliberately been made so weak economically, by being carved up into many separate countries, that they are not able to sustain out of their own resources the machinery of independent government, the cost of which cannot be reduced beyond a certain minimum. I recognize the impossible position in which they were placed when the transfer of power took place. Their frontiers were not of their own choosing, and they were left with an economic, administrative and educational system which, each in its own way, was designed to perpetuate the colonial relationship.

Ghana's case was no different, but we are making decisive efforts to change the pattern and are determined to retain our independence of policy and action. I regard as culpable the insidious reluctance of these states to formulate an independent policy even though it may involve the loss of the contributions which were offered in exchange for continued conformity to the policies of the colonial powers. Equally reprehensible is the refusal to give recognition to the nature of the new imperialism that is using them as pawns in keeping Africa divided, as a means of aborting total independence and maintaining neo-colonial hegemony. Worse still are the deceits in the pretended willingness of some leaders to co-operate on certain levels of African affairs, while actually conniving with the colonial powers to mislead the efforts at mutual African assistance and unity. The perfidy of these artifices cannot be too strongly denounced for their fatal implications in the betrayal of African freedom. They bring in question the patriotism of the leaders employing them and give rise to suspicions of their sincerity and honesty. If they had had to fight a stern battle for their independence, they might have valued it more.

A point in our history has been reached where Africa's interests must be the prime concern of Africa's leaders. The safety and progress of every one of our states can be safeguarded only by the acceptance of this precept, which can best be promoted by our unalloyed unity. This means that where associations linking African countries with European powers cut across basic African interests at any level and offer impediments to the goal of union, they must be discarded, and rejected where they are offered. In all relations with the world overseas, the key consideration must be not merely the superficial or even intrinsic advantage of such relationships for the given African country but the obligation to the African continent as a whole. However much we may protest our loyalty to the cause of African freedom and our united destiny, our affirmations will be without value unless we accept this approach as the cardinal guide to our actions.

States emerging from the tutelage of other colonial powers have not always understood Ghana's attachment to the Commonwealth and the sterling area. That is because the loose, *ad hoc* nature of the structure is not correctly comprehended by those who have been or are members of a more formal association. It is difficult for those not accustomed to a *free* connection with Europe to appreciate that the Commonwealth is an association of sovereign states, each of which is free from interference from the others, including the United Kingdom. Each decides for itself its own foreign and domestic policies and the pattern of its government, as provided in the Westminster Statute of 1931, which laid down that: 'Dominions are autonomous communities within the British Empire, equal in status, in no way subordinate to one another in their domestic or external affairs though united by a common allegiance to the Crown, and freely associated as members of the British Commonwealth of Nations.'

Some of the nomenclature is outmoded but the principle of sovereign identity of the members of the Commonwealth is more meaningful than ever. Members, however, have the right to criticize each other, and do. For example, events in the Union of South Africa and the whole subject of *apartheid* came under heavy fire at the Conference of the Commonwealth Prime Ministers in May 1960, and in 1961 South Africa left the Commonwealth.

There is no compulsion to remain within the Commonwealth, or even to become a member. Burma exercised the right to sever her relations with the Commonwealth on becoming free in 1947. Other states, like Canada and Australia, acknowledge the British Crown as Head of State. India, Pakistan, Ceylon and now Ghana, choose to maintain Republics.

There are mistaken claims that the French Community, by virtue of the changes that have been wrought in its original intentions through the greater panoply of powers vested in the new African states (which are the result of popular pressures), is taking on the character of the Commonwealth. The resolution from the recent meeting of the Brazzaville Group at Bangui, calling for the transformation of the Community into a French-speaking association patterned on the Commonwealth, does not comprehend the essential uniqueness of the Commonwealth. The fact is that, in the circumstances of having to dissolve an existing association to replace it with a new one, constitution-making will have to be invoked. This will at once instil a principle which is entirely out of keeping with the whole idea of the Commonwealth, which is not governed by any constitution. It grew out of the association of the white dominions within the British Empire and has adapted itself, with customary British flexibility, to the continuing evolvement of political independence among the non-European members.

Nevertheless, if the United Kingdom opts into a close European federation by attaching to the European Common Market, the position of Ghana, as a member of the sterling area, would be prejudiced, and we might be forced to withdraw from the Commonwealth to safeguard our trading position. It seems anomalous, therefore, that the new African states at this time, when the French Community is in decline and the unity of the

Commonwealth in question, should seek to bind themselves once more into a European political association which can only intensify their economic dependence on France.

It is significant that the word 'Eurafrica' has come into use in connection with the European Common Market negotiations. It sums up the dangerous conception of a close, continuing link between Europe and Africa on neo-colonialist terms, which must be cemented in any political formation such as that envisaged in the Bangui resolution.[1] The newly emergent states do not make it a principle to break off all relations with their former colonial masters. In the context of a united Africa these relations would take on new and more dignified forms. Even at this time, there may be certain advantages in maintaining a link which history has forged. No question of dictation, however, must arise. The new states must ensure that such relations are the result of a free choice freely negotiated, in which they can treat with the European power just as with any other state in the world with whom they may wish to promote friendship. Nonetheless, however loose such a relationship may be, if it should tend in the slightest degree to impinge upon the African state's relations with other African states, its retention becomes indefensible. Pan-Africa and not Eurafrica should be our watchword, and the guide to our policies.

What is at stake is not the destiny of a single country but the freedom and destiny of the African continent, the unalterable prelude to African Union and the fullest development of the many countries comprising the continent. Just as we are alive to the dangers of a world which is half-slave, half-free, so we are alert to the perils of an African continent split between states that are wholly sovereign and states that are only half-independent. Such a pattern can only impede the real independence of Africa and its transformation into an industrialized continent exercising its rightful influence upon world affairs.

None of us should be under any illusion about the difficulties that lie ahead in the forging of continental government. Enemies of African unity will multiply their endeavours to deflect us from our course. Their device is the creation of discord

[1] Resolution at the Conference of Brazzaville States held at Bangui from 25–26 March 1962.

and distrust in order to keep a wedge between us. Besides the open methods of division, the impact of rising nationalism and independence has encouraged the more subtle velvet-glove weapon of flattery of our national egos. Play is made upon our vanities, the importance of each of us is magnified at the expense of others. We are subjected to the insidious suggestion that a certain African state is anxious to exalt itself to the place of the retired colonial power; that some African states have a large mouth, open and ready to swallow their neighbours. Appeal is directed to our personal ambitions and we are reminded that in a union of African states there will be room for only one Prime Minister, a single cabinet and a sole representation at the United Nations. Hints are spread around that some states, on account of their size and magnitude of population, are more qualified than others to play the role of leadership in Africa and to be its mouthpiece. There is a tendency to divide Africa into fictitious zones north and south of the Sahara which emphasizes racial, religious and cultural differences.

The basic fallacy of these persuasions, dangerous to the independence of Africa in their shrewd exploitation of our pride and vanities, is the deliberate distortion of our vision of African Union. We do not intend a relationship of unequal partners. We envisage the African Union as a free merging together of peoples with a common history and a common destiny. As with other existing unions, the size and resources of countries joining the African Union will be irrelevant to the choice of union leadership. In America, the President is not chosen from the largest of the states. Both President Eisenhower and President Truman came from among the smaller states.

In the early nineteenth century Simon Bolívar, the great liberator of the South American colonies from Spain, had a vision of a Union of South American States as the precursor to the economic development of the South American continent. Unfortunately for the subsequent history of these lands, he was not able to bring his farsighted idea to triumph over the personal ambitions and jealousies of contending individuals and forces. We have seen the unhappy results of this failure in the dissidence and sloth in which the South American countries were sunk for so many decades. It is only today, against the pressures of popular discontent and welfare aspirations, that they are making some headway on the road to development. Unless, however, they can come together in a union such as Bolívar envisaged, their rate of development can never reach anywhere near those of the integrated, planned economies of the U.S.S.R. and China.

The United States of America, but for the firm resolve of Abraham Lincoln to maintain the union of the states, might well have fallen into a disintegration which would have barred the way to the tremendous acceleration of development that an enormous agglomeration of land, resources and people made possible. Lincoln plunged into a civil war to maintain the union as the only logical base of viability. Slavery and its abolition was a secondary, subservient consideration, though the advantage of free labour in a growing industrial economy, making for lower working costs and greater productivity, were impressing their reasoning upon the entrepreneurs of the North.

Here, then, is the lesson for Africa, and our choice. Are we to take the road of national exclusivism or the road of union?

In the British West Indies at this time we are witnessing a sorry spectacle of political jugglery which refuses to subordinate selfish 'big island' interests to total West Indian welfare within federation. Inter-island rivalries and jealousies, adroitly stirred by designing politicians, local racial dissensions which have been deliberately fostered to break down a one-time at least superficial cosmopolitanism in such multi-racial islands as Trinidad and Jamaica, the skilfully exploited fears of the predominant East Indian population of the South American mainland territory of British Guiana of being swamped within federation by the total African-descended population, the complacency of island leaders, have all played their several parts in interring the still-born federation.

Federation of the British West Indian territories, leading eventually to a wider unity with those under other suzerainties, is the only answer to the present poverty and stagnant agricultural societies of the Caribbean world. The islands are less numerous and scattered than those of Indonesia, where the central government is reaching out to bring them all within a centrally directed state. Unless they succeed in coming together within a federation more strongly knit under a firmer central authority than the first attempt, the islands of the West Indies can have a future no different from that of the 'banana republics' of Central America, notwithstanding Trinidad's oil and asphalt industries and Jamaica's bauxite extraction and secondary manufactures. For these are, anyway, all foreign-owned and controlled, and the illusion they give of 'industrialization' must disintegrate before the perennial problems of over-population in islands like Jamaica and Barbados, unemployment in all of them, and the steadily rising inflation which has become a noticeable feature of West Indian economies.

Meantime, separate and inwardly split into minuteness by political friction and group animosities, they are unable to give support to the African struggle for freedom and unity, in spite of the bonds of race and sympathy that exist.

Vanity and narrowness of outlook were what kept the leaders of the original states of North America from uniting for a long time. They were finally overwhelmed by the exertions of the people and the emergence of leaders of stature, maturity and farsightedness. No one today doubts that the welfare and prosperity of the United States would never have been achieved if each state still cherished its petty sovereignty in splendid isolation. Yet in those days there was perhaps less obvious reason for South Carolina to join New Hampshire as members of a continental union than there is today for Ghana and Nigeria, Guinea and Dahomey, Togo and Ivory Coast, Cameroon and Mali, and others, to form themselves into a Union as a first step to the creation of a union of all the states of the African continent.

That is why any effort at association between the states of Africa, however limited its immediate horizons, is to be welcomed as a step in the right direction: the eventual political unification of Africa.

The Central African Federation was never to be confused with these free associations of Africans expressing their own desire to come together. The Federation of Northern and Southern Rhodesia and Nyasaland was forced upon the Africans of those territories by the white settler minorities, with the consent of the United Kingdom Government, in the hope that they would be able to extend their combined hegemony over a dominion freed from the supervision of Whitehall, and to spread the intensive racial practises of Southern Rhodesia to the other parts.

There is a strong financial and ideological connection between South Africa and the Rhodesias which extends through Portuguese Angola and Mozambique. There is talk of a secret military pact between Portugal and the Union of South Africa. The military machine that is being built up by South Africa presents a most threatening danger, not only to the struggle for independence in Central, East and South Africa, but to the safety of the already independent African states. It is unfortunate that the United Kingdom, even though South Africa has withdrawn from the Commonwealth following the heavy censure of her *apartheid* policy from the majority of the members, continues to give support to the Union's policy of military preparedness.

We cannot afford either to ignore the sinister chain of interests which unites events in the Congo and Angola to East and South Africa. These interests are also connected with the East-West battle for world supremacy and the frenzied efforts being made to drag the newly emerging countries of Africa into the orbit of the cold war. The contest for ideological influence over the new states of Africa is throwing into confusion and complicating even more what is already a complex enough struggle for freedom from imperialist political and economic dominance and the unification of the continent. Any difference, any kind of fissure among Africans is seized and turned to the imperialist and cold-war interests. The Congo offers perhaps the most striking example of how tribal dissensions and political careerism are exploited in order to fragment united territories and exacerbate divisions. The aim of the marionette control of local careerists like Moise Tshombe, besides the maintenance of economic power, is to cut across the African determination to secure continental unity in full independence. It was unfortunate that the United Nations was manoeuvred into a position where at one time it appeared to be weighting its influence against the legitimate Congolese Government on the side of those who were responsible for throwing the country into upheaval and for the murder of Patrice Lumumba.

We must be forgiven, I think, if we also see some connection between events in the Congo and Angola and N.A.T.O. The dominating powers joined in this organization – Britain, France, the United States – are all influenced by financial, industrial and military considerations in maintaining in Africa regimes that will support their interests. The means used for doing so are, if the evidence is to be believed, dubious in the extreme. It would be difficult to convince most people of what can only be described as the criminal intent behind certain actions that are employed to upset the stability of states trying to sustain their national unity and integrity against subversive forces. It has been left, however, to a publication linked with N.A.T.O. to reveal the strategy of the *coup d'etat*, which is recommended for use out of the 'search for alternative methods of violence'. This publication, the *General Military Review*, published in its October 1957 issue an article by a Captain Goodspeed, on this subject, in which he advised that:

> Insurgent leaders should endeavour to ensure that public opinion is inflamed against the government prior to the *coup*. Carefully selected acts should be performed which will provoke official reaction, and this reaction should be presented to the public in the worst possible light. There is probably no better way of achieving this than by a judicious assassination or two.
>
> The general public, from the very inception of the *coup*, should be kept informed, not necessarily of what is actually going on, but at least of what the rebels wish them to believe.
>
> The object of this is to influence the public in those courses of action desired by the insurgents, and it is not necessary therefore that the broadcasts correspond to the real situation.

This exposure must surely give credence to the publication of plots that governments in Africa have uncovered from time to time, aimed at assassinating the leaders and overturning the state.

As we examine the multifarious dangers to which the new states and the freedom fighters of Africa are exposed, the more it becomes certain that our best, indeed our one, protection is in unity. For it is that very unity which all the imperialist designs and actions are intended to prevent. It should, therefore, be glaringly obvious that these designs can only be circumvented by achieving the end they are planned to frustrate. At present, an apparent diversity of view among the leaders of some of the

African territories draws a façade of disharmony across the fervent will to unity that pervades the rank and file of the large nationalist movements throughout the continent. It is the idea of the universality of freedom that has impelled the struggle for independence. And just as the vast masses of the peoples of Africa instinctively absorbed the notion of freedom's indivisibility, so, in contradistinction to those unpatriotic leaders who ally themselves with foreign interests rather than support Africa's continental cohesion, they spontaneously understand and uphold the need for African union. Their Africanism is a more solid reality, for they have not been seduced by the sophistries of assimilation into an alien culture and foreign ideological identity. There is a bond of unity here that cannot be disregarded. It must be used to mould the cause of African Union and carry us forward to its attainment and the exorcism of every vestige of imperialism from our continent. Our course is clear. We must beware of the gift of fictitious independence and refuse the falsities of encumbered foreign alliances. We must examine carefully praise from questionable sources and give to the people guarantees of our sincerity in every way. We must stand firmly together against the imperialist forces which are engineering our division and seeking to make Africa a war-ground of contending interests. For it is only in the African association of unity and not in a rider-horse relationship with the very powers that are planning our balkanization that we can counteract and surmount this machiavellian danger.

A Union of African States must strengthen our influence on the international scene, as all Africa will speak with one concerted voice. With union, our example of a multiple of peoples living and working for mutual development in amity and peace will point the way for the smashing of the inter-territorial barriers existing elsewhere, and give a new meaning to the concept of human brotherhood. A Union of African States will raise the dignity of Africa and strengthen its impact on world affairs. It will make possible the full expression of the African personality.

CHAPTER NINETEEN

AFRICA IN WORLD AFFAIRS

IT IS impossible to separate the affairs of Africa from the affairs of the world as a whole. Not only has the history of Africa been too closely involved with Europe and the Western hemisphere, but that very involvement has been the driving force in bringing about major wars and international conflicts for which Africans have not been responsible. Africa has too long been the victim of disruptive aggression, which still attempts to make a hunting ground of our continent.

Our interest, therefore, in the maintenance of peace and the elimination of the forces which daily threaten it, is very real indeed. Hence, our co-operation in any living organism that can be counted on effectively to promote international peace, provided it does not invade our independence of action, is assured. At the moment there exists only the United Nations Organization which offers, with all its defects, the possibility of working towards a peaceful world.

When the United Nations Organization was founded in 1945, Asian and African nationalism was of little consequence. Since then, however, so many former colonies have achieved independence that Afro-Asian countries now form the most influential single group within the United Nations.

At the end of 1961, African states occupied more than a quarter of the seats. The proportion might rise to almost a third as the entire African continent becomes free. This possibility was certainly in the minds of those at the Lagos conference when they passed a resolution calling for a specifically African group at the United Nations.

But the dramatic increase in the international importance of independent Africa, though it may at first sight appear to demonstrate strength, in fact reflects weakness, since it is based in the fragmentation of the continent into many states, few of which are really viable.

The two most powerful countries in the world are the U.S.S.R. and the U.S.A., with populations of 215 millions and 185 millions respectively. Both have one representative each at the United Nations, as entities; though the Byelo Soviet Socialist Republic and the Ukrainian Soviet Socialist Republic, units of the U.S.S.R., are each represented since Laos and Cambodia were admitted. India, with her population of 460 millions, also has only one representative. When the People's Republic of China is admitted, its mighty population of over 640 million people will doubtless have a single representative. There is no reason, therefore, why Africa, with its approximately 300 million people, once united, should not send a single representative to the United Nations. A single representation, resting on the strength of a whole continent, would be more positive in its influence than all the separate representations of the African states put together.

Although confidence in the United Nations has suffered several shocks since its foundation, and particularly of late in connection with the Congo crisis, it remains the only world organization in which the many problems of the world have a chance of finding reasonable solution. It must, therefore, be supported by all interested in the preservation of peace and the progress of human civilization.

We in Ghana showed our faith in the organization when we responded at once with troops to support United Nztions intervention in the Congo in 1960. The reason why we did not withdraw our troops when several other countries did, was because we felt that by doing so we would weaken the authority of the United Nations and leave the way open for the intensification of intervention from just those forces we are anxious to oust.

Recently, in January 1962, Ghana was elected to serve for two years as a non-permanent member of the eleven-nation Security Council. We welcomed the opportunity to take our share of responsibility in the United Nations, though this does not deter us from pressing for certain changes in the administrative

structure which we consider necessary if it is to function as a more
objectively serviceable organ of world peace.

The United Nations, in its present form, does not reflect true
conditions in the world at this time. Today, more and more
countries are assuming the dignity of sovereign states out of a
colonial status which previously made them nothing but
appendages or vassals of imperialism. It has not, however,
eliminated the view that the powerful nations (and some who
regard themselves as still powerful even though events have
proved their brittle vulnerability) have a right to set the pattern
for the budding nations and even to interfere nakedly in the
internal affairs of these struggling states.

In the past might meant right. The idea that right presides in
might still persists. Indeed, it has achieved its fateful acme in the
contest between the two colossi, who seek to draw the rest of the
world into their opposing camps. However, the very fact of a
progressively enlarging world, which is altering not only in the
number of independent nations but in kind, is having its impact
in creating a fringe bloc of states which, though individually
unimportant, collectively are able to exert an influence on the
international scene which is unprecedented.

Their common concern with the anti-colonial struggle and
the continuing liberation of subjected territories is forcing the
United Nations to abandon its temporizing methods for more
positive measures in connection with arbitrary rule in Africa, as
well as the extension of aid to the less developed parts of the
world. The constant whittling at South Africa's resistance
resulted in the visit in May 1962 of a United Nations special
mission to the trust territory of South-West Africa to investigate
allegations of slavery and maltreatment. Another delegation
from the United Nations special committee on colonization
visited East Africa to enquire into conditions in Mozambique
from freedom fighters who had been forced into exile in
Tanganyika and elsewhere. A seventeen-nation sub-committee
which sent a mission to Central Africa to examine the tenability
of Central African Federation, recommended its breaking up, as
it imposed 'no freedom' measures on the majority population. It
found that the proposed new constitution for Northern Rhodesia
was 'basically undemocratic and discriminatory'. The principle

of 'parity' made a sham of democracy by providing 70,000 non-Africans with fifteen seats in parliament and giving the same number to 3,000,000 Africans.

Nothing like this busy concern with the African surge for freedom could ever have happened without the concerted pressure of the newly independent states within the world organization of nations.

And they are able to operate their decisive influence because many of them adhere to a policy of non-commitment to either of the East-West blocs, a policy of neutral non-alignment, but not of passivity. They exercise their right of free choice in supporting those acts which they consider will help to maintain the peace on which their continuance as independent nations rests.

When the United Nations came into being, the old order still existed and its rules made concessions to the prevailing assumption of the priority of the great powers. It is now necessary that recognition be given and concession made to the novel factor of a growing number of new states unwilling to be swallowed up by the older, powerful ones. Thus, at the Conference of Non-Aligned Countries, held in Belgrade in September 1961, I suggested that three deputy secretary-generals should be appointed, one from the East, one from the West, and the third from among the uncommitted nations. This would reflect the main streams of current political thought, restore confidence in the secretary-generalship, and enlarge the objectivity of the secretariat.

I also proposed the setting up of an executive body, elected by the General Assembly, whose duty it would be to ensure that the decisions of both the General Assembly and the Security Council were faithfully and promptly put into effect. For it cannot be denied that decisions are not always readily executed. An effective secretariat is essential to the proper functioning of the United Nations and the energetic implementation of decisions.

Ever-darkening clouds over Angola, South-West Africa, the Rhodesias, Congo, Laos, Korea, and over Berlin, gravely over-cast the international sky. It is significant that so many uneasy centres are in Africa and Asia. For where they are not the direct outcome of Western imperialist manœuvrings, they are engaged with an issue arising from the conflict between the two great power blocs of East and West, with which the peace of the world is dangerously tied up. These two blocs are each committed to its own political and economic ideology. Both are militarily powerful, and each is suspicious of the thoughts and actions of the other. The failure to reach any agreement over such fundamental issues as disarmament and the testing of nuclear weapons seems to hold out little hope for the future.

A new and vigorous approach to the problem of peace and war is needed. The time has come when the destiny of mankind should cease to hang so dangerously on the aims and ambitions of the great powers. In recent years I have travelled extensively in America, in the Soviet Union, in Europe, India and China, where I have spoken to men and women in all walks of life. Everywhere, I have noticed a deep longing for peace. This universal, but often inarticulate, desire for peace must find expression and exert its proper influence on the conduct of world affairs. For peace is indivisible. Disagreement between East and West, for example over Laos or Berlin, can threaten the security of the whole of the rest of the world.

These were the kind of considerations behind the Belgrade Conference of the Non-Aligned Countries, held in September 1961, which 25 countries[1] attended. At Belgrade, we did not intend to form a third power bloc, but we did hope by our solidarity to constitute ourselves into a distinct moral force which might hold the balance of power between East and West in the cause of peace.

At that time the United States was spending an estimated $47,966 million a year on defence and armaments alone, more than half the entire national budget. In 1960 the Soviet Union spent some 96,100 million roubles on defence, out of a national budget of 745,800 million roubles. In a declaration issued at the end of the Belgrade Conference, the United Nations was asked to convene either a special session of the General Assembly

[1] Afghanistan, Algeria, Burma, Cambodia, Ceylon, Congo, Cuba, Cyprus, Ethiopia, Ghana, Guinea, India, Indonesia, Iraq, Lebanon, Mali, Morocco, Nepal, Saudi Arabia, Somalia, Sudan, Tunisia, United Arab Republic, Yemen and Yugoslavia. There were observers from Brazil, Bolivia, and Ecuador.

to discuss disarmament, or to call a world disarmament conference.

When the non-aligned nations talk of disarmament they are not merely concerned with the destructiveness and madness of the armaments race. They are thinking of the vast possibilities now denied the people of the less-developed areas for increased standards of living, the development of agriculture and industry, the planning of cities, the abolition of illiteracy and want, and the curing of disease. It has been estimated that one-tenth of the expenditure involved in armaments would be enough to raise the whole of the less-developed world to the level of a self-sustaining economy. The influence of the uncommitted nations must be exerted to the full to restore a proper sense of values to the world.

As a contribution to this end, the Ghana government set aside £50,000 for an Assembly held in Accra in June 1962, and attended by representatives of all organizations throughout the world whose aim is the ending of the threat of nuclear warfare and the establishment of universal peace. At the meeting of the Preparatory Committee for this 'Accra Assembly', held in Zagreb, Yugoslavia, in March 1962, it was agreed that the following subjects should be discussed: the reduction of international tensions; methods of effective inspection and control in disarmament; the transformation of existing military nuclear materials to peaceful purposes, and the prevention of the spread of nuclear weapons; economic problems involved in or arising from disarmament; and the examination of such fundamental problems as hunger, disease, ignorance, poverty and servitude, with a view to utilizing for social purposes resources now misused as a result of the armaments race.

The three basic aims of Ghana's foreign policy are African independence, African unity, and the maintenance of world peace through a policy of positive neutrality and non-alignment. The first two aims are inextricably bound together, since until we are free from foreign domination we cannot be completely united. Yet united action is essential if we are to achieve full independence. The third aim is closely associated with the other two. Living as we do under the constant threat of universal destruction, the more unaligned nations there are, the wider the non-committed area of the world, the better the chances of human survival. By moral force, if not by material strength, the non-aligned nations must exert their influence to save the world from ultimate disaster. The unity of Africa and the strength it would gather from continental integration of its economic and industrial development, supported by a united policy of non-alignment, could have a most powerful effect for world peace.

I do not believe it is possible for a state, in the world today, to secure its safety by withdrawing from international affairs and refusing to take a stand on issues which affect peace and war. This would be to follow a policy of negative neutralism which is tantamount to a fatal belief that war between the great powers would bring misery and destruction only to those who participated in it. Since war, if it comes, is likely to destroy most of us, whether we are participants or not, whether or not we are the cause of it, negative neutralism is no shield at all. It is completely impotent and even dangerous.

The participants in the Belgrade Conference held this view. They agreed it was 'essential that the non-aligned countries should participate in solving outstanding international issues concerning peace and security in the world as none of them can remain unaffected by, or indifferent to, these issues'.[1] They considered that the further extension of the non-committed area of the world constituted the only possible alternative to the policy of the total division of the world into blocs, and the intensification of cold war policies.

A free and united Africa would contribute greatly to the strength of the non-committed area. While the enormous obstacles that still stand in the way of African freedom and unity must not be under-estimated, account must be taken of the ever-growing strength of our cause. For the opposition to colonialism, both moral and material, is greater in the world today than it has ever been, and it is becoming more powerful all the time.

It is significant that, at the fifteenth session of the General Assembly of the United Nations, a 'Declaration on the granting of Independence to Colonial Countries and Peoples' was adopted. Not only was colonialism condemned, but colonial powers were asked to begin preparations at once for the liberation

1 Declaration issued at the end of the Conference, in October 1961.

of all territories still under their rule. This declaration was strongly supported at the Belgrade Conference, though it has yet to be implemented.

United States spokesmen have often declared their condemnation of colonialism and latterly have affirmed their support of African independence. We must hope this means that determined efforts will be made to halt the imperialist interventions of the Western bloc in Africa. The Soviet Union, by the very nature of its state and constitution, is a supporter of independence. We can count, also, on large numbers of well-wishers in Britain and in other colonial countries. The days of colonialism in Africa are numbered, despite the military reinforcements Portugal has hurriedly packed into Angola, and the imperialist and cold-war machinations in the Congo; despite the latest suppressions of the nationalist movements in the Rhodesias, the gruelling enforcement of *apartheid* in South Africa, and the frenzied manœuvres of neo-colonialism in Africa. Sooner or later, and I think it will be much sooner than the world thinks, all these frantic efforts to save imperialism in Africa will be swept into the debris of history.

Along with them will go the fascist dictatorships in Europe that are so finely balanced on the prolongation of colonialism, which, in the case of Spain, provided the military means for the seizure of power; with the concurrence of a democratic world more concerned at the time with supporting reactionary ruling cliques as a bastion against Communism than with the issue of popular liberty. In the present, there is a positive revolutionary connection between Captain Galvao's exposure of Portuguese atrocities in Angola after his plucky break for freedom and the intensification of nationalist activities in the Portuguese colonies. These, in turn, are undoubtedly having their reaction upon the intellectual and working class revolt in progress against the dictatorship in Portugal. The weakening of Portuguese fascism simultaneously at the metropolitan centre and in the colonial periphery can start off a chain of events which might successfully engage Portuguese forces split between the metropolis and the colonies, provided there is no interference from the neo-colonialist and cold-war elements. There is the danger that South Africa's military forces may be brought into play to prevent the extension of the colonial revolt to its own and its neighbours' borders.

The freedom fighters of Africa must prepare themselves for this danger, which also threatens the independent states, who can meet it effectively by unifying their military command and foreign policy, and uniting with the liberation movements through a concerted strategy. The dangerous potentials herein envisaged are a graphic illustration of the direct bearing of imperialism on international affairs through its instruments, colonialism and neo-colonialism. It can be readily seen that imperialism is a fundamental cause of war. An iniquitous system which has generated intense rivalries and conflicts between nations that erupted into open warfare on a major scale in the scramble to secure 'a place in the sun' of colonial supremacy, it has today spawned the neo-colonialism which is as busy as ever in creating clashes among the nations. In their eagerness to exploit the resources of the overseas territories, they engage in wicked policies that bring a serious threat to the peace of the world. Their grabbing involves them in a constant scramble, like crabs in a pot, climbing over each other's backs in order to get the biggest helping. More often than not this scramble ends in physical fighting, with the loss of countless innocent lives.

When we in Africa denounce imperialism and the recent off-shoot, neo-colonialism, we do it not only because we believe that Africa belongs to the Africans and should be governed by them, but also in the interest of world peace which is so essential to our development and freedom. By abolishing imperialism in all its forms, the world will be rid of many of the present areas of conflict.

It is in the same interest of world peace that we also advocate unity. A united Africa would be able to make a greater contribution towards the peace and progress of mankind. For one thing, it would resolve the problems of those arbitrary frontiers erected by the colonial powers, and so eliminate irredentist dissensions. There would be no foreign military bases on African soil. With a united foreign policy and a common defence plan, there would be no need for them. In the concourse of African union, no African country would be left in a position of solitary weakness in which it could be bullied into allowing them. Any kind of military pacts or alliances with outside powers would be unnecessary. Our united strength would be sufficient to deter any would-be aggressor, since an attack on any African country would be regarded as an attack on the Union.

The maintenance of military forces imposes a heavy financial burden on even the most wealthy African states. We all need every penny we can get for development, and it is suicidal for each of us, individually, to assume such a heavy burden when the weight could be lightened by sharing it among ourselves. I do not imagine that France would have dared to attack Bizerta if we had been united. Nor would she explode atomic bombs in the Sahara in spite of urgent and repeated African objections.

World peace today needs Africa's total independence, needs Africa's unity, as positive contributions to an elimination of the elements engaged in creating the conditions for war. Some of these elements are connected with the supply of materials for and promotion of the manufacture of the most lethal weapons of destruction yet devised. To ensure the continuance of this supply, Africa is being drawn into the danger zone of war. In Angola, the Rhodesias, in South Africa, a menacing military machine is being built up, aimed at destroying African independence and maintaining the servitude of millions of Africans to white supremacy, in conditions of slavery.

World peace is not possible without the complete liquidation of colonialism and the total liberation of peoples everywhere. The indivisibility of peace is staked upon the indivisibility of freedom. And this indivisibility extends to minorities within independent states who are segregated from the body politic. Wherever there is the possibility of conflict arising out of discriminations and the refusal of human rights, the peace of the world is threatened.

Hence it follows that, if the true interest of all peoples is pursued, there must come an end to all forms of exploitation and oppression of man by man, of nation by nation; there must come an end to war. There must result peaceful co-existence and the prosperity and happiness of all mankind.

The balance of forces in the world today has reached such a stage that the only avenue open to mankind is peaceful co-existence. The alternative to this is chaos, destruction and annihilation. However, in terms of the African Revolution, we cannot speak of a balance of forces or even of co-existence as long as the problem of colonialism remains unsolved. Until colonialism and imperialism in all their various forms and manifestations have been completely eradicated from Africa, it would be inconsistent for the African Revolution to co-exist with imperialism.

CHAPTER TWENTY

EXAMPLES OF MAJOR UNIONS
OF STATES

THERE are in the world several unions of states which can offer examples or case studies for the political unification of Africa: the United States of America, the Union of Soviet Socialist Republics, Australia, Canada, Switzerland and Venezuela. Each of them came into being at different historical periods, but all aimed at giving greater protection to the uniting states against internal and external disintegrating pressures; and at providing within the union the conditions of viability and security which would lead to faster economic evolution.

The first of them was the United States of America, whose constitution has, with modifications and adaptations, provided a pattern for most of those which followed. James Bryce, a famous English jurist who died in 1922, in his *Studies in History and Jurisprudence*, defined the most perfect form of a federation of states as that which delegates to a supreme federal government certain powers or functions inherent in themselves or in their sovereign or separate capacity. In its turn, the federal or union government, in the exercise of those specific powers, acts directly on the individual citizen no less than upon the communities making up the federation. The separate states retain unimpaired their individual sovereignty in respect of the residual powers unallotted to the central or federal authority. The citizens of the federated states owe a double allegiance, one to the individual state, the other to the federal government.

By the constitution adopted in 1787 and put into effect in 1789, the original thirteen members of the United States of America, each wholly independent of the other, formed a federal republic by a voluntary combination. This formation strengthened and centralized the confederation and perpetual union that had been established under the confederation articles accepted in 1777 and operated between 1781 and 1789. The constitution recognized a common citizenship for the whole union, and gave powers to the federal government to exercise such authority as was expressly delegated to it. These powers which are extremely wide, are set out under Article One Section 8 of the constitution as follows:

The Congress shall have power to lay and collect taxes, duties, imports and excise, to pay the debts and provide for the common defence and general welfare of the United States; but all duties, imports and excise shall be uniform throughout the United States;

To borrow money on the credit of the United States; to regulate commerce with foreign nations, and among the several states, and with the Indian tribes; to establish a uniform rule of naturalization, and uniform laws on the subject of bankruptcies throughout the United States;

To coin money, regulate the value thereof, and of foreign coin, and fix the standards of weights and measures;

To provide for the punishment of counterfeiting the securities and current coin of the United States;

To establish post-offices and post-roads;

To promote the progress of science and useful arts, by securing for limited times to authors and inventors the exclusive right to their respective writings and discoveries;

To constitute tribunals inferior to the Supreme Court;

To define and punish piracies and felonies committed on the high seas, and offences against the law of nations;

To declare war, grant letters of marque and reprisal, and make rules concerning captures on land and water;

To raise and support armies, but no appropriation of money to that use shall be for a longer term than two years;

To provide and maintain a navy;

To make rules for the government and regulation of the land and naval forces;

To provide for calling forth the militia to execute the laws of the Union, suppress insurrections and repel invasions;

To provide for organizing, arming and disciplining the militia, and for governing such part of them as may be employed in the service of the United States, reserving to the states respectively, the appointment of the officers, and the authority of training the militia according to the discipline prescribed by Congress;

To exercise exclusive legislation in all cases whatsoever, over such district (not exceeding ten miles square) as may, by cession of particular states, and the acceptance of Congress, become the seat of the government of the United States,[1] and to exercise like authority over all places purchased by the consent of the legislature of the state in which the same shall be, for the erection of forts, magazines, arsenals, dockyards and other needful buildings; and

To make all laws which shall be necessary and proper for carrying into execution the foregoing powers vested by this Constitution in the government of the United States, or in any department or office thereof.

Apart from allocating certain special powers to the federal government, the United States constitution lays down certain specifics in regard to migration of persons, the inviolability of habeas corpus except 'when in cases of rebellion or invasion, the public safety may require it', export taxes and duties, inter-state duties, the avoidance of preference in the regulation of commerce or revenue as between the ports of the different states, the appropriation of moneys from the federal treasury, as well as a number of other matters.

The constitution can be amended by approval of two-thirds of both houses of Congress, or 'on the application of the legislatures of two-thirds of the several states, shall call a convention for proposing amendments, which in either case shall be valid to all intents and purposes, as part of this Constitution, when ratified by the legislatures of three-fourths of the several states, or by conventions in three-fourths thereof, as the one or the other mode of ratification may be proposed by Congress'. No amendment, however, can, without its consent, deprive any of the states of its equal suffrage in the Senate.

Three distinct authorities have been entrusted with the powers of the central government: executive, legislative and judicial. The executive head is the President, who is elected for a term of four years by electors chosen for that purpose from each of the

---

[1] That is, the District of Columbia, in which Washington, the capital, is situated.

states. He chooses and dismisses his own cabinet, members of which are responsible to the President and not to the Legislature. In case of his resignation or death, the Vice-President, *ex officio* President of the Senate, assumes the presidency. The presidential succession is regulated by an act of 1887. Beginning with the Secretary of State, the succession goes according to the seniority of the departments.

Legislative power is vested in a Congress consisting of two houses: a House of Representatives, composed of representatives in numbers proportionate to the population of each state. They hold their seats for two years. The senior house is the Senate, having two members from each of the states, elected for six years, but in rotating thirds. The supreme judicial authority is vested in a supreme court, which consists of a chief justice and eight associate justices, all appointed for life by the President, subject to confirmation by the Senate. The task of the Supreme Court is to balance the rights of the citizens with the interpretation of the constitution.

Defining briefly the nature of the Soviet Union, the constitution sets out its role as the determinator and director of the union economy, in which it safeguards 'the small private economy of individual peasants and handicraftsmen based on their own labour and precluding the exploitation of the labour of others'. It also protects the personal property right of citizens in their incomes, the savings from them and their personal effects, including houses, and the right to inherit such property.

The Soviet Union consists of sixteen sovereign republics and some hundred autonomous republics, autonomous regions and areas. The first Soviet constitution, adopted in 1924, revised in 1936 and subsequently amended in certain respects, guarantees equal rights for all citizens regardless of race or nationality. Every citizen of a Union republic is also a citizen of the U.S.S.R., giving dual citizenship.

The Supreme Soviet is the highest organ of power. It is elected every four years and consists of two chambers: the Council of the Union and the Council of Nationalities, both of which have equal rights, and must approve legislation before it becomes effective. Election to the Council of the Union is by direct vote on the basis of one deputy for every 300,000 of the population.

The Council of Nationalities is elected on an equalitarian basis of twenty-five deputies for each Union republic, eleven from each autonomous republic, five each from the autonomous regions and one from each autonomous area. The Supreme Soviet meets at least twice a year for about ten days, but a small number of members is elected to carry on its work between sessions. This is called the Praesidium. It does the major part of the work of the supreme authority, but its actions must be ratified by the Supreme Soviet. The Supreme Soviet, at a joint sitting of the two chambers, appoints the Council of Ministers of the U.S.S.R., which includes the heads of the various state committees and also the chairmen of the Councils of Ministers of the Union republics, by virtue of their office. The division between All-Union ministers and republican ministers is defined by the constitution.

The powers of the All-Union government are specifically defined and include foreign affairs; defence and security; finance, money and credit; the use of the land and its resources, which are nationalized; the planning, administration and super-vision of the Union economy; education and health; the judicial system and procedure; weights and measures; marriage and family; rights of citizens and aliens; and many other matters. Outside of the spheres of central authority set out in the con-stitution, the Union republics exercise independent authority and are in great measure responsible for carrying out their parts of the unified state programme. Specifically, the U.S.S.R. protects the sovereign rights of the Union republics, whose territory may not be altered without the consent of the republic concerned. Since February 1944, each republic has the right:

(1) to have its own national army formation;
(2) to enter into direct negotiations with foreign governments, to conclude agreements with them and to have diplomatic and consular representation abroad; and
(3) to sever relations with the Union and secede from it. (This right was a cardinal right granted in the first constitution, but is now more clearly defined.)

Each Union republic has its own constitution, which takes account of the specific features of the republic and is drawn up in full conformity with the constitution of the U.S.S.R. In the event of divergence between a law of the Union republic and a law of the Union, the Union law prevails. Laws of the Union are published in the languages of all the Union republics.

The right to nominate candidates for election belongs to the various social organizations and societies: the Communist Party, trade unions, co-operatives, youth organizations and cultural societies. However, only the Communist Party is tolerated, all other organizations being classified as non-party.

The U.S.S.R., beginning with four republics, now comprises sixteen. Few would have thought that so many different peoples at various levels of social, political and economic development, could have been welded into the mighty power which the Soviet Union has become in a comparatively short space of time. Similarly, in the case of North America, the original thirteen states have grown to fifty and 1787 constitution, with various amendments, still operates in the United States.

There is, however, a significant difference between the union of the American states and that of the Soviet Socialist Republics, in the historical circumstances that secured their combination. Though originally conceived as a free union of sovereign states, the United States of America, in its present form, was not achieved as a free and voluntary union, but was imposed as the result of the North's victory over the South in the civil war. The right to secede was brought into the open when some states broke away in 1861, and President Lincoln, in order to maintain the unity of the nation, began the civil war against the secessionists.

Though the seceding states wanted to break up the Union because of the North's growing opposition to slavery, Lincoln, writing to Horace Greeley, editor of the *New York Herald Tribune*, in 1862, declared that 'my paramount object is to save the Union, and not either to save or destroy slavery. If I could save the Union without freeing any slave, I would do it; if I could save it by freeing all the slaves, I would do it; and if I could do it by freeing some and leaving others alone, I would also do that'.[1] The war was won and Lincoln was able to assert most solemnly 'that I did all in my judgment that could be done to restore the

[1] Abraham Lincoln: *Life, Public Service and State Papers.*

Union without interfering with the institution of slavery. We failed, and the blow at slavery was struck.'

The survival of the Union, however, required the abolition of slavery. One was incompatible with the other, supporting our Pan-African stand that complete freedom is imperative for African unity. Within the United States, the continuance of the Union paved the way for America's vital industrial advance:

> The rich section, which had been kept back in the general development by a single institution, and had been a clog on the advance of the whole, had been dragged up to the level of the rest of the country. Free labour was soon to show itself far superior to slave labour in the South. . . . The power of the nation, never before asserted openly, had made a place for itself; and yet the continuing power of the states saved the national power from a development into centralized tyranny. And the new power of the nation, by guaranteeing the restriction of government to a single nation in central North America, gave security against any introduction of international relations, international wars and continued war taxation into the territory occupied by the United States.[1]

Thus the American nation emerged stronger out of the civil war to continue its road to its present eminence as the foremost free enterprise state in the world.

In the Soviet Union, the story was different. There the right of secession was the crucial testing point of the Treaty of Union. Lenin made this clear in the assertion that:

> Just as mankind can achieve the abolition of classes only by passing through the transition period of the dictatorship of the oppressed class, so mankind can only achieve the inevitable merging of nations by passing through the transition period of complete liberation of all the oppressed nations, i.e. their freedom to secede.[2]

On this, the third All-Russian Congress of Soviets amplified Lenin's standpoint in its declaration of 24 January 1918 that:

[1] *Encyclopaedia Britannica*, 1947. Article on The History of the United States of America, Vol. 22, p. 810.

[2] Lenin: *Selected Works*, Vol. V, pp. 270–1.

the Soviet Republic is established on the basis of a free union composed of free nations. In order to avoid misunderstanding on the question, the declaration offers to the workers and peasants of every nationality the right to make their own decisions in their own authorized Soviet congress: do they wish, and on what grounds, to participate in the federal government and other federal Soviet institutions.

The strength of the Soviet Union has been proved in the furnace of war. Even under the impact of fascist savagery, it remained unbroken.

The union of Canada came into being as an effort to resolve the Anglo-French racial differences between the provinces of Upper and Lower Canada, which were being fanned by the rivalries between England and France. Though united in one legislature after the conferment of self-government under a governor, a deadlock was reached in government, and a union was mooted. On 1 July 1867 four provinces united. They were Upper Canada (now Ontario), Lower Canada (now Quebec), Nova Scotia and New Brunswick. With the new era that was opening in America, following the civil war, the union of the Canadian provinces 'offered the sole hope of successful growth'. Rupert's Land was added in 1869 by purchase from the Hudson Bay Company, and British Columbia joined in 1871. The British Government transferred to Canada in 1878 all of British North America except Newfoundland.

Theoretically, the executive consists of a governor-general and privy council, but in practice it is a cabinet under a prime minister. The governor-general is appointed for five years to represent the sovereign in all matters of federal government. There is a House of Commons elected by the different provinces according to population. Lieutenant-governors of the provinces are nominated by the governor-general. All local legislation is carried on by the provincial parliaments of single houses, except in the case of Quebec, which has two. The federal parliament has jurisdiction over all matters not specifically assigned to the local legislatures.

In the Commonwealth of Australia, the federal parliament exercises jurisdiction over those matters expressly assigned to it by the constitution. The States retain control, accordingly, over

those subjects that are not withdrawn by constitutional defini-
tion. Nevertheless, the central authority is quite extensive,
ranging over trade, industry, criminal law, taxation, quarantine,
marriage and divorce, weights and measures, legal tender, copy-
rights and patents, naturalization and aliens. The federal
principle of equal representation of the states is practised by the
election of six members from each of the six states to the Senate,
for a period of six years, half retiring every three years. Election
to the House of Representatives is on a population basis, with
not less than five members from each of the States.

If union did not bring to Canada and Australia, for example,
the tremendous surge forward that it gave to the United States
and the Soviet Union, it is because other factors were not equal.
Though Canada is considerably bigger than the United States,
her territory includes large stretches of wasteland where civilized
habitation has so far proved impossible. Australia, on her side,
has a great belt of arid country in the interior, and the population
is more or less confined to the coastal areas. Both Canada and
Australia are thinly populated and are encouraging a policy of
immigration from Great Britain and Europe.

Though both dominions remain tied to the British Commonwealth, Canada's contiguity with the United States has brought
her within the orbit of American monopoly capitalism, which
today has major investments in the growing Canadian economy,
to the chagrin of certain critics. Wool and gold helped to
accumulate early capital in Australia; but industrialization did
not really get under way on a large scale until fairly recently.
Here, again, American monopoly is sinking in its teeth. In
Canada, there is still a certain amount of racial friction between
the French and English communities and this is aggravated by
the interference of the Roman Catholic Church.

A federal form of government operates in Venezuela, and the
provision of the constitution adopted in 1936 vests legislative
power in a national congress of two houses: the Senate and
Chamber of Deputies. It meets every year at Caracas. The
Senate consists of two members from each of the nominally
independent, self-governing states. This gives forty members,
elected by the state legislatures for a period of four years.
Election to the Chamber is by direct vote of a suffrage limited to

Venezuelan males, literate and over the age of twenty-one, in the proportion of one deputy for every 35,000 of population. Each state is entitled to send at least one deputy. The presidential term is for five years and, constitutionally, the President cannot immediately succeed himself. The President is assisted by a cabinet of ministers and the governor of the federal district. The nominally autonomous state governments consist of legislative assemblies composed of deputies elected by ballot for a period of three years, and for each a president and two vice-presidents chosen by the legislative assembly for a period of three years.

It has been said that Switzerland is a model of federal government. It consists of twenty-two sovereign states or cantons. Two legislative chambers constitute the apparatus of government. They are the Senate or Council of States, in which each canton has equal representation; and the National Council, chosen on the basis of one member to every 20,000 of the population. The two bodies form the Federal Assembly. An Executive Council of seven members is elected by the Federal Assembly for a period of three years, and one of its members is chosen annually, also by the Federal Assembly, to be President of the Council. His powers are no greater than those of his colleagues, although he is President of the state and represents the nation on all ceremonial occasions. The constitution provides that not more than one councillor can come from any one canton, which carries the federal principle into the structure of the executive. The Federal Council is responsible to the Federal Assembly, but it does not resign if its policy is rejected by the legislature. Of a coalition character, it more nearly represents a council of permanent heads of department than the cabinet of a parliamentary system.

In order to improve effectively and quickly the serious damage done to Africa as a result of imperialism and colonialism, the emergent African States need strong, unitary States capable of exercising a central authority for the mobilization of the national effort and the co-ordination of reconstruction and progress. For this reason, I consider that even the idea of regional federations in Africa is fraught with many dangers. There is the danger of the development of regional loyalties, fighting against each other. In effect, regional federations are a form of balkanization on a grand scale. These may give rise to the dangerous interplay not only of power politics among African States and the regions, but can also create conditions which will enable the imperialists and neo-colonialists to fish in such troubled waters. Indeed, such federations may even find objection to the notion of African unity. We must look at the problem from the point of view of its practical and immediate objectives. For example, whereas it may be inexpedient geographically and otherwise for Ghana to join an East African Federation, there would be no difficulty for Tanganyika, let us say, joining a political union of Africa. We must endeavour to eradicate quickly the forces that have kept us apart. The best means of doing so is to begin to create a larger and all-embracing loyalty which will hold Africa together as a united people with one government and one destiny.

CHAPTER TWENTY-ONE

CONTINENTAL GOVERNMENT
FOR AFRICA

WE have seen, in the example of the United States, how the dynamic elements within society understood the need for unity and fought their bitter civil war to maintain the political union that was threatened by the reactionary forces. We have also seen, in the example of the Soviet Union, how the forging of continental unity along with the retention of national sovereignty by the federal states, has achieved a dynamism that has lifted a most backward society into a most powerful unit within a remarkably short space of time. From the examples before us, in Europe and the United States of America, it is therefore patent that we in Africa have the resources, present and potential, for creating the kind of society that we are anxious to build. It is calculated that by the end of this century the population of Africa will probably exceed five hundred millions.

Our continent gives us the second largest land stretch in the world. The natural wealth of Africa is estimated to be greater than that of almost any other continent in the world. To draw the most from our existing and potential means for the achievement of abundance and a fine social order, we need to unify our efforts, our resources, our skills and intentions.

Europe, by way of contrast, must be a lesson to us all. Too busy hugging its exclusive nationalisms, it has descended, after centuries of wars interspersed with intervals of uneasy peace, into a state of confusion, simply because it failed to build a sound basis of political association and understanding. Only now, under the necessities of economic stringency and the threat of the new German industrial and military rehabilitation, is Europe trying – unsuccessfully – to find a *modus operandi* for containing the threat. It is deceptively hoped that the European Community will perform this miracle. It has taken two world wars and the break-up of empires to press home the lesson, still only partly digested, that strength lies in unity.

While we in Africa, for whom the goal of unity is paramount, are striving to concert our efforts in this direction, the neo-colonialists are straining every nerve to upset them by encouraging the formation of communities based on the languages of their former colonizers. We cannot allow ourselves to be so disorganized and divided. The fact that I speak English does not make me an Englishman. Similarly, the fact that some of us speak French or Portuguese does not make us Frenchmen or Portuguese. We are Africans first and last, and as Africans our best interests can only be served by uniting within an African Community. Neither the Commonwealth nor a Franco-African Community can be a substitute.

To us, Africa with its islands is just one Africa. We reject the idea of any kind of partition. From Tangier or Cairo in the North to Capetown in the South, from Cape Guardafui in the East to Cape Verde Islands in the West, Africa is one and indivisible.

I know that when we speak of political union, our critics are quick to observe an attempt to impose leadership and to abrogate sovereignty. But we have seen from the many examples of union put forward, that equality of the states is jealously guarded in every single constitution and that sovereignty is maintained. There are differences in the powers allotted to the central government and those retained by the states, as well as in the functions of the executive, legislature and judiciary. All of them have a common trade and economic policy. All of them are secular, in order that religion might not be dragged across the many problems involved in maintaining unity and securing the greatest possible development.

We in Africa who are pressing now for unity are deeply conscious of the validity of our purpose. We need the strength of our combined numbers and resources to protect ourselves from the very positive dangers of returning colonialism in disguised forms. We need it to combat the entrenched forces dividing our continent and still holding back millions of our brothers. We need it to secure total African liberation. We need it to carry forward our construction of a socio-economic system that will support the great mass of our steadily rising population at levels of life which will compare with those in the most advanced countries.

But we cannot mobilize our present and potential resources without concerted effort. If we developed our potentialities in men and natural resources in separate isolated groups, our energies would soon be dissipated in the struggle to outbid one another. Economic friction among us would certainly lead to bitter political rivalry, such as for many years hampered the pace of growth and development in Europe.

At present most of the independent African States are moving in directions which expose us to the dangers of imperialism and neo-colonialism. We therefore need a common political basis for the integration of our policies in economic planning, defence, foreign and diplomatic relations. That basis for political action need not infringe the essential sovereignty of the separate African States. These States would continue to exercise independent authority, except in the fields defined and reserved for common action in the interests of the security and orderly development of the whole continent.

In my view, therefore, a united Africa – that is, the political and economic unification of the African Continent – should seek three objectives:

Firstly, we should have an over-all economic planning on a continental basis. This would increase the industrial and economic power of Africa. So long as we remain balkanized, regionally or territorially, we shall be at the mercy of colonialism and imperialism. The lesson of the South American Republics *vis-à-vis* the strength and solidarity of the United States of America is there for all to see.

The resources of Africa can be used to the best advantage and the maximum benefit to all only if they are set within an over-all framework of a continentally planned development. An over-all economic plan, covering an Africa united on a continental basis, would increase our total industrial and economic power. We should therefore be thinking seriously now of ways and means of building up a Common Market of a United Africa and not allow ourselves to be lured by the dubious advantages of association with the so-called European Common Market. We in Africa have looked outward too long for the development of our economy and transportation. Let us begin to look inwards into the African Continent for all aspects of its development. Our communications were devised under colonial rule to stretch outwards towards Europe and elsewhere, instead of developing internally between our cities and states. Political unity should give us the power and will to change all this. We in Africa have untold agricultural, mineral and water-power resources. These almost fabulous resources can be fully exploited and utilized in the interest of Africa and the African people, only if we develop them within a Union Government of African States. Such a Government will need to maintain a common currency, a monetary zone and a central bank of issue. The advantages of these financial and monetary arrangements would be inestimable, since monetary transactions between our several States would be facilitated and the pace of financial activity generally quickened. A central bank of issue is an inescapable necessity, in view of the need to re-orientate the economy of Africa and place it beyond the reach of foreign control.

Secondly, we should aim at the establishment of a unified military and defence strategy. I do not see much virtue or wisdom in our separate efforts to build up or maintain vast military forces for self-defence which, in any case, would be ineffective in any major attack upon our separate States. If we examine this problem realistically, we should be able to ask ourselves this pertinent question: which single State in Africa today can protect its sovereignty against an imperialist aggressor? In this connection, it should be mentioned that anti-*apartheid* leaders have alleged that South Africa is building a great military force with all the latest weapons of destruction, in order to crush nationalism in Africa. Nor is this all. There are grave indications that certain settler governments in Africa have already been caught in the dangerous arms race and are now arming themselves to the teeth. Their military activities constitute a serious threat not only to the security of Africa, but also to the peace of the world. If these reports are true, only the unity of Africa can prevent South Africa and these other governments from achieving their diabolical aims.

If we do not unite and combine our military resources for common defence, the individual States, out of a sense of insecurity, may be drawn into making defence pacts with foreign powers which may endanger the security of us all.

There is also the expenditure aspect of this problem. The maintenance of large military forces imposes a heavy financial burden on even the most wealthy States. For young African States, who are in great need of capital for internal development, it is ridiculous – indeed suicidal – for each State separately and individually to assume such a heavy burden of self-defence, when the weight of this burden could be easily lightened by sharing it among themselves. Some attempt has already been made by the Casablanca Powers and the Afro-Malagasy Union in the matter of common defence, but how much better and stronger it would be if, instead of two such ventures, there was one over-all (land, sea and air) Defence Command for Africa.

The third objective which we should have in Africa stems from the first two which I have just described. If we in Africa set up a unified economic planning organization and a unified military and defence strategy, it will be necessary for us to adopt a unified foreign policy and diplomacy to give political direction to our joint efforts for the protection and economic development of our continent. Moreover, there are some sixty odd States in Africa, about thirty-two of which are at present independent. The burden of separate diplomatic representation by each State on the Continent of Africa alone would be crushing, not to mention representation outside Africa. The desirability of a common foreign policy which will enable us to speak with one voice in the councils of the world, is so obvious, vital and imperative that comment is hardly necessary.

I am confident that it should be possible to devise a constitutional structure applicable to our special conditions in Africa and not necessarily framed in terms of the existing constitutions of Europe, America or elsewhere, which will enable us to secure the objectives I have defined and yet preserve to some extent the sovereignty of each State within a Union of African States.

We might erect for the time being a constitutional form that could start with those states willing to create a nucleus, and leave the door open for the attachment of others as they desire to join or reach the freedom which would allow them to do so. The form could be made amenable to adjustment and amendment at any time the consensus of opinion is for it. It may be that concrete expression can be given to our present ideas within a continental parliament that would provide a lower and an upper house, the one to permit the discussion of the many problems facing Africa by a representation based on population; the other, ensuring the equality of the associated States, regardless of size and population, by a similar, limited representation from each of them, to formulate a common policy in all matters affecting the security, defence and development of Africa. It might, through a committee selected for the purpose, examine likely solutions to the problems of union and draft a more conclusive form of constitution that will be acceptable to all the independent States.

The survival of free Africa, the extending independence of this continent, and the development towards that bright future on which our hopes and endeavours are pinned, depend upon political unity.

Under a major political union of Africa there could emerge a United Africa, great and powerful, in which the territorial boundaries which are the relics of colonialism will become obsolete and superfluous, working for the complete and total mobilization of the economic planning organization under a unified political direction. The forces that unite us are far greater than the difficulties that divide us at present, and our goal must be the establishment of Africa's dignity, progress and prosperity.

Proof is therefore positive that the continental union of Africa is an inescapable desideratum if we are determined to move forward to a realization of our hopes and plans for creating a modern society which will give our peoples the opportunity to enjoy a full and satisfying life. The forces that unite us are intrinsic and greater than the superimposed influences that keep us apart. These are the forces that we must enlist and cement for the sake of the trusting millions who look to us, their leaders, to take them out of the poverty, ignorance and disorder left by colonialism into an ordered unity in which freedom and amity can flourish amidst plenty.

Here is a challenge which destiny has thrown out to the

leaders of Africa. It is for us to grasp what is a golden opportunity to prove that the genius of the African people can surmount the separatist tendencies in sovereign nationhood by
coming together speedily, for the sake of Africa's greater glory
and infinite well-being, into a Union of African States.

INDEX

AFRICA AND ITS ISLANDS

DATE DUE

APR 1 5 '66			
MAR 1 3			
APR 3			
MAR 4 1968			
APR 1 1968			
NOV 4 1969			
MAY 2 5 1970			
APR 2 1971			
APR 1 1974			
GAYLORD			PRINTED IN U.S.A.